Seekers
A Twentieth Century Life

We are all Seekers

Made weak by time and fate, but strong in will
To strive, to seek, to find, and not to yield.

Tennyson's Ulysses

Ask and it shall be given you; seek and ye shall find,
Knock and it shall be opened unto you.

The Bible, Saint Matthew, 7,5

Subject to human error and illusion, and learning how to share!

Everything we know is subject to error and illusion ...

Recognition of error and illusion is all the more difficult in that error and illusion are not recognised as such ... We should learn that the search for truth requires seeking ... The ideas that I defend here are not so much ideas I possess as ideas that possess me ... To understand (*comprehend*) means to intellectually apprehend together, *comprendere*, to grasp together (the parts and the whole, the multiple and the single) ... Henceforth, we have to learn to be, to live, share, communicate, commune as humans of Planet Earth ... It is the combination of entropy, order, with chaos, disorder, in our thinking that makes for human creativity.

Edgar Morin, UNESCO, Seven Complex Lessons for the Future, Page 17

Morin also emphasises the necessary interaction of entropy, order, and a creative chaos in our survival. We have so much to learn from his complex combination.

Seekers

A Twentieth Century Life

Memories of People and Places, 1918-2013

Michael Barratt Brown

SPOKESMAN

First Published in 2013 by Spokesman
Russell House, Bulwell Lane,
Nottingham NG6 0BT, England
Phone: 0115 9708381 Fax: 01159420433
e-mail: euro@compuserve.com
www.spokesmanbooks.com

ISBN 978 0 85124 825 7

A CIP Catalogue is available from the British Library

Printed by Russell Press Ltd. (www.russellpress.com)

Contents

Acronyms

AML	Allied Military Liaison
BFI	British Film Institute
BRPF	Bertrand Russell Peace Foundation
CEO	Chief Executive Officer
CND	Campaign for Nuclear Disarmament
COBSRA	Council of British Societies for Relief Abroad
DIUS	Department for Innovation, Universities and Skills
EEC	European Economic Community
ELF	European Labour Forum
END	European Nuclear Disarmament
FAU	Friends' Ambulance Unit
FWVRS	Friends' War Victims Relief Service
GLC	Greater London Council
GLEB	Greater London Enterprise Board
LSE	London School of Economics
MBE	Member of the Order of the British Empire
MEP	Member of the European Parliament
MERRA	Middle East Relief and Refugee Administration
MHFAU	Mobile Hygiene and First Aid Units
NAAFI	Navy, Army and Air Force Institutes
NATO	North Atlantic Treaty Organization
NFFC	National Film Finance Corporation
NGO	Non-Governmental Organisation
OCN	Open College Network
RAMC	Royal Army Medical Corps
SACMED	Supreme Allied Commander of the Mediterranean Theatre
SOE	Special Operations Executive
TWIN	Third World Information Network
UK	United Kingdom
UN	United Nations
UNRRA	United Nations Relief and Rehabilitation Administration
USA	United States of America
WEA	Workers' Educational Association

Acknowledgements

Successive versions of this book have been read and commented on by a loyal team of advisers, and my friends and family – Liz Barratt Brown, Victoria Bawtree, David Browning, Catherine Cameron, Simon Caulkin, Bos Dewey, John Halstead, Robin Murray, Hugo Radice, Nancy Worcester and Peter Parker. They have made important corrections of fact and judgement and suggestions for improvements, and I am most grateful to them. The errors that remain are mine. Especially helpful were the suggestion of Catherine Cameron that I should put an historical introduction to each chapter and Hugo Radice's corrections of my memory of the founding of the Conference of Socialist Economists. I have also had helpful advice on family matters from my two sons, Christopher and Richard Ronald. Finally, I owe a very great debt of gratitude to Tony Simpson and Abi Rhodes at *Spokesman* and the Bertrand Russell Peace Foundation, who have so competently seen the book through its several stages of publication. I have to add a special word of thanks to my granddaughter Sarah for all her help in taming my unruly computer, especially in reproducing the photos. Finally, I owe a special word of gratitude to John Halstead, who took over my piles of diaries and unorganised papers, and arranged them in chronological order and delivered them to the archivist at Sheffield University Library.

In supplying photographs for the book I have to thank Liz Barratt Brown, Victoria Bawtree, Claire Bown, David Browning, Catherine Cameron, Simon Caulkin, Tamara and Deborah Coates, Bastien Gomperts, John Halstead, Liz Jackson, Alastair MacColl, Beth Murray, Richard Ronald, Ricky Wilkinson, for pictures of themselves, and sometimes of their relatives and friends, and also David Hukin for his photograph of Harold MacMillan, reproduced from the Oxford University magazine. Most of the other pictures are from my own collection, including those on the book's covers, taken by my friend Henry Grant, and now preserved in the Museum of London.

Prologue

In July 2012, I was browsing in my brother's library at his farm in Mallorca, and came across the autobiography of John Buchan titled *Pilgrim's Way*. It is not really so much the story of Buchan's life, but of the famous people he got to know and the places where he met them. They ranged from King George V of England to Prime Minister Ramsay MacDonald, from Cecil Rhodes of Africa to Lord Milner, from Marshall Foch to Premier Laval, and included very many others.

It occurred to me to write something myself about important people I had met and their countries. Buchan's *Pilgrim's Way* assumed that he had a clear destination. My idea was much more tentative and I have adopted the title of *Seekers*, which is how my Quaker ancestors described themselves, searching for the way. Perhaps none of my friends and acquaintances quite ranked in importance along with Buchan's, but they included some I had conversations with – Harold Macmillan, Archbishop Temple, Marshal Tito, Mahatma Gandhi, Sir Cyril Pickard, Bertrand Russell, Joseph Needham, Ahmed Ben Bella, Benjamin Britten and two Mayors of New York City. The people I was thinking of were friends who had all made a major contribution to the lives of the people where they worked – in England, Scotland, India, China, Africa or America. They were all seekers for the way, not just one simple way, but a very complex one – and complex means woven together.

It so happened that I was writing this autobiography on the evening when we were listening to Daniel Barenboim conducting and then explaining the meaning of Beethoven's eight symphonies. Beethoven, Barenboim insisted, was not so much telling us how the world was, and certainly not of some divine providence, but searching always for the true objective of human beings. Nothing could have been closer to my own thoughts, and in concentrating the story on my friends, I recalled my mother's favourite quotation – from Hilaire Belloc:

> *From quiet home, and first beginning,*
> *Out to the undiscovered ends,*
> *There's nothing worth the wear of winning*
> *But laughter and the love of friends.*

So it is to my friends and family that this book is dedicated.

My family has now grown to quite a size – children, grand children and great grandchildren. I will start with my brother Hilary's daughter – my niece, Liz, her husband Bos, and their children, Barratt and Eliza; then there are my sisters, Deb and Bridget and their children, Humphrey and Giles, and their wives, Sarah and Alison, and their children, Becky and JJ, and John and Jane, and the next generation, Janet, married to Mark, and Sarah and Fiona, married to Glen, Nicola and Stewart. There is my daughter Debbie and husband Bjorn and his son, Afon.

Then there are my sons, Christopher, Richard and Daniel and their wives, Sue, Rachel and Bobby, Christopher's children, Ivan, Lorna, and Ken, their spouses, Teresa, Bryan and Alice, and the next generation, Daisy and Oliver, Benjamin and Rebecca, Thomas and Ted. Then Richard's children, Elliot, Angelica and Lewis; Angelica's husband Jos and their two children Sasha and Sienna; finally, Daniel's ex-wife Bobby and their children, Sarah and Claire, and Claire's children, my ninth and tenth great grandchildren, Emma and Ruby. I hope that I haven't forgotten someone.

* * *

Felix, qui potuit rerum cognoscere causas
(Happy is he who understands the causes of things)

The Sheffield University motto, after Virgil, which is why I am a seeker for the way.

* * *

There is another, more personal autobiography available in the 'Life Stories' series at the British Library, in an interview with Louise Broder which I made in 2010. But there are some personal items in this book, about my father and mother. There is an appreciation of my first wife, Frances, after I left her. I have included a long note about my wife Eleanor, following her death in 1998. There are references throughout to Annette, who was with me in 1940-41 and again 65 years later, in 2005-2012, and I have written at length about her in the Epilogue.

My Gurus: Gilbert Murray and Joseph Needham

Michael and The Northern College, painted by Pat O'Neill

Preface

A Century of Convulsion and Rapid Change

Time present and time past
Are both perhaps present in time future
And time future contained in time past.
T.S.Eliot, *The Four Quartets*

What do I remember of my past as I see it now in the present and why should I recall it? What importance does it have for the future? Time is a slippery thing. We give it and take it. We have London time, set by the sun rise at the meridian of Greenwich, and British summer time an hour earlier, and continental time an hour later, and all the times round the world to the international date line. How many different kinds of time we recognise! Time flies, time is running out, 'time and tide wait for no man', I haven't time, it saves time, time is money, serving time, wasting time, 'the times are out of joint', my time is come.

As I look back over 90 years, the sense of time and the urgency of time are weakened. That must be a good thing. Everything was speeded up in the Twentieth Century, the turnover of capital, the pace of work, the growth of the plants and food we eat, even the way people talk. It is good to slow down, not to be in such a hurry, not always going on to the next thing. I can ruminate now, and think about what I have done with my life. Because this is an autobiography, or at least something autobiographical, I am writing about myself. I can do this because human beings, perhaps alone among animals, have consciousness. Chimpanzees can also recognise themselves in a mirror, but humans can stand outside their being and think about their existence from outside. 'Exist' from the Latin means stand outside. From this arises all Hegel's argument about the 'Other', 'in itself' and 'for itself', which I have never been able fully to understand. Looking back now on my past I have in some ways to consider myself a different person. In the famous phrase of Heraclitus, 'No man descends twice into the same river'. The man changes and the river changes.

The words we use about ourselves are very revealing. I say that I am in some ways still the same 'person', though this in origin refers to the *persona*, the mask that I present to the world. I say that I still act 'in character', though this comes from *charaz*, a pointed stick in Greek that makes a certain impression, and, as one would say, 'makes a definite point'. What then about my true self, my 'identity', meaning literally what stays the same? We conjugate, meaning yoke together, the verb 'to be' from the Sanscrit *bhu* for 'to grow', as follows:

I am, meaning in Sanscrit *asmi* 'I breathe' (even though I am now a bit 'asthmatic' –
the same word);
Y(th)ou are (art), Sanscrit *asti*, other than me (*ti-tutoyer*)
S(h)e is, meaning stands (from the same Latin word *sto* as in ex-ists, stands out).

Am I the same as I was? In what ways have I changed? Because I am human, I
can look at myself and write about myself. When I say that I can stand outside
myself, I am not distinguishing mind and body, as if I was looking at a carcass. It
seems that all of 'me' is looking at all of 'me', but at different stages of
development. 'Me, me, me!' – it is the second sound that infants produce after
'ma ma' and common to all Indo-European languages, as I learnt long ago from
Frederick Bodmer's *The Loom of Language*. Teaching and writing have always been
my release, but all conscious thinking must imply the use of words. Dreams don't
always have words, but must imply them. Julian Jaynes, in his book *The Origins of
Consciousness,* has written about this, arguing that consciousness comes from
reasoning (which we share with the chimpanzees), but human consciousness
comes from the use of words, language, *logos,* 'the word' in Greek, from which we
derive 'logic'.

'In the beginning was the word and the word was with God and the word was
God' is how the fourth Gospel according to St. John begins. This is pure Greek
religion, the metaphysics of Zeno and the Stoics of the Fourth Century BC, as I
was taught by Gilbert Murray to understand it in his *Five Stages of Greek Religion.*
In the Hebrew Book of Genesis of the Old Testament, we read: 'The Lord said
"Let there be Light, and there was Light"'. But the Word was already there in the
beginning.

It is the Word, the logos of the Cosmos, the reason of the world or the mind of
Zeus, that we are presented with in Greek religion. The human soul is a fragment
of the divine. If you know yourself, as Socrates, following Zeno, taught, and then
act in accordance with the nature of your true self, you comply with the divine
will, 'whose service is perfect freedom'. This is how the *Book of Common Prayer* has
it in the Morning Prayer, 'The Second Collect, for Peace'. I don't believe in an
immortal soul or a 'divine will', but I try to follow Socrates. How much of
Christianity draws upon Greek religion is a subject I will discuss later.

I bring all this up here at the very beginning of this memoir, because it seems
to me looking back over more than ninety years that, while I have grown in size
and then wisened, grown in knowledge and perhaps in understanding, and then
become forgetful, I have a strong sense of my identity, of what remains the same.
My opinions and judgements have changed, and if I am criticised for that I would
answer with Maynard Keynes, 'When circumstances change I change my mind.
What do you do?' What is important to me is that I do not think that I have acted
different parts, except when deliberately acting in plays. I may have dissimulated
out of politeness or fear, but I do not think that I have dissembled. I have

behaved badly, as I see it (not only as society sees it) and I will say something about that. I have often been angry and irritable, though never for long. But I have always been open. I could not ever have sustained a double life, as those have done who were engaged on espionage. I am a bad liar and when I committed adultery I had to own up, and I had a second marriage for over fifty years in which the plight of my troth was perfectly kept, and without any kind of difficulty.

Now that I am alone without my beloved Eleanor and then without my lovely Annette, I know that I have turned in on myself. Oh! These wonderful metaphors of language! I have my family around me and wonderful friends about whom I will write. But there are so many hours of the day and the night when I am now alone. Writing up these pieces of autobiography over the last three years is a reflection of that fact and of my desire to recall how it once was. I have still, I expect, some years to live and I have begun to wonder about things left undone that I should do before it is too late. I fear that I am forgetting things and that makes me untruthful. The Greek for truth is charmingly *aletheia* meaning 'not forgetful'. One of the things I should do therefore before it is too late seemed to be to write something about my life, not just as a personal confession but as a political statement.

In fact, I believe it to be more important that I should make a political statement than a personal confession, because there are so many events of the last ninety years that I have witnessed or been involved in that have been buried by the passing of time, which I think need to be remembered. The reason for the forgetting is generally just amnesia, but some things have been carefully forgotten, if not having the truth deliberately suppressed. Some were bad things such as the hopelessness of years of mass unemployment in Britain in the 1930s, the hunger and poverty of millions even in the rich countries in the first half of the century, the heartless dispatch of hundreds of thousands of young men to their deaths in the First World War, the Holocaust, the deliberate bombing of civilians by both sides in the Second World War, the deployment of nuclear weapons, the denial of all human rights to half the world's people in the colonies, the brutal suppression of their attempts to free themselves, the using up of finite energy resources to increase economic growth, and the use of starvation and corruption as instruments of public policy.

Some, however, were good things such as the struggle of working people to form trade unions and establish a Party of Labour, the attempt in the Soviet Union to build a socialist commonwealth, the heroic resistance to oppression of men and women in colonies and occupied territories, the experiments in workers' self-management in Yugoslavia and Cuba, the mass protests at nuclear armament, the increasing public responsibility for universal health provision, education and care of the very young and the elderly, the growing demand for environment-friendly and people-friendly production of consumer goods.

These lists of bad things and good things do not appear at the top of most of the items recorded for us in the public memory as presented by the media. We are flooded with terrible stories of human violence and war but rarely with the loving care and demonstrations for peace that occur at the same time. And almost never are we asked to consider why human beings fight but are also capable of co-operating happily. Yet that is the most important question that has engaged me in my lifetime. Not that I will write here only about politics. There will be much of human interest woven in with the politics, and I hope that what I say will not be only for what Nietzsche called 'ears related to our own'. While I was writing at first primarily for my family and friends, I am hopeful that others who share some of my several interests will feel inclined to browse in these pages.

I have started here with some thoughts about time, and what we remember as time passes, because memories are fickle. While I have been writing about my life, I picked up a book about time by Jay Griffiths, entitled *Pip … pip … A Sideways Look at Time*, in which she reviews the many meanings we give to time and makes an interesting suggestion. For men time is like an arrow, as the astro-physicist Arthur Eddington saw it, because of 'the one-way property of time, which has no analogue in space'. But for women Griffiths believes that time is circular. The signs for men and women are different – respectively the arrow and the circle, the blade and the chalice.

It is Old Father Time whose chronicles and chronometers record our passing days and as the Great Reaper at the close will cut us down, while Mother Earth holds us in her arms and suckles us. Once every month the moon circles the earth and the female body responds. Our lives are divided up by celestial time, not only by the day and night and by the lunar months, but by the year of the earth's rotation around the sun, with the solstices and equinoxes. Farmers, many of whom especially in the Third World are women, share women's concern with cycles of time, and have given to our language that phrase about 'getting round to it some time', as they do the round of their stock and fields, the 'daily round, the common task' of John Keble's *Christian Year*.

Only the week is a human invention. The ancient Chinese and Egyptians had ten days, ten fingers to count on. The Sumerians over 4,000 years ago gave us not only the 60 minute hour and 24 hour day, but a seven day week with one rest day, the sabbath in Greek and Hebrew, the Lord's Day. Why seven? That started with the observation of the sun and the six nearest planets, 'seven for the seven stars in the sky', and we can tell this from the names of the days – in English, Sunday, Mo(o)nday, Satur(n)day, and then we have the Norse names, but in French there is Mardi for Mars, Mercredi for Mercury, Jeudi for Jupiter, Vendredi for Venus. One by one the religions have taken them over. Seven seems to have been a magic number for measuring time, distance and collectives. We still say that 'she is in her seventh heaven', and Christ, when asked 'Shall I forgive him till seven times?', said '… till seven times seven'. We keep a thing seven years, count the seven ages of man, suffer from seven deadly sins, have seven golden candlesticks, wear seven veils and seven league boots, tell of a man with seven wives and 'seven maids with seven mops'. Lawrence of Arabia wrote *Seven Pillars of Wisdom*, John Berger wrote *A Seventh Man,* while William Empson offered seven types of ambiguity – always sevens.

An important aspect of time is waiting, both deferring action and expecting it. But waiting has the other sense of serving. 'They that wait upon the Lord shall renew their strength', in Isaiah's words, reveals the connection. Quakers practise this waiting in their silent meetings and gain strength from the practice, as I know from my own experience. It is a good corrective for men who can't wait. Much of the time of women, who have historically been servants of their men, consists in waiting – as waitresses, ladies-in-waiting, expectant mothers, attending to patients, mothering, charring (originally taking your turn), in Waitrose – and then in meditation, in dream-time, where myths are made. Women are the great writers of fiction and I notice a growing practice in novels of starting at the end and circling back to the beginning. A beautiful example is Arundhati Roy's *The God of Small Things*. I shall start at the beginning but I shall circle round before coming to the end.

One interesting thing about time is having a watch. I can remember the first watch my parents gave me with a leather strap when I went to my boarding school. I was not at all well organised and often forgot to wind it up each evening and had to ask others what time it was. I suppose I had a watch at Oxford, but I have no memory of it. When I arrived in Egypt I found a fine Swiss watch, which was *wasserdicht* (waterproof) so I swam with it on in the Gezira swimming pool and wore it for at least thirty years. Then after several cleanings, our watch-mender in Chesterfield told me that it was beyond repair. Eleanor my wife gave me hers, which she had bought at the same time in Cairo. She had a beautiful gold watch, given to her on her 21st birthday by her parents, which she had not taken to the Middle East, and she wore that thereafter.

I always had an expandable metal strap on my watch and this broke when we were in China. I went to a supermarket in Shanghai to buy a new one, because I had been told that the strap was made in China. The salesman refused to sell me a new one and insisted on repairing the old one. This took him some time and I got worried that I should miss our coach. Very reluctantly, he sold me a new one, which has lasted to this day – 25 years. Unfortunately, the watch itself has recently started going wrong. I have twice bought cheap battery driven ones, while mine was being mended, and each time the strap has broken, where it is attached to the watch. I bought my present watch in Kings Norton with Annette five years ago, and have just had to have the strap replaced and a new battery inserted. Nothing is made to last for any time these days. But I was talking about my time.

'Once upon a time; and a very good time it was' is how James Joyce opens his self-portrait. It fits very well for my own life, and I have to add, as most storytellers do, 'a long time ago'. For indeed 95 years seems a long time. I have had a good time in my life, but the years of my childhood and youth, as I look back on them, seem idyllic. I was born on the Ides of March, when Julius Caesar was warned of his imminent death. I have lived for many more years than his 56, but done far less. Why should I write about them? I suppose it is because I think that I have a good story to tell. This is not, however, primarily an essay in autobiography. My mother always warned me that it would be very self-indulgent, and some contemporary autobiographies have confirmed her view for me. It is rather an attempt to record for my grandchildren and for others who might be interested what it was like to be born in the first quarter of the Twentieth Century and to have lived through the last three quarters and the beginning of the next quarter in a relatively wide range of experiences.

This book, however, is chiefly a book about ideas as well as actions, about the development of my ideas over time – on history, politics, economics, literature, art, music – about emotions, my loves, as well as about happenings, about how to put my ideas into practice. I don't want to pretend to any great originality. I think about ideas according to the origin of the word, in Greek, as ways of seeing – 'in my mind's eye' to use that lovely metaphor, but it is an essential part of our human nature to be a social being so that this book is not about a lone hermit dreaming of new worlds in some desert cave. Language is the product of human relations, of seeing and conversing with others. A solitary being, an 'idiot' in Greek, would not speak, like monks who have taken the vow of silence. But I am not just a social being. I am a political being. The word derives from living in a *polis*, a Greek city-state, where the affairs of the city are the business of all free men. I have always regarded the affairs of the society I live in as my business. This book is inevitably, therefore, a political statement as much as a personal statement.

I do not know when my life will end, but I have continued writing into the year 2013. Many people said that 'the world changed' on September 11th 2001. I have to say that in many ways it seemed to me to start on another cycle of violence that took us all back to 1914-18.

The world is changing rapidly and we need to learn lessons from the past. We give names to past periods of history, and in this periodisation the epithets we attach to the periods are interesting. Such epithets tend to be what one would properly call 'political'. Eric Hobsbawm began his Nineteenth Century with the *Age of Revolution* and ended it with the *Age of Empire,* but for J.L. Marvin it was *The Age of Hope,* and when Gladstone died, in 1898, he said that he had 'presided over a revolution'. It seems that since then the speed of change has accelerated.

I have on my shelves a little pamphlet which is the Romanes Lecture delivered in Oxford on 14 June 1935 by Professor Gilbert Murray. From the inscription on the cover it appears to have been given to me by his wife, Lady Mary Murray, at Christmas that year. It is entitled *Then and Now: The Changes of the Last Fifty Years.*

He describes the 'Victorian Age' in which he grew up as an age of cosmos, well ordered and peaceful. He was, however, a long way from being a typical Victorian. He was a radical and a humanist, as I shall discuss later. Nor were Victorian Liberals all of a piece. Before being accepted by Lady Mary into the Howard household at Castle Howard, Gilbert Murray had to pass the tests with Lady Carlisle of all the following: Temperance, Home Rule, Women's Suffrage, Free Trade and general radicalism.

Perhaps the most remarkable aspect of the Victorian order was that the state hardly impinged on the lives of the law abiding and was to be recognised mainly in the postman and the occasional policeman and in celebrations of royal occasions. There was no requirement of military service. No licences were required for a car or driving tests, no passports were needed for travel abroad and no limits on changing money. Foreigners, moreover, could spend their lives in Britain without permits or informing the police. The state imposed some rules on employers regarding hours of work and safety in factories. Income tax of a few pence in the pound was levied and children had to be sent to school up to the age of 13.

After 1914 all this was to change. The state moved into every area of people's lives and began to spend not 10% but 30% of the nation's income. But despite all this Gilbert Murray could only describe the Victorian age of cosmos as having descended by the 1930s into chaos and disorder – twenty-five million dead in the World War, mass unemployment, wheat being burnt in Canada, herring thrown back into the sea in Scotland, all to keep the price up, the conquest of the air used for aerial bombardment, the rise of dictators and no international organisation capable of restraining them, a servile and licentious press, and everywhere a loss of confidence and a decline from reason into all sorts of unreason – faith healing, psychiatry and xenophobia.

And so it went on after the 1930s. I have called it a 'century of convulsion' as well as of rapid change, 'convulsed' in its literal sense of pulled hither and thither. In writing about the first half of the century, Murray, the great Greek scholar, compared his age with the years of collapse of Greek civilisation after 5th century Athens and, to Lady Mary's discomfiture, he would have included Christianity among the other unreasoning forms of Greek religion that followed. Lady Mary was an active Quaker and as such a dear friend of my parents. When she wished Gilbert to give one of his books to me and my first wife, Frances, on our engagement, he selected *Stoic, Christian and Humanist,* his latest, and we overheard the following amusing exchange, which I tell in more detail later:

> Lady Mary: 'No, Gilbert, I do not think thee should give them that book; it might undermine their faith.'
> GM: 'If their faith is so easily undermined, it is not worth holding.'

I still have the book duly inscribed and dated 11 May 1940, and I notice that GM signed it for me and for Frances Russell, her mother's name, as her mother was

Bertrand Russell's first cousin. I do not recall whether Frances read it, she was not at all religious, but Lady Mary was not far wrong. I was deeply impressed. Although I had been in the Society of Friends for four years, and quite happy in it, I responded warmly to the Stoic faith, particularly in its Comtian form, which emphasised the long millennia of social living that had made human nature co-operative as well as competitive. Without any supernatural support, I accepted the idea of being as good as one could be from one's nature, in whatever one was doing. I was not moved by hope of reward, certainly not of one in the 'hereafter', though it was nice when I got rewarded and irksome when I didn't, but not too worrying. When I decided, in the end, to become a teacher, it seemed to me to be of immense importance that I should be a good teacher, like a good carpenter or a good doctor. On leaving the Society of Friends, some years later, I found in the humanism of Murray's Comteian beliefs, deeply rooted as it was in Greek Stoicism, my spiritual home.

I was convinced at the same time by GM's rejection in those essays of any expectation of an afterlife. My father had told me that he held no such belief. But I was surrounded by people, whom Murray described as having a clear conviction of the supernatural, which he could not share, although he was visited by a priest on his deathbed, at the request of his daughter. I along with many others do not believe that GM died a Catholic. In calling himself 'religious', he used that word not in any dogmatic sense, but in the sense that he makes clear in his *Five Stages of Greek Religion,* of having 'a consciousness of a vast unknown' beyond our reasoning. That is quite different from believing in some afterlife. But I am assured by his grandson, Sandy, that the priest who came to him at the request of his Catholic daughter, as he was dying, blessed him and administered extreme unction on the grounds of his recognition of that vast unknown.

Murray's vision in his lecture of the condition of his times is, of course, an exaggerated one, both of the positive order of the Victorians – it was a highly repressive order for the poor at home and the colonial peoples abroad – and of the negative disorder of the 1930s. But, at the end, he does offer to the youth of his day the 'outline of a great crusade, the prospect of a heroic future'. I underlined these words in my copy at the time, and also his earlier words with which he sets out the tests to be applied to a social order:

> 'first how far it protects the weak, reduces human suffering, and encourages a spirit of good will in daily life; and secondly what heights it reaches or is capable of reaching in the things of the intellect and the spirit.'

Murray concluded that:

> 'Our age comes very high indeed in the first, and surely high also in the second – an age of magnificent achievement, of far more magnificent possibilities, though threatened by grave dangers and deep-rooted flaws to be overcome.'

I see that I have placed a tentative question mark in the margin of my copy at the claim to 'magnificent achievement', but I think I was at that time inspired by the idea of a 'great crusade' and 'a heroic future'.

I feel the need, moreover, to defend Gilbert Murray and his generation of English liberals (small 'l') from the traducing they have suffered at the hands of conservatives like Correlli Barnett. In the chapter 'Audit of War' at the beginning of his *The Collapse of British Power* (and expanded later into a whole book of the same title), Barnett blames 'the moral change' which followed Wellington's victory at Waterloo and changed the British character from being 'thoroughly hard-nosed and aggressive in foreign policy', of which Barnett approves (he must be pleased with Mr Blair) into one that Barnett finds 'left them fatally unprepared to meet the challenges of the determined imperialists guiding the nations in the Twentieth Century'. This 'moral change' he blames on both 'the nonconformist sect, which converted generations of the lower middle classes and "respectable" working classes' and on 'the Church of England public school, which by 1900 had re-made the crudely *arriviste* middle classes and the old upper classes alike according to the ideal of a Christian gentleman'.

I have no desire to defend the latter. In my education I fear that I imbibed some of its arrogant elitism. But the former I will defend to the death, partly because I was brought up in such a sect and owe much that is best in my character to that upbringing, especially my pacifism, which is what Correlli Barnett so hates and despises. Mainly, I will defend the nonconformist sect in Britain not only for its pacifism but also because it has been the foundation of such real democracy that we have, and of the Labour and trade union movement that has nourished that democracy. When I come to write about the influence of William Temple on my formation, I will quote at some length what he said on this aspect of the English democratic tradition. My father taught me to see in John Ball, John Bunyan, William Blake and William Morris the roots of democracy and of the idea of progress towards an earlier dreamed of English Utopia. John Ruskin once said, 'I do not live because I learn. I learn because I live'. And it keeps me going on learning – always seeking.

It must be hard for anyone born in the second half of the twentieth century to imagine what it was like to live in the first half. This was overshadowed by the two World Wars – 1914-18 and 1939-45. We called the first 'The Great War' until the Second came. Those who were born in the first half of the century, as I was, were haunted by war and by the fear of war. Yet, it seems that by living with this fear we became inured. It is very noticeable that, while Americans have been overwhelmed and disoriented by the terrible bombing of New York and Washington on 11 September 2001, Europeans who had experience of war, or knew of it from their parents, have remained quite calm, even though all expected that the next target for Al Qaida would be in Europe. We all thought, before 1940, that the German bombing of London would be a much worse experience than it proved to be. Of course, I was lucky. Although I was in London in the East End where the bombing was worst, I survived – like the overwhelming majority. But it made me hate war, the misery and destructive violence of it, from actual experience, where I had only had the lessons of a loving family before.

I was in every way lucky – not only in that I survived two world wars but in my endowment and in the place of my birth. This continuing contrast of happiness and fear gives me a certain perspective, but it must be recognised as a very narrow perspective. It is that of a man, from a cultural minority, born into a middle class, relatively well-to-do, nonconformist English family. This meant in effect living in a small and prosperous island off the north-west coast of one of the less populated continents of the world. When I was growing up, we still thought of Britain as the centre of a great empire, whatever attitude we took to that fact, and I was brought up to feel less than proud of it. As a boy I read Rudyard Kipling's *Kim* and learnt that the 'Great Game' was keeping the Russians out of India. The British were as ruthless in suppressing colonial revolts as the Russians in Chechnya or the Americans in Yugoslavia, and both of them in turn in Afghanistan. For just a little time in the middle of the Twentieth Century, it seemed that we might begin to settle international problems by peaceful means, but it was not to be. I shall have to explain why not.

What sort of time is my time? My life began and was ending with the bombing of Afghanistan. The British occupied that country in 1919 and were repelled, as they had been in 1842, but part was incorporated into India (now Pakistan) then under British rule and, throughout the 1920s and 30s, there were British forces in Egypt and Palestine and other Arab lands. As children we learnt to support King Amanullah who sought to create a strong democratic state in Afghanistan, but was soon toppled because of his friendly relations with the newly established Soviet Union. My wife Eleanor's brother-in-law, Paul Terry, resigned as a pilot in the Royal Air Force because he did not approve of bombing Arab villages. The RAF under the formidable command of Lord Trenchard opposed the banning of aerial bombing, which was being discussed in the League of Nations in the 1930s, because such aerial control was necessary, he believed, to maintain law and order, without the costly deployment of ground forces. That sounds familiar. I feel no prouder of being British under the leadership of Mr Blair, who has led the country into five wars – in Yugoslavia, in Afghanistan, in Iraq, in Libya and in Sierra Leone. One wonders, where next?

For reasons that must be to do with my Quaker upbringing I never felt proud to be British, rather half ashamed. When in my youth I read in novels by Rider Haggard of forced labour in the Empire, by Margaret Mitchell of slavery in America, by Conrad of racial prejudice, by Trollope of contempt for Jews, by Galsworthy of the horror at marriage to an infidel, I was amazed. Were we not all human? Perhaps because Quakers have no dogma, but just a belief in 'that of God in every man', they are supremely tolerant. It makes for easy living, but also for some smugness. I think of the word 'divine' in its original Greek sense of the god of daylight (diurnal), as being clearly seen, not anything supernatural. The Greek meaning of seeking was not of beauty but of what was right (well designed). When the Quaker school in York which I attended had to be evacuated from fear of invasion, in 1939, the Catholic Ampleforth College received them. They did not receive the Anglican school in York, St. Peter's. I always supposed that the Quaker's lack of dogma protected them, and felt rather pleased about it. Although I knew that we were different from most other people in England, I didn't feel at all excluded, perhaps rather superior. Some questionnaires ask you to state your race. I enter 'human'. I don't want to be thought of as 'Caucasian' any more than as a 'Brit'.

There is a saying of Theodor Adorno's: 'It is part of morality not to be at home in one's home'. This was applied to exiles such as Joseph Conrad, James Joyce and Henry James who were supposed to have deeper insight into the human condition as a result of their exile. E.H.Carr wrote a book about 19th century Russian exiles, called *Romantic Exiles*. Edward Said, himself an exile, wrote much about the trauma of homelessness. I have often thought of myself as an outsider. I think it has made me what some colleagues, professors, readers and senior lecturers at Sheffield University once, apparently, said of me, when I was nominated for a chair, but turned down: 'The man is not clubbable'. Although I love company and good talk, I took it as a compliment.

I had very good friends at the University – Royden Harrison, John Halstead, Bob Heath, Teodor Shanin, Bill Carr – but when some said that I was not 'clubbable', I think they meant that I did not fit into the *mores* of the Senior Common Room. There, much of the talk among the members was of what they had done in the War, an unwelcome surprise to me as a pacifist who could not join in. I alienated some by having a 'posh' car, an *Alvis* open tourer, which I had bought with some money my Aunt Fran had left me. I also always dressed very neatly in a suit and tie, with polished shoes. It would have been insulting to dress carelessly among my coal-mining students who all came in their best Sunday clothes for their educational day release. I don't think that I missed anything, and in some circles not being a professor was a positive advantage. I did attend a select Extra-Mural dining club, but once only, and at Extra-Mural gatherings I felt happiest among the Irish and Scots – and not only for their drinking habits.

There are several strands woven together in the meaning of being outside home and the loss of homeland. There is, first, the horror of ethnic cleansing and religious or political persecution, which results in a life in refugee camps and the breaking up of family and friends. This may last for years, but even when exiles settle in a new land there is evidently a deep sense of loss and a desire to return 'home'. This surprises me because 'home sweet home' has always been where my loved ones were. Only those who have lived and worked on the land for generations, and own it as their own, will feel deprived by the loss of place. Most people move away from 'home', when they marry or change jobs, and this may take them to countries other than that of their birth, where they may think of themselves as expatriates but not necessarily exiles.

When I say that I am 'not at home in my own home', I mean that I do not feel strongly English or British. This is partly due, as I say, to my inherited pacifism. I do not feel that British is best, or that Europeans have any right to superiority. I feel no loss of pride if England loses at cricket or football. I feel guilty that we have a lousy Health Service, but that is because I am sorry for the patients and think that I might have done more to preserve it, and this is, anyway, nothing to do with nationalism. I can, however, understand the love of a peasant for his land, because I know how it feels to have laid every stone in the walls and paths, planted every tree and bush, made the vegetable beds and fruit cages and sown the lawns in our Derbyshire garden and rebuilt a ruined farm, together with Eleanor my love, and I wanted to stay there until I died. Some of my family and friends were nearby. It was a terrible loss to have to leave. But I cheerfully left the first beautiful home and garden and orchard that Eleanor and I made together from an old Essex alehouse and nearby cottage. I was young then, but I left again, much later, with Annette. My point is that 'home' does not mean for me a national home. This is probably just because I have always had a secure family home. I can then try to understand those who have lost, or never had, such a home, looking, as both the Jews and the Arabs do, for the security of a land that they can call their home.

In writing about my own life I have had to think hard about the old problem of nature and nurture. It has become fashionable to attribute all our behaviour to the genes we inherit. I have never accepted that view of the matter and was glad to hear that in the human genome only 30,000 genes were found and not the 300,000 that some were expecting. The idea of 'selfish genes' determining our behaviour seemed then that much less likely. I had always imagined since I read Marx and Engels on dialectics that development followed from the interaction of seed and soil, the varied response of seeds to different soils. As a gardener, that made sense to me. I have to add, after reading *Is there a God gene?*, that the evident differences in character between pairs of identical twins, brought up together, the one extrovert and the other introvert, does suggest a genetic origin, but why the author sees extroverts as more 'mystical' than introverts I don't understand.

I have an ebullient spirit. I have never had a bout of depression. I felt very lonely in 1936 in Germany. I should not have done. I perfected my German, I learnt to ride performing horses, I learnt how to pole vault. I was certainly frightened by the rise of the Nazis to power, but in our *Landschulheim* we had no *flaggenparad* in the morning, but only classical music, mainly Bach played on the piano by the music master. One of the teachers, the French teacher, gave me a book by Albert Coue, and I learned to recite each morning, 'Every day and in every way, I am getting better and better'. It didn't, frankly, do me much good but, fortunately, I found a girlfriend. I was given the job in my English class of producing Shaw's *Pygmalion,* and I fell in love with the girl who played Eliza Dolittle. At the end of term I took her in my little car for a short tour in Germany before I went to Berlin to the Krauses, about whom more later. Making lady friends, as well as good male friends, has perhaps been my saving grace, though it has got me into trouble.

I have always felt happy with the body and mind that I inherited, and believed strongly in my capacity to make a success of all the enterprises I have undertaken,

Michael in the 1960s

without ever embracing Sartre's idea of an absolutely free individual. But what of the soil? I have mentioned my privileged upbringing. I knew that there was a really nasty world outside my happy home, and I inherited a powerful sense that being so fortunately placed I had a duty to do something to make the world a better place. How far have I fulfilled it? I have always done my Quaker duty of giving a tenth of my income to charity, but that is not enough. It is what you give your life to that is important, as I learnt early on from reading John Ruskin's *The Crown of Wild Olive* and *Unto this Last.* I did what I thought was right but what mattered was that I enjoyed doing it. The world has certainly changed but, in most ways, it seems not for the better. When I write about my pacifism I will say something about what makes men fight, and it is mainly men, but yet capable, also, of co-operating peacefully. There is evidently a spectrum in our characters ranging from aggressively competitive to pacifically co-operative, with men on average more competitive and women more co-operative. It is through the combination of both characteristics that humanity has survived, and the current excess of competitiveness may not be sustainable. And women would end wars tomorrow if it was in their power to do so.

Ruskin College, Walton Street, Oxford

CHAPTER 1

Birmingham and Oxford
in the 1920s-30s

The period covered by this chapter is from 1918 to 1929. In 1918, the Great War was still raging with horrendous losses of life on both sides. In 1916, conscription for military service had been introduced in Britain, and those who opposed this like my father and Bertrand Russell were imprisoned. There were severe food shortages, owing to German U-boats sinking ships in the Atlantic carrying grain supplies. Zeppelin raids on British factories had begun in 1917. The war ended with an Armistice in 1918, but many shortages continued. The US and European economies soon recovered, with the exception of Germany, which was reduced by the victorious Allies to near starvation conditions. In 1921, Ireland was divided between the mainly Catholic south, which became Eire, and the mainly Protestant north, which remained in the UK. In 1924, a Labour Government under Ramsay MacDonald was elected with a small majority.

In 1917, Lenin in Russia had brought together a Communist Party which dominated the newly created Soviet Union. The Labour Government in Britain was brought down in 1926, in part because of supposed Soviet influence on Labour – in a faked 'Zinoviev letter'. The coalminers in Britain declared a General Strike in 1926, which was supported by the railwaymen and some other trade unions, but failed to achieve its objective of higher wages and more trade union power. A Conservative Government under Stanley Baldwin returned Britain to the Gold Standard to hold gold to underwrite the value of the pound sterling. In 1928, all women over 21 were allowed to vote and, in 1929, a second Labour Government was elected. This collapsed in the worldwide economic crisis of 1929, which had begun in the USA, and the Labour Government was replaced in 1930 by a National Government of all parties under Ramsay MacDonald as Prime Minister.

I once told my mother that I was writing an autobiography. She warned me that that would be very self-indulgent. 'But, mother,' I said, 'I have such a wonderful opening sentence: I was born during a Zeppelin raid, while my father was in Wormwood Scrubs'. 'Only, Michael dear,' she replied, 'it is not true: the raid was over, and your father had been given one week's compassionate leave to be moved to Canterbury Gaol'. 'Thank you, mother,' I said, 'that gives me a whole chapter to write about Quaker honesty!'

My father was certainly an important person by any standard. He was born in Leeds in 1887. His father was Alfred Kemp Brown. These Browns came from a long line of Quakers, going back to George Fox, living over the years in Yorkshire, Hertfordshire, Essex and Sussex. My father's mother, Emma, was a Barratt, from a Quaker farming family in Lincolnshire. The Browns had married into other Quaker families, not only into the Kemps of Lewis, but the Grovers of

North View.   **South View.**

VIEWS OF CANTERBURY. I & II.

The Pilgrim Way. I.

Knight & Squire & Reeve, Pardoner & Friar,
They're a motley crowd of pilgrims in
Geoffrey Chaucer's Tale,
In the Tabard Inn at Southwark you will
find them by the fire
With a shout for good St. Thomas & a toast
of Kentish ale.

O the Pilgrim Way is a merry way, & it
winds across the Downs,
And we are bound on pilgrimage to
Canterbury Town.

Socialist & Anarchist, Catholic & Quaker,
We're a motley crowd of pilgrims, when you
come to write the Tale,
But we're vowed to Lady Peace, and we never
will forsake her,
So here's to good St. Thomas & Canterbury
gaol!

O the Pilgrim Way, etc...

The Pilgrim Way. II.

I think that in this place we are not alone
Here died the rebel priest who dared in vain
Defied his King for conscience, & was slain
Ingloriously, upon the altar stone.
And hither to his tomb in centuries gone
Came knights & squires in many a Pilgrim train
To heal their bodies & their spirits' pain,
And paid their vows, silently one by one.
The Pilgrim Way still wanders over the Weald,
Here a great highroad, there a grassy line
The sheep have followed, passing from field
to field,
Then lost in some deep wood without a sign.
But we have rediscovered it, & we yield
Our pilgrim offerings at thy quiet shrine.

Views of Canterbury Gaol and poems by Alfred Barratt Brown

FATHER OF LIGHTS

Here in my prison cell the Sun has been
A kindly visitor to cheer my mind
Quietly he creeps the window-bars between
And slowly steals along the wall to find
My face, and finding, gently touches me
With a warm sense of joy; then passes on
To other cells, and leaving silently
With a consolatory kiss — is gone.
Father of lights! in this I see thy love
But Thou art ever here. No prison bars
Can hinder Thee, and Thou dost not remove
Thy Presence like the Sun and the other stars.
Thou dost abide. We are not bound but free
And strange new liberty we here have won,
Who know the Light that comes to all from Thee,
In solitude our great companion.

Pentonville — August 1916

HEIMWEH

Dart of a swallow across the blue
Speeding home to his mate in the nest.
So does my heart fly home to you.

(Domine, cor inquietum est!).

Canterbury — May 1919

TO MICHAEL

Hebrew = Like to God

Michael, little Michael, four months old today,
Why is thy father all this while away?
Has he forgotten his little baby son?
Mother shall tell thee, so listen little one.

Once there was a Michael, an Archangel he,
Fought a great dragon, and won the victory:
Still there are dragons for all of us to slay
And father is in prison fighting one today.

Fighting to save thee and other little ones.
Michael and all angels — from bayonets and guns,
So that *you* shall not be made to
fight and kill each other.
(St. Michael and All Angels, guard him
   and thee and mother)

Michael the Archangel prayed to God for grace,
Prayed that he might have a smile like God
   upon his face,
Michael, little Michael, with thy merry little nod,
Smile upon thy mother with the smile of God.

Michael, little Michael, four months old today
Why is thy Father all this while away?
No, he's not forgotten his little baby son
Soon he will be coming back, so sleep,
   my little one.

Wormwood Scrubs Prison — June 1918

Father's poem to Michael and Geoffrey Morland's music

A.B.B.

dedicated to Michael Barratt Brown by the Composer.

words by A. Barratt Brown.
　　　Wormwood Scrubs. July 1918
music by Geoffrey Morland.
　　　Dorchester. Christmas 1918.

Arundel, and the Barratts into the Horners of Nottingham, which is why my brother Hilary and sister Bridget were given, respectively, those as their second names, Grover and Horner. We always had a painting of Arundel's Swanwick Mill in our living room; it is now in the library of my brother Hilary's farm at Pedruxella, Mallorca. Jemima Horne, who married a Grover, was the daughter of Joshua Horne, the Swanwick miller on the Duke of Norfolk's estate at Arundel – a Quaker working for the aristocracy! Our painting was done by a John Thompson, but Constable did a famous painting of the same mill.

My father studied at Bristol University and Oxford, and got his first job as a lecturer in Psychology at Birmingham University, and was made Vice-Principal of Woodbrooke, the Quaker College. My father was a conscientious objector. He declined to accept absolute exemption from military service granted to some who refused conscription on religious grounds, because he objected to the War not only on religious grounds but also on political grounds, as a member of the Independent Labour Party (ILP) and, along with his friend, Bertrand Russell, campaigned against conscription as an active member of the 'No Conscription Fellowship'.

I was born on the Ides of March 1918, during a Zeppelin raid on the Austin Works. My mother's sister, our Aunt Fran, was with my mother for my birth. There was a serious milk shortage in 1918 because of the u-boats sinking grain supply ships crossing the Atlantic, and Aunt Fran had to scour the farms near Birmingham to get milk for my mother and me. My father came from prison to be present at my birth, and wrote a little poem in prison about me, comparing me rather fulsomely to the Archangel. The poem is reprinted here from my father's *Songs of a Gaolbird*, together with the opening bars of Morland's music that went with it. My father had to go back to prison after a week.

My father spent two-and-a-half years, 1916-1919, in four separate gaols – Dartmoor, Wormwood Scrubs, Pentonville and Canterbury. He wrote a series of poems, *Songs of a Gaolbird,* while in prison, scratched out on pieces of lavatory paper, which my sister, Deborah, and I found and had printed for private circulation with some of our father's drawings and other poems and writings. We had it reprinted in 2013.

My chief memory of Woodbrooke is of the drive into the College from the Bristol Road, a long drive which passed the college and the Principal's lodgings, where we lived, and ended in a wooded lane. Each morning I remember that, at the age of three, my father gave me a jug to take to the Bristol Road. There I met the milkman and climbed on to the milk cart drawn by a horse. When we got to our house, the milkman ladled milk out into my jug from a large churn on the cart, and I had to carry the jug very carefully into the kitchen, rinse a cloth out under cold water and spread it out on top of the jug to keep the milk cool. It was typical of my father that he trusted me with this task. It must be said that he also one day left me outside the bank in my pram and went back home, only to be sent back by my mother. I was apparently found laughing at some ladies who were wondering who had left me. By the side of the kitchen in our house there was a greenhouse, where I could pick the ripe tomatoes. In the grounds, there was a lake, and I remember paddling on the lake in a little boat with my father. When my sister Deborah was born, I heard her wailing in the bedroom upstairs, and I ran up, crying, 'Tom pusscat upstairs!', until my father explained that I had a little sister.

Indeed, father was somewhat forgetful. He took a hat and a tightly rolled umbrella with him every morning when he left home. Caps or hats were universal before the 1939-45 War, and father wore a large brimmed trilby hat. Once, I remember, he was looking for his umbrella everywhere, when mother pointed out that he had it hanging from his arm. 'Thee is hopeless, Barry dear!' she said. 'One day thee'll lose thy head.' 'I'll send thee a trunk call!' came the reply, quick as a flash.

My father was a very considerable scholar with a fabulous memory. He is said to have read *The Times* to his ill mother at the age of three, and could recite the whole of Hamlet and most of the poems in Palgrave's *Golden Treasury* to us. His father was a biblical authority, and taught my father Greek, Latin, Hebrew and Aramaic. When my father went to prison, he was told that he could only take a bible, but he took five, one in each of those languages, and an English Bible designed for the clergy, with blank pages on which to write sermons. On these my father noted the different translations in each language. This bible is still in the library at Friends House in London.

Grandpa Brown travelled all over the world in the service of the Society of Friends collecting many souvenirs. These included 'five smooth stones from the brook Hebron' such as David used in his sling to slay Goliath. My sister Deb still has this collection. When I knew Grandpa Brown, he lived in Letchworth Garden City. He was mainly of interest to me because he had a crystal wireless set and earphones, on which I could hear music. I clearly remember going out of the house to check that there were no wires coming into the living room. When we moved to the Old Malt House in Westcote Barton, Oxfordshire, Grandpa gave us a then very advanced set with an earth and aerial, and valves and Le Clanche batteries, which needed recharging. It was the music that I loved to hear. The talk was generally beyond me.

In the summer after I was three, my father was appointed Vice-Principal of Ruskin College, Oxford, and we went to live in The Red House on Cumnor Hill, just outside Oxford to the south-west. In 1921, there was a drought, and I remember looking with my father into our well, from which we pumped water for use in the house. The water could only just be seen at the bottom of the well. Our next-door neighbour up the hill was A.D. Lindsay, Master of Balliol College. Usually, he and my father went into Oxford on their bikes, but sometimes on very wet days they shared a Hansom cab. I thought Professor Lindsay was a very frightening person with a loud Scottish voice, but his son, Michael, though much older, played with me. My father got much support from Lindsay in getting Ruskin students into University activities, and Lindsay presided over the opening of the new Ruskin buildings, which my father succeeded in raising finance for. That he raised the money in the economic crisis of the 1930s was a considerable achievement.

My father knew very well the story of the founding of Ruskin College and the agreement of John Ruskin in old age to associate his name with it. My father was a great admirer of Ruskin, and had a complete collection of his works at the top left-hand corner of the bookshelves in his study. I inherited these books, and kept them on the top left-hand shelf of my 'best books' case in Robin Hood Farm. When I was about 16, my father gave me Ruskin's *Unto this Last* to read, and I absorbed Ruskin's virulent attack on the capitalist system for the rest of my life. In addition to a great interest in architecture, I also developed my life-long admiration for Gandhi when I saw that he had found *Unto this Last* in South Africa, in 1904, and translated it. More recently, I was fascinated to discover that Derek Wall quoted Ruskin as a 'proto-Green' in his *Green History Reader*, published in 1994. What happy introductions from my father!

Our house was near to the top of Cumnor Hill, just opposite a wood yard. Steam engines pulled tree trunks up the hill to be sawn in the yard. My mother taught me what they were saying as they came up the hill. On the steep part, near the bottom, she said that they were saying, 'Can I do it? Can I do it? Can I do it?' Then, as the slope eased, it became 'I think I can, I think I can, I think I can!' Finally, on the level bit as they approached the yard, they said, 'I've done it, I've done it, I've done it, I've done it!' I really liked that, and stood outside our gate whenever the engines came up with their loads so that I could hear them.

I loved the garden at the Red House. I kept a tame rabbit, and in the orchard we picked apples, which we kept in the attic. I was very sorry to leave after three years and to go to live in the Principal's lodging at Ruskin College in Oxford's Walton Street. Sanderson Furniss, who was the Principal of the College, became too blind to continue, and my father was made Acting Principal and, two years later, Principal. The best thing about Ruskin for me was the long passage to my father's study. My father had had constructed for me a shelf on which I could put my train set – rails, station, shunting yards and fields with animals grazing. I could also go down the passage on my 'kiddy-car' and out into the students' lodgings to their bathroom where I could turn round and come back.

At about six I started to go to the kindergarten of the Girls' High School in Oxford. I was astonished to find that most of the children could not read – something I had been able to do from the age of three or four. The teacher was Miss Aubrey Moore and she had cats which did performing tricks in cages at her house. On my sixth birthday, or perhaps my seventh, I went down to the College bicycle shed, where I guessed that there was a bike for me. There was and I hopped on and went down the hill on it beside Ruskin College. I did not know how to stop, but very fortunately landed up, or rather down, in a pile of saw dust in the woodyard of Hinkins and Frewin at the bottom of the hill. The men there took me home. My mother was appalled, but my father most congratulatory, showing me how to use the brakes – typical of my father who later taught me how to swim by throwing me into the Cherwell, holding on to a rope which he pulled in, to help me dog paddle back to him on the steps of the bathing place. I had no fear of water after that!

From my bedroom at Ruskin I could climb on to a flat roof and look into the main hall, the Buxton Hall. One evening, I climbed out and saw a very large crowd in the hall and a young man presenting a bunch of flowers to a lady who stood up and began to speak. As I couldn't hear what she said, I went back to bed. Many, many years later I read a biography of Marie Stopes and found that she went to Oxford at about the time we were living in Ruskin College. She was refused permission to speak in the Town Hall, and the University closed all its schools to her. So, my father evidently made the Buxton Hall

Gandhi visited millworkers in Darwen, Lancashire, 1931

available. If this was her meeting that I watched, then the real surprise is that the young man presenting the flowers and taking the chair was Evelyn Waugh, before he became a Catholic. It was typical of my father's progressive views that he would make Ruskin open to propaganda for contraception, but he also knew that Marie Stopes's father was a Quaker!

My father had more difficulty when, in later years, Communists and Fascists wanted to use the Hall for their public meetings. He decided to let it be used by both, so long as no uniforms were worn and there were no 'bouncers' ejecting people who asked questions. As far as our family was concerned, the Buxton Hall was a place where we could have parties and hear concerts from performers especially invited by my father. I remember the Spooner sisters singing, daughters of Professor Spooner, famed for his 'spoonerisms' such as 'The Fast and Merry Road', not Marston Ferry, and Frank Howes, *The Times* music correspondent and his wife, and a small opera company.

There were some very famous people invited by my father to Ruskin when I was young. In 1930, when Mahatma Gandhi attended the Commonwealth Conference, I sat on Gandhi's (very sharp) knees to be told that I should remember all the little boys in India whose fathers were in prison, just as my father had been, for holding and expressing views that challenged the government. When I went to lecture in India many years later, this story got me entrée to all sorts of interesting people. Then, on another occasion, I was carried on Paul Robeson's shoulders and discovered what lovely firm curly hair he had. My father took me to Stratford to see his performance of Othello. A little less

*Paul Robeson sings with
US shipyard workers, 1942*

famous was Kenneth Lindsay, MP for Oxford University, who carried me round Oxford on his shoulders while canvassing. Much later, during the London blitz in 1940-41, I met up with Kenneth Lindsay again and showed him round some of the air-raid shelters where I was working with the Friends' Ambulance Unit, ending up our tour with a drink at the Prospect of Whitby in Shadwell.

When I was about ten, my father took me to Bertrand Russell's school at Beacon Hill in his brother's house in Sussex. I was shown into a room where an oldish man was sitting on the floor with some children. I was amazed to learn that this was the man my father called 'the greatest philosopher of our time'. Russell called for me to sit by him on the floor, and after he had settled the other children with books to read, he turned to me and said, 'Now, Michael, what is the biggest problem of your life?' I thought for a minute, and said, 'I am very small!'. 'That doesn't matter,' Russell replied. 'It is between here and here that matters,' and he put one hand below his chin and the other above his head, and I noticed that on a quite small body, he had a big head. I also looked in a mirror afterwards and saw that my head was about the same size as other boys' heads. This was all very reassuring. Russell left his wife Dora shortly afterwards, and my mother didn't want me to see the person she called 'Bertie' any more. I told my mother that Dora was 'a silly old cow!' and I did not blame him for leaving her. Many years later, I read that before their separation, Dora had had another affair and Bertie, to protect her, had pretended that the child of that affair was his.

Bertie's marriages were not a success, until the last one, to Edith. When I met his first wife, Alys Pearsall Smith, near Leith Hill in Surrey, I rather liked her. She was a Quaker, whose brother wrote two lovely books, *Trivia* and *More Trivia*. But Bertie really deserted Alys for seven years to write *Principia Mathematica*. I met Dora's son, John, who was a friend of my first wife, Frances, at Dartington Hall school; a very sad man who inherited the peerage, but was seriously ill. And I met Bertie's third wife, Patricia Spence, when they lived near Oxford. She was the historian Conrad's mother. I saw something of Edith in connection with the Russell Foundation and liked her. But Bertie's lover, Colette O'Niel, her name as an actress, whom both my father and I really liked, he never married, but kept contact with all his life. This was 'Conny', as my father called her, Lady Constance Malleson, married to Miles Malleson. There is a letter in Bertie's papers to Conny, written in 1916, in which he complains about a heavy day with the Quakers at a meeting of the No Conscription Fellowship but adds, 'Barry [that is my father] is alright; he has a sense of humour'.

My father was not himself musical, but was determined that his children should be introduced to music at an early age. So, he bought a pianola, with a box full of rolls to play. I can well remember, aged about four, sitting on his knees and pretending to play the piano keys, while my father pumped away at the pianola. We also had a phonograph and records. My father's favourite was of master Hugh Clough, a chorister, singing 'Oh, for the wings of a dove!' Mine was a jazz song – 'In eleven more months, and ten more days, they're going to let me loose! I shall be out of this calaboose!' – and Debussy's children's songs, especially the 'Teddy Bears' Picnic'.

In the years before we had radio, let alone television, we entertained ourselves with imaginary games, play acting and dressing up. Often the game was to guess what was being acted - silently in 'dumbcrambo', with speech in 'charades'. Another version was called 'animal, vegetable or mineral' and you could ask questions of the actors to guess what they were acting. Our father was immensely imaginative and often extremely funny, even a little bawdy, as when he referred to the tarts of Tartini and translated the Cat and Fiddle – the pub on the Derbyshire hills above Buxton, as *la Caton fidele*, the faithful tart. But he really shocked our maiden aunts when he mis-pronounced Rimsky-Korsakov as 'Ripsky corsets off'. He was a great one for inventing doggerel to explain complex English words. One, I remember, went as follows:

> *Moses supposes his toes to be roses,*
> *But Moses supposes ERRONEOUSLY*
> *For nobody's toeses are composed of roses.*
> *As Moses supposes his toeses to be.*

My mother seemed to spend a lot of time having more children, but my father always had time for us, as we grew up. My great love was for our nanny, Con, and I can still think of sitting on her lap at Ruskin in the windowsill of the nursery. She left us to marry a defrocked clergyman. I felt a prejudice for such persons for a long time afterwards. The picture of me aged five at that time is from a miniature painted by Con's artist sister, Jeannie *(see page 38)*. There will be much more to say about my father in the next chapters. My mother was very caring to me. I had psoriasis on my legs for many years and she put a tar ointment on them every night. I am afraid that I was disrespectful. She once said to me, 'Michael, I know thee knows more than I do, but I know better!' Certainly, it was true that at 12 I knew Latin and Greek and thought her French poor, but she employed a French nanny and insisted that I read a chapter of *Tartarin de Tarascon* with her every day. I tell my grandchildren to see that their children learn a second language very early. It did me much good. My French is still usable, and I found no difficulty in learning German, even teaching in a German *landschulheim*, and

Mother and me

Grandpa Cockshott and me

later mastering Serbo-Croat with, I was told, a Bosnian accent. Spanish and Italian were easy, so like Latin. Portuguese more difficult.

I used to go shopping with my mother in Oxford, and looking back at that time I realise how much has changed in 90 years. Some shops have the same names, Sainbury's, for example, but my favourite shop, Woolworths, with nothing costing more than sixpence or a shilling (5p today), has gone. I could buy a book for a shilling there. Woolworths introduced a weighing machine. You could weigh yourself for a penny and a deep voice spoke your weight. Three other boys and I decided to get onto the weighing stand together, and the voice said 'one at a time, please!' A very fat man got on and received the same response. A grocer's shop really sold things 'in gross'. Butter or lard was cut up according to what you had asked for, and then wrapped up for you. Sugar or salt was sold in the same way, weighed out and put in a paper bag for the quantity you wanted. Milk and cream came from churns to go into jugs or bottles which you brought with you, as I had found in the Bristol Road in Birmingham. As I wrote this, a TV programme was describing 'The Secret Life of Rubbish', unfortunately only too obviously disastrous for the survival of the planet, as we throw away more and more wrapping and bags.

Con was not my only nanny who I fell for. My mother made a funny comment about Nellie the nursemaid we had in Southport who always woke me up with a big kiss. Nellie got married, and my mother said that she had asked her how she liked married life. Her answer, she told me, was, 'Oh, it's loovely, but it ain't half rude!'

As I look back on my childhood, my mother introduced me to many nursery rhymes which I still remember:

> *Ride a cock horse to Banbury Cross*
> *To see a fine lady ride a white horse*
> *With rings on her fingers and bells on her toes*
> *She shall have music wherever she goes.*

> *Baa, baa black sheep, have you any wool?*
> *Yes, sir, yes, sir, three bags full.*
> *One for the master, one for the maid,*
> *And one for the little boy who lives down the lane.*

I always wondered who that was.

And from Lewis Carroll:

> *Humpty Dumpty sat on a wall.*
> *Humpty Dumpty had a great fall.*
> *All the king's horses and all the king's men*
> *Couldn't put Humpty together again!*

And from Edward Lear:

> *The Owl and the Pussy Cat went to sea*
> *In a beautiful pea green boat.*
> *They took some honey and plenty of money,*
> *Wrapped up in a five pound note.*
> *The owl looked up to the stars above,*
> *And sang to a small guitar,*
> *'Oh, lovely Pussy, Oh, Pussy my love,*
> *What a beautiful Pussy you are,*
> *You are,*
> *You are!*
> *What a beautiful Pussy you are!*

I remember all these lines because Annette sang these nursery rhymes when she could remember little else. Such is the peculiarity of an Alzheimer's memory. But, she especially loved cats.

In 1928, women under 30 were allowed to vote in elections. It was called the 'Flappers' vote', and my mother gave me a toy to illustrate it. There were four cut-out wooden figures on a board, in the centre a young lady, and round her the three candidates for the premiership in the election – Stanley Baldwin, Lloyd George, and Ramsay MacDonald. Each candidate was articulated and attached by a string to a knot with a weight under the board. If you swung the weight round, the candidates' figures bent and bowed in turn to the flapper in the centre. When the weight settled, the candidate facing the flapper was the winner. Of course, I always tried to make Ramsay the winner! Much later, it was my mother who introduced me to Bernard Shaw's *Intelligent Woman's Guide to Socialism, Capitalism, Sovietism and Fascism*. This book impressed me greatly in the 1937 edition which she gave me. I re-read the latest 2012 edition, with a foreword by Polly Toynbee, and refer to it later.

Michael aged 5 from a miniature by Jeannie McConell

CHAPTER 2

Oxford, the Cotswolds
and Lancashire, 1930s

The period covered by this chapter is from 1930 to 1935. After 1930, the UK and world economies recovered slowly, but in the weakened economic state of Germany, in 1931, Hitler moved, eventually, to seize power. In the same year, Japan under military leadership occupied Manchuria. Mussolini had come to power in Italy in 1922, so that the democratic world was faced by three dictatorships. A League of Nations was formed with headquarters in Geneva to try and solve international problems peacefully, but it had little effect on the dictators.

A Next Five Years Group was formed in the UK, in 1934, to bring together proposals for democratic planning in the UK as an answer to both fascist and communist planning controls.

In 1934, a Peace Ballot was organised in Britain, which attracted several million signatures for peaceful solutions to international problems, but preparations in the UK for possible war had already begun and were generating economic activity. At the same time, a revolution was taking place in road and air transport. By the late 1920s, Ford in the USA was selling 15 million cars a year and Morris in the UK several hundred thousand. In 1927, the American airman, Charles Lindbergh, flew across the Atlantic, and Amy Johnson from Britain flew non-stop to Australia in 1930. British Overseas Airways was formed in 1935 to take over UK companies that were already flying regularly to the USA, Africa, India and Australia.

My mother was worried, when we moved to Ruskin in 1935, at the lack of gardens and country for us children to play in. The Worcester College gardens were next door, but you had to walk through the College to get to them and they were sometimes closed. So, when I was seven, my parents bought a house in Oxfordshire half-way up the road to Banbury, The Old Malt House in Westcote Barton. We went there at weekends and in the holidays. I loved it. I could climb over the style opposite us, and run past the grazing sheep to the stream below. There I could sail model boats and catch minnows, which I kept in the water tank in our attic. I fed them on ants' eggs, which I found in our garden, until one fish died and my mother smelt it in the drinking water, and the fish had to go back into the stream.

I was very keen on cycling all around Oxfordshire, between the Banbury and Woodstock Roads, among the Tews, and even up to the Rollright Stones above Long Compton. On Saturday in the summer my father played cricket on the ground at Steeple Barton. He went by car and I used to see if I could keep up with him on my bike. The ground was surrounded by trees, and one Saturday there was a horrible accident. A sudden thunderstorm came over, and lightning

Old Malt House

struck one of the trees and killed a spectator, who was standing under it. From then on we rushed back home if we were outside in the thunder.

The Old Malt House had an outside lavatory, which my father called the House of Lords. He placed a stick on the path leading to it, which naturally he called 'Black Rod', to indicate whether it was occupied. The lavatory had an Elsan bucket underneath, which was emptied once a week. The seating was peculiar. There were two openings side by side, and when my sister and I could not find our parents, they were sitting together on the lavatory discussing private matters out of our hearing.

Apart from the fascinating students of my father's, including a Japanese student who played the piano and sent us all to sleep, and the local foundryman who had a steam driven car, the most interesting person I got to know in the village was the then composer of *The Times* crossword puzzles (perhaps the first?) In his study he had shelves all round it with different patterns of crosswords on them, which he would fill in with words and then write out the clues. I remember that he asked me for the name of another Burton that was not on the Trent, and was very impressed when I said, 'On the Water'. I got an extra slice of his wife's delicious parkin for that!

My father wore his scholarship very lightly. He was a cheerful character, who celebrated the 'laughter of Christ', which he descried in the New Testament. He was in many ways a practical man, a keen gardener, who liked to grow his own vegetables. One day, at the Old Malt House, as I wrote in my seven-year-old diary, 'Daddy gave us an "orful" shock'. He arrived in a Morris Cowley car, WL 391. He had come from the Morris Garages in Oxford with an engineer, the only instruction he received. The engineer returned to Oxford by bus, but only after helping my father to manoeuvre the car across the yard into the space under my playroom that became our garage.

My father was very particular about the petrol he bought for the car, which made my friends laugh. It had to be either ROP (Russian Oil Products) or NBM (National Benzole Mixture), the first for obvious political reasons, the second because it came from coal and so helped the coalminers. The car had a 'Stepney' to attach to the wheel if it had a punctured tyre – Stepney, not from East London, but from South Wales where the factory was that made them.

By the garage there was a washroom, and on Monday I had to light the fire under the boiler and help our cook, Mrs Churchill, to wash the dirty linen. It cleaned my grubby hands marvellously. My playroom upstairs looked out on an apple tree and I could climb out onto its branches. I can see a painting of this tree on the wall above me as I write, and I have reproduced a painting of it here with the house behind.

After we had the car, our first visit was to my father's artist friend, Hilda Strange, on the Isle of Wight. Her husband was a scientist working in his back yard on ways to convert seaweed into petrol. Tragically, he blew himself up while making an experiment. In the light of the interest, over eighty years later, in 'the great green hope: seaweed that could help save the planet', (*Guardian* 01.07.2013, page 9), this was not only a personal tragedy, but a human disaster. Our family were just very saddened for Hilda. We could not know that his death halted seaweed research for many years.

We made many trips across England, even to Scotland, generally in the autumn, to the trade union conferences, which my father had to attend. This led to our holidaying near them – Scarborough, Blackpool, Plymouth, Brighton, and Edinburgh. But there were two regular annual trips, to Southport, to my mother's Cockshott family at Christmas, and to my father's sister, Kath, and uncle Percy Davies and family at Easter at St Anne's on Sea. We stopped for a picnic lunch between Nuneaton and Eaton, which pleased my father's sense of humour.

On one journey going to Scotland, we stopped for the night at a farm in Yorkshire on the way. It was summer and very sunny and the car was open. We got very brown, and when the farmer saw us sitting under a haystack having our tea, he said, 'Ee! Anoother dip and they would have been dark!' Before we went to bed, mother and father went off for a walk and disappeared behind a hedge. I got in a panic that they might have another child. We could hardly afford the four of us as it was.

My grandmother, Jane Cockshott, was of Irish/Scottish descent, from Fergusons and Kents. Fergusons had a bad reputation – 'Feargus swore a feud against the clan MacTavish, to murder and to ravish'. I still wear my mother's Ferguson clan tartan scarf. I have got it on as I write. The Kents were Protestant Irish. Mother's uncle was the Master of the Galway Blazers, which I understood was a hunt, and he once started to tell me a story of how he fell off his horse at a high fence, but started to talk about something else before he had finished the story, which seemed to me to be typical of the Irish! Mother had two Kent cousins who lived on the High Street in Waterford, and she told a funny story about them. Apparently, the head of the Guinness family, Lord Iveagh, had a large house in the street and thought that it would be nice if all the houses were repainted, and proposed to offer some financial help. He called on mother's cousins at the front door announcing his name, whereupon the cousins said that they received tradesmen at the back door. To Iveagh's credit, he went to the back door, and they agreed about the painting. I once told this story to an Irishman, who said that he could cap it. When Lord Iveagh was seventy, he held a dinner party at Iveagh Castle, so he was told, and all the landowners were invited, however small their landholding. They sat at the top table, while the other plebeians were seated at long tables below, and that is where the chairman of the Guinness brewing company, Arthur Saunders, found himself! Such is the nature of British class society!

The Cockshotts lived in a house in Queen's Road, Southport, with a gate and formal garden and trees in front and garages and outhouses in a yard at the back opening onto a mews. My grandfather Cockshott was a remarkable man, a foundling, as I understood. Found on the steps of a Liverpool church, he was adopted by the Cockshott family and brought up in Preston. He was largely self-educated, having got himself into a school by learning a poem and reciting it a great speed, which he told me he thought would impress the headmaster. By the time I knew him, he was one of the most distinguished solicitors in Southport and chair of the local hospital board. Each morning, he was collected by a client, Lord Hesketh, in his Rolls Royce to take him to his office in Southport's Houghton Street. Grandpa sent all his children – women as well as men – to boarding school and university, a remarkable thing to do at the end of the nineteenth century. That is how my mother met my father at Oxford.

Grandpa's eldest daughter, our Aunt Winnie, became a don at St. Hilda's College, and wrote a brilliantly researched book on *The Pilgrim Fathers,* first published by Methuen in 1909, reissued in paperback in 2000. When the 1914 war came she enrolled in a Voluntary Aid Detachment (VAD) and nursed soldiers invalided to Malta. After the war, Grandpa persuaded her to take a law degree and join his practice. Like so many other women at that time, she and her sister Frances lost their men in the fighting and never married. They really adopted our family, and Aunt Winnie encouraged me greatly in my history studies after I got polio, and probably helped to pay for them at Oxford.

Grandpa Cockshott was a staunch Conservative, with a drawing of Lord Curzon on the wall at the end of his long dining room table, but he tolerated my father's socialism because of my father's enthusiasm for adult education, which Grandpa shared. Grandpa lent me books on religion and wanted me to study them, and once, when he visited us in Oxford, he asked me to go to a meeting at which Frank Buchman, the leader of the so-called 'Oxford Group', was speaking, at Lady Margaret Hall. Grandpa said that he had observed many religious revivals in his time, and was anxious to see and hear this one. We went, and outside the Hall found a large crowd and lines of parked cars. Grandpa's comment was 'It was Dean Inge who said, "There wont be a queue at the Golden Gate!"' Before Buchman had completed his oration, Grandpa decided to leave, to avoid the crowd – embarrassing for a young boy, but sensible! Grandpa always took a pear on these trips, which he carefully peeled with a silver knife and shared, and put the peel neatly back in the bag.

The other regular visit, besides going to Southport, was to go at Easter to visit Uncle Percy and Aunt Kath and the Davies family, in St. Anne's-on-Sea and then go on to Heys Farm outside Clitheroe, where they managed a Youth Hostel. The house at St. Anne's was right by the sea. We had to sleep with our windows open and, one year, a high tide and strong wind sent spray from the waves on to the beds of my sister and me. Uncle Percy did not think that was anything to worry about. The farm had beautiful views over the valley to Pendle Hill, where George Fox had preached, and rolling moorland to walk on. Uncle Percy seemed to us to be a very important person. One of his favourite injunctions was: 'Eat slowly! Only men in rags, and gluttons old in sin, mistake themselves for carpet bags, and tumble victuals in!'.

Percy Davies was the owner of a textile business in Darwen, but was an active Labour Party member. He had given up nursing a safe Manchester seat to Sir Oswald Mosley, who many years later became the British Fascist leader! Uncle Percy failed to get elected for Skipton in 1945, and was made a peer by Clement Attlee and given a government job as Lord Darwen. He became chairman of the National Peace Council and sponsored a pamphlet on Tito's Yugoslavia, which I wrote with Dr. Doreen Warriner. She was an academic economist, the daughter of a Yorkshire coal and steel owner, but revealed very progressive views when I took her round activities in Yugoslavia organised by the United Nations Relief and Rehabilitation Administration (UNRRA).

As well as visiting my father's sister Kath and Uncle Percy, one year we went to the second wedding of Uncle Bevan Witney, who had married my father's other sister, Edith. She had died before I was around, but her daughter Joyce became a good friend, sharing my Communist sympathies. In my diary describing this event I have made a drawing of a red squirrel which we saw on a tree on our way. I doubt if I saw many more after that until we went to our house in Scotland, in 1969.

Uncle Bevan was an engineer and aroused my father's disapproval by driving an engine in the General Strike. I remember the 1926 strike because one of the Ruskin students went on horseback in a demonstration and he put a red light at night on one of the horse's back legs. Uncle Bevan's second wife was a lovely lady and they had a son who became the head of the old public Royal Mail. Joyce sent me copies of letters sent to her mother from my father in prison. They have the most moving description of the few minutes when the sun could be seen passing his prison window, reminiscent of Oscar Wilde's *Ballad of Reading Gaol*, which father used to read to us with tears in his eyes. The letters were marked first by the sense of comfort that my father experienced from awareness of a presence in his thoughts that he called 'God', and second by the revelation of extraordinary sympathy for conscientious objectors shown by both gaolers and prisoners alike. The drawing and verses, 'two views of Canterbury', are taken from my father's prison diary (*see page* 26).

We moved from Ruskin to North Oxford when I was 11, and The Old Malt House was sold. The new house in Summertown was spacious. It had a living room, dining room and study with a porch onto the garden, a kitchen with separate outside door and dining space for the cook and house maid, and upstairs there were bedrooms for all four children and our parents, and for a nanny, a bathroom and a bedroom for the staff above the garage. When I went to boarding school my room was used as a workroom with the treadle Singer sewing machine in it. Some time in the summer a Miss Mundy came on holiday from Australia, where she was the Lady in Waiting to the Governor's wife, and worked at the machine. She made clothes, lengthened my sisters' dresses, turned sides to middles on our sheets and other such tasks. My father called her 'Gloria', making a pun of the rather appropriate Latin tag, 'Sic transit gloria mundi'.

The house had a good walled garden with fruit trees on one wall. It was very close to the school we all attended, the Dragon School, where we studied classics and the usual subjects but including wood work and much physical training (PT) and games – rugger, cricket and swimming. From the school two wide fields stretched down to the River Cherwell where we swam. My sister Deb was a first class scrum half at rugby. She was a real 'tomboy' who shared with me all our ventures on the scaffolding of the new houses being built near us.

My father went to work on a fixed wheel bicycle, jumping on from a step at the back. Next but one to our house there was a Professor of Logic, Professor Joseph, who also cycled to work. My father found him one day, pumping up a tyre, and noticed that the front tyre was flat, but he was pumping air into the back tyre. My father pointed this out to him, and got the reply from the Professor of Logic, 'Oh, but don't they communicate?'

In the slump of the 1930s, we had many coal miners coming from South Wales, looking for work with the Morris companies. I think that they must have put a mark on the gate to our house, because we so often had miners calling, hoping for a cup of tea, which my mother always had available and a cheese sandwich for them. Professor Joseph was a keen gardener, and one day I noticed that he was shovelling manure that had been delivered outside his house, and a miner hoping for work was asking if he had another job. I heard the Professor's answer, 'Well, if you call it a job, I am the Professor of Logic at the University'. I thought that that was very funny.

Opposite our house in Northmoor Road lived Basil Blackwell, the bookseller and publisher, with his family. I became a great friend of Basil's son Richard, and fell in love with his daughter Penelope. At election times the only houses in the road decorated with yellow for Labour – Laburnum blooms – were ours and the Blackwells. After a few years the Blackwells moved to a large new house on the Thames west of Oxford, and I spent many happy days and weekends canoeing up the Thames with Richard past the 'ten or twelve' poplars at Binsey, which Gerard Manley Hopkins celebrated in a famous poem. Mrs Blackwell was a particularly warm lady, and Basil was only too happy to encourage us to climb up the ladders and browse among the books in his huge library, just as we did later in his bookshop in Oxford, where I spent many hours just reading without having to make a purchase.

When the Blackwells left Northmoor Road, their house was taken by Professor Tolkien and his family. One day, my father told me that Professor Tolkien wanted to read some of his stories to some local children, and suggested that I should go. I went and found the stories unutterably boring – all funny names and no action. A few weeks later, my father told me that Professor Tolkien had some more stories. I am afraid that I said something very rude, which I think I had read coming from F.R. Leavis. 'Oh,' I said, 'Not more fucking elves!' My father was shocked. 'Where did you learn that word?' he asked. I said that I regularly went to Acott's music shop in Oxford to listen to jazz records, and the latest one had the following refrain:

> *Poor old Mose is dead! Oh fuck, fuck, fuck it!*
> *He's kicked the bucket!*
> *Poor old Mose is dead!*

My father was appalled. But I didn't have to listen to any more of Tolkien's stories.

When the Blackwells left Northmoor Road I began to see much more of Tom Maitland and started going regularly to his house in Headington. We played all sorts of outdoor games and excavated a 'house' in the bank under the hedge that formed the boundary then to Pullens Lane. We also acted plays which we made up and performed to Tom's parents, including an adaptation of Sherriff's *Journey's End*. Mr Maitland had been part owner of a large textile company at Broughty Ferry in Scotland. Mrs Maitland was a musician and secretary of the Holywell

Dragon School

Musical Society in Oxford. She was a friend of Sir Hugh Allen who conducted the Bach Choir in the Sheldonian Theatre in Oxford. Tom and I often saw him at meal times. He was a most irascible man who terrified me, but he brought lovely people to the Maitlands. Two of these were Adila Fachiri and Jelly d'Arányi, nieces of Joseph Joachim, the violinist.

In the last holiday we had before leaving the Dragon School, Tom and I went with Tom's parents to Scotland, and after a visit to Broughty Ferry, where Mr Maitland taught us how to use golf clubs, we went to Oban. The Maitlands had hired a sailing boat and crew for a cruise in the Hebrides. Tom and I learnt how to sail her in various weathers and we circled the islands of Rhum and Eigg and Skye. We swam in jellyfish-full lochs and did paintings of the islands. 'Rhum to the left and Eigg to the right over the sea to Skye', speeding on the 'bonnie boat', 'to carry the lad who was born to be king', as the song to Prince Charles Stuart has it.

Many years later, Tom and I had another sailing holiday, just before the Second

World War, when Tom went to North Africa with his tank regiment and was killed. I always looked back on that holiday in Suffolk with special pleasure. We stayed in the Maitland's house in Aldeburgh and sailed on the river. One day we were beached on a sandbank and were told that we would not get off for a year, until there was another such high tide. Luckily, we did get off at the next high tide. I recalled that time at The Maltings, when I met Benjamin Britten and Peter Pears, taking them to a wartime shelter concert in the London Blitz.

My last year at the Dragon School I had to polish up my Greek and Latin verse writing to enter for an Eton scholarship. I was not good enough, but my friend Tom got a scholarship and went to Eton. I then wanted

Michael aged 11

to try for Rugby, but my father had other ideas, and I am very glad that he did. I got a scholarship to Bootham, the Quaker school in York.

I went away to school at thirteen and a half, and was happy to do so. I was very fond of my parents and my father had given me much good and loving advice. They had instilled in me a kind of independence that enabled me very easily to make good friends, as this memoir will reveal. I was always happy at boarding school until the end, and could keep in touch with my parents with weekly letters, no more. My parents did once come to visit me at school, but I don't think more often than that.

In my last term at the Dragon School, I was chosen to play the part of Johnny Moreton in the Kidlington Pageant, complete with wig and breeches, as in the picture. The play was built round a re-enactment of the scene in the painting; 'When did you last see your father?' Puritan roundheads question the young boy about his Cavalier father's absence. The boy says he last saw him in the 'Tower', which to him is not the Tower of London, but what he calls the trunk, which his questioners are sitting on. I am standing by my mother, who in the play was acted by Felicity Fennell from Whitham Abbey. I became a skating partner to my sister in the play, until she became a very much better dancer on skates than I was. I was given the part because of the big parts I had played in Dragon School plays, including Bolingbroke in Shakespeare's *Richard II.*

My Quaker pacifism came into sharp conflict with the church services at the Dragon School and the celebration of VC day in honour of an old Dragon, called Smyth, whose anniversary of winning the Victoria Cross we recognised every year. I was always very moved by Laurence Binyon's verses 'For the Fallen', which are still read out on every Remembrance Day. But my attitude to religion reached the point that I did not take it very seriously. I did like the hymns, especially Bunyan's 'To Be a Pilgrim' and Blake's 'Jerusalem', and I enjoyed reading the lessons.

At the Dragon's we all had to learn poems to recite, and the headmaster, A.E. Lynham, (we called him 'Hum' because he made us hum) gave me special instruction in reading the lessons, so that as a result I got big parts in the school plays. I remember especially that he taught me never to exaggerate, but, like an organ grinder, to let the poem take its own rhythm. I think that I neglected such instruction about reciting with my own children, but I now suggest to my grandchildren that they should give their children not only a second language to learn, but also exercises in reciting. Being able to recite in public is not only good for the memory, but greatly enhances your self-confidence, especially if you are going to be a teacher.

Johnny Morton.

CHAPTER 3

Bootham School,
York in the 1930s

This chapter covers the period 1930 to 1935. Recovery from the slump of 1930-31 in the US and UK was slow. Quaker businesses reached a remarkable height of influence in the 1930s, in banking, brewing, chemicals, and most particularly in chocolate and cocoa. Quakers also owned the Daily News, the leading Liberal newspaper of the day. The Daily Herald was the organ of the Labour Party, and the one that came to our house. The media was spreading its wings. Silent films, which had begun to appear in 1909, became 'Talkies' in 1930, and a succession of musicals and comedies came out of Hollywood each year. British films, especially documentaries, appeared on the screen in the 1930s. In 1935, Stalin began his purge trials of rival leaders in the USSR, but a physiology conference was held in that year in Moscow under the leadership of Ivan Pavlov, which my second wife-to-be, Eleanor, attended. Russian novels and histories became widely popular. A quite rebellious attitude emerged among young people, especially in boarding schools, from which I was not immune. The Emery brothers were expelled from Wellington for their radical views and writings.

My father was an active Quaker who was the author of one of the annual Swarthmore lectures – his was on 'Democratic Leadership' – and also of a kind of modern Quaker manifesto, *The Naturalness of Religion*, written jointly with his friend Professor John Harvey. My father encouraged me to go to Bootham School in York, the same Quaker school where he and his father had been before me and where my son, Richard, followed me. York is a beautiful city, and I could walk along the top of its ancient walls, look out of my study window over the house roofs to the Minster, and sit in the cool shadows under its arches and stare at the great North Chancel 'Five Sisters' window. During the War the window glass was buried for safety's sake, and the window then reconstructed with funds from women's organisations in the UK. They are listed in a tableau by the side of the window.

My first nights in a boarding school were a bit scary. As the new boy to the dorm I had to run the gauntlet, crawling under the eight beds while their occupants stood up with knotted towels to beat me, as I crawled from bed to bed. I realised at once that, if I put my arm out first, it would take the blow, and I could get to the safe cover of the next bed before I took the body blow. There were also inter-dorm raids, and I was given the duty of door guardian. I had to bring my knotted towel on an invader entering. Any poor boy caught had his 'pipes' (stomach) tickled until he screamed for mercy; this in a Quaker pacifist school! The first person to enter on my guard proved to be Mr. Heyhoe, the gym master, whom I hit smartly on the head. Fortunately, he just laughed. He was a very friendly fellow, married to a beautiful lady. In the showers after games we sang rude songs about staff members. We called women 'hags', and sang 'Heyhoe's hag is a chorus hag'. One of our masters was called 'Victor', and we believed that he had his eye on the prettiest of our serving maids. So, we sang, 'It's a bit thick of Vic – to squeeze Louise!'

Teachers sometimes crept up to a dorm door, waiting for something to punish, and we cried, 'they also serve who only stand and wait!' (quoting Milton's sonnet). For punishment we were 'served rounds', which meant running so many times round the playground, or 'lines' of so many words correctly spelt, or 'sums' to add up correctly – no corporal punishment! And my jogging, spelling and arithmetic all benefited me for a life-time. There were some very strict rules – no playing cards, no visits to the cinema, no alcohol or smoking, and meeting with girls at the Mount, the sister school, only with York Quaker families, but I found nothing to complain of there that I could not arrange for my convenience.

The school introduced me to the Rowntrees, especially to Arnold Rowntree, chairman of the chocolate company and also of *The Daily News*. Arnold's son Michael became my best friend at school, later with me in the Friends Ambulance Unit (FAU). Michael went with the FAU, in 1939, with their vehicles to Finland in the Finnish and German war against the Soviet Union. They suffered some heavy bombing from the Russians, and Michael wrote to me saying that he had been really frightened. They were captured by the Russians and repatriated to the Middle East, where I caught up with Michael again, before he joined the Hadfield-Spears Medical Unit with the Free French Forces in the campaigns in North Africa, Italy and France. Back in England at the end of the War, Michael worked on the *Oxford Mail* and finally became a director of the Friends Provident Insurance Company and chairman of Oxfam. I wrote his obituary for *The Guardian.*

I once asked Arnold why I could only buy Rowntree's chocolate in the North, north of the Trent, and Cadbury's in the South. Arnold's answer was, 'Well, once a year we have a luncheon meeting in the Station Hotel at York'. 'Who are "we"?' I asked. 'Ah!' he replied, 'The Quaker chocolate companies – Rowntree's, Cadbury's, Fry's, Terry's, Jacobs – and at some point in our meeting, someone says, "same as last year?" and we agree.' 'Is that why Quaker firms are so profitable?' I asked, a bit cheekily. 'No!' Arnold replied. 'That is because honesty is the best policy!' and I remembered that my father had told me that Rowntree's had originally been grocers, who established the practice of fixing the price of their goods and had no bargaining. Quakers had gone into brewing beer – Truman, Hanbury, Buxton, Stopes, all Quakers, to wean people off the dangers of gin drinking, and then, when beer still led to drunkenness, they switched to cocoa.

Arnold Rowntree was a big man in every sense, with an extraordinary feeling for his religious convictions. At Bootham we all attended the Quaker Meeting in York on Sundays, and I remember one occasion when Arnold fell to his knees, saying, 'Oh Lord! Thou must have read in *The Manchester Guardian* yesterday?' Michael and I burst out laughing. On Saturdays, Arnold played tennis on the

Rowntree court with William Temple, who was then Archbishop of York, in a foursome with Michael and me. The two portly gentlemen served the most terrific serves and left Michael and me to continue the rallies. Every summer Rowntree's arranged a visit to the chocolate factory and gave the school a strawberry party. The head boy had to make a speech thanking Arnold. One year, when I was present, the head boy, Stoughton Holborn (Stoho), made a speech based on Lewis Carroll's 'Jabberwocky', ending up with his arms around Arnold's shoulders declaiming:

Come to my arms, my beamish boy!
Oh, frabjous day! Callooh! Calay!
We chortle now with glee,
As we circle round the tum-tum tree.

The head master was not amused, and Arnold looked embarrassed!

William Temple, who was one time President of the Workers' Educational Association (WEA) when my father was the Treasurer, was a good friend of my father's and sometimes stayed with us in Oxford. He was a very large man, and I remember once at a lunch-time my mother saying, 'William, dear, will thee have the hot or will thee have the cold?' Temple's mother was a Quaker, and 'thee-thouing' came natural. Temple replied, 'I will begin with the hot and go on to the cold'. The whole Barratt Brown family said to themselves 'FHB!' (Family Hold Back!) Temple stayed with us once and told us lovely bedtime stories. One I remember was about his sending his laundry to be washed when away from home, and getting his surplice back, marked 'To one bell tent!' He told us one very memorable story about St. Augustine walking along the shore of the Mediterranean Sea, considering the nature of the cosmos, when he came upon a little child digging a hole in the sand to allow the sea to flow into it. Augustine asked the child what he was doing, and the child replied 'letting the sea run into this hole in the sand!' 'You can't get the whole sea into that little hole of yours,' said Augustine. 'No more can you get the whole of the cosmos into that little brain of yours!' replied the child. We liked that story.

William Temple taught us a charming little rhyme:

The rain it raineth every day,
On the just and unjust fella.
But mostly on the just, because
The unjust has the just's umbrella.

William Temple had a great influence on my thinking, especially his book, *Christianity and Social Order*, published in 1942. This is a forthright statement of socialist principles supported by Christian authority. The equality of all human beings is given religious power and is argued to justify trade union organisation and the ending of the so-called public schools and other private discrimination in favour of the rich. It was an extraordinary book coming from an archbishop and was very much in tune with the mood of the country, as it was developing during the anti-fascist war. Any idea of returning to the inequalities and unemployment of the 1930s was becoming totally unacceptable among large sections of the British public, and Temple was reflecting that fact. But his support for workers' education gave the message particular force.

William Temple's nephew Freddie was in the Friends Ambulance Unit (FAU) with me, and helped us to sort out a crisis of governance, to put the Executive into the hands of elective members of the Unit. I was then the editor of the FAU Newsletter, and I began my subsequent editorial with a quotation from Shakespeare:

> *Now is the winter of our discontent*
> *Made glorious summer*
> *By this son of York!*

I saw Freddie many years later with his Quaker wife, once again repeating the liaison of an Anglican bishop with a Quaker wife, like his grandfather. Freddie became a London suffragan bishop, and then Bishop of Tewkesbury. But by the time I saw him he had, very sadly, become totally blind. He still had all the playful humour that I remembered from our FAU days.

William Temple was not a pacifist, indeed he disagreed strongly with pacifist arguments, but he was a very progressive thinker. There is a nice story of the Soviet ambassador in London, Ivan Maisky, meeting William Temple and Stafford Cripps both in mufti and coming away convinced that Cripps was the Archbishop and Temple the left-wing politician.

One summer holiday, after I had taken my Matric exams, I went with Michael Rowntree to an international Summer School in Germany organised by the lady who became Sir Michael Sadler's wife, Miss Pegler. My understanding of German was not very good and I found the French girls silly. I fell in love with an English girl, Joan, and we decided to go midnight bathing in the Ammersee. I climbed up an outside pipe to the girls' bedroom and got her down to swim. I helped her back again, but we were caught by Michael Rowntree's elder sister, Tessa, who was a teacher at the School. Michael was having an affair with Olive Layton, and Tessa commented that at least her Michael was not 'furtive in his amours'. We all went from the school to a performance of the *Passion Play* at Oberammergau. Hitler himself was present, and I found it particularly frightening when the whole audience joined with the actors in crying, *'Am Creuz mit hiem!'* as Christ was condemned to the cross. I saw much more of Joan at the School, and visited her in Surrey at her home later, but somehow the passion had faded in England.

The following summer I got polio. I was going to act the part of the Queen in a performance of *Richard of Bordeaux,* which was to be shown in Germany by an English public school cast. I had to go to rehearsals at Bryanston School. The night before I was due to go, I said goodbye to my father and he winked very cheerfully at me. I asked him if he always winked with his left eye. He said that he did not think so, and winked with the right eye. When I woke up next morning I had a headache and thought about my father's winking. I tried winking with both my eyes and to my horror found that I could only wink with my right eye. I rushed to the mirror to confirm this and saw that the left side of my mouth was twisted. Our doctor, Gerald MacMichael, called in Professor Cairns, who declared that I had polio and must stay in bed for some weeks. No *Richard of Bordeaux* to act! Other boys with whom I had been swimming in the Cherwell also had polio, and one of the Mitchison boys died from it.

Our family went on holiday and my Aunt Fran came to look after me. After a time I was allowed to read and I remember that I read *Anthony Absolute,* and fell in love with the heroine, whose name, as I recall it, was Dolores de la Fuente de Carlos y Someruelos. I was able later to join the family briefly in Cornwall, and then went for convalescence with my Aunt Winnie to a hotel on Dartmoor. I had been told to give up my classical studies, and I talked at length with her about studying history on long walks over the moors with the hotel's Alsatian dog. I also went riding each day, which was quite marvellous. It so happened that the actor John Laurie (see *Dad's Army*) was staying in the hotel with his wife, and kept us amused with his Scottish stories. I was not allowed to go back to school for that term, but began studying history with Dorothy Sheepshanks, a Somerville don, friend of my mother's, and aunt of the boy who had bullied me at the Dragon School – until I did his homework for him. After my new studies I even took the entrance exam for Balliol College, and was told to try the next year.

During this time my father was working with Clifford Allen (CA) and others, including Lord Horder, the King's doctor, on preparing the Next Five Years' Group. CA suggested that Lord Horder should be consulted about the results of my polio. I saw him. He refused to take a fee and proposed that I should see Dorothy Collier about a possible operation, a decompression of the seventh nerve, the one affected. I saw her and went into University College Hospital for the operation, and was visited there very thoughtfully by Arnold Rowntree and my current girlfriend, Jo Richardson. I saw Dorothy Collier several times after the operation and found her very engaging. She was a Catholic with wide literary interests outside her medical speciality. She gave me Gerard Manley Hopkins' poem 'The Wreck of the Deutschland' to read. I committed it to memory, and can still recall the first lines:

> *Thou mastering me*
> *God! giver of breath and bread;*

World's strand, sway of the sea;
Lord of living and dead;
Thou hast bound bones & veins in me, fastened me flesh,
And after it almost unmade, what with dread,
Thy doing: and dost thou touch me afresh?
Over again I feel thy finger and find thee.

And I would think of that painting by Michelangelo on the roof of the Sistine Chapel in the Vatican, of God holding out a finger to Adam, reproduced on the wall of the building that held the League of Nations in Geneva. Of such rich memories life is constructed. But I did not become a Catholic. I met Dorothy again in Cairo, where she was a colonel in the Royal Army Medical Corps. Her operation was not really successful, though over the years the twist in my mouth appeared reduced, partly by my growing a beard.

I came under the influence of three very important people in my life at Bootham. The first was Neave Brayshaw who introduced me to the mysteries of Gothic architecture, in buildings both in and around York and in France where he took a party of us to visit cathedrals – Chartres, Rheims, Rouen, Senlis and Notre Dame de Paris. I learnt to draw archaeological features – capitals and bases, towers and spires – so that, when we were interviewed about career choices, I was told that I should be an architect. My son Richard did become one, but I was then set on joining the Civil Service, which seemed to me to be the height of ambition.

I don't know why, but we called Neave 'Puddles', and used to imitate his stammer, especially in our visits to churches in 'Upp-per Per-Poppleton and Lower Per-per Pop-Poppleton'. There were competitions as to who could best imitate his rendering of:

Say not the struggle nought availeth,
The labour and the wounds are vain,
The enemy fainteth not nor faileth,
And as things have been, they remain!

I have needed that 'say not' sentiment these last few years, as I watch all that I have ever struggled for – peaceful solutions to international relations, a National Health Service, comprehensive schools, and full employment – falling to the enemy.

Neave Brayshaw also encouraged me to read about Quakerism in several books he had written and in some of the writings of George Fox. The result was that, by the time I was 18, I was anxious to apply to join The Society of Friends. Because of our long Quaker ancestry, we could become 'birthright Friends', but my father believed strongly that we should make a deliberate decision. So, I was duly 'visited' by two elders of Oxford Meeting, our doctor, Henry Gillett and

Liesl Joachim, niece of the musician and aunt of my first wife to be – Frances Lloyd. I don't remember anything of the discussion, but I do remember what Liesl gave us for lunch. I came out in a violent rash of urticaria. My father advised me to consult Henry Gillett who said it would be from the tinned salmon Liesl had given us, and I would be fully recovered the next day. My father's comment was that it was a 'bad omen!' and indeed I had left the Quakers for the Communist Party within ten years – along with several of Henry's children.

After Neave Brayshaw, the second major influence on my life at Bootham was Philip Corder who taught us English literature, and from whom I got an abiding love of Shakespeare. My voice broke very late – at about 17 – and I was small. Because of my training in acting at the Dragon School in Oxford, I was given leading female parts in plays at Bootham, a boys-only school then. I played Jessica and Miranda, but the most demanding part, after that of the daughter in *Tobias and the Angel*, was of Cleopatra in Shaw's *Caesar and Cleopatra*. The part of Caesar was taken by John Kay, the French master, and I plucked up courage in a rehearsal, to say 'Please, sir, would you mind shaving?' 'I am sure that Caesar didn't shave!' came the reply. 'Perhaps, Cleopatra didn't mind being scratched,' I said. 'OK!' John Kay replied, 'You may kiss me on the cheeks!' Philip Corder had the part of Pothinus and overheard this exchange, which made him laugh. The major influence of Philip Corder on me, however, was imparting his interest in Roman archaeology. He left Bootham to become curator of the Archaeological Society. While still at the school he was working on a 'dig' at a Roman villa in Langton near Malton in North Yorkshire, and he took parties of us from the school to work there. It taught me much about the technique of archaeological investigation.

My experience of taking female roles in school plays gave me an idea. I was passionately fond of American cinema musicals, especially Fred Astaire and Ginger Rogers. But Bootham boys were not allowed to go to the cinema, and on Saturday afternoon, reeves (prefects) stood outside the local cinema to see that no boys went in. There was, of course, then no television. I had been taught to walk like a girl, and I had a collection of girls' clothes and shoes. I decided to go to the cinema dressed as a girl. I put a selection of things in the basket of my bike in the cycle shed, changed there, and went out of school past the Sanatorium, where no one challenged me. I got to the cinema, walked past the reeves, bought my ticket and went in. It worked and I did it several times. One time I nearly got caught. I wore glasses to increase my disguise, and they made things look larger. I paid for my ticket with a florin, which I thought was half a crown. When this was pointed out, I said 'Oh, sorry!', just by a reeve, who looked at me queerly, but did not dare to challenge me. On another occasion, I had to go to the toilet, and guessed correctly that the Ladies' would have cubicles and not urinals.

The third influence was that of Leslie Gilbert, who taught sixth form history. I got polio in the summer holiday when I was 17, and missed a term at school.

When I returned, the doctors had advised me to give up classics as too much of a strain on my brain, and do 'something easier like history!' I was not much impressed by the argument, but followed the advice. Leslie Gilbert had a remarkable record of teaching students who went on to be distinguished historians – AJP Taylor, Frank Thistlethwaite, Christopher Butterworth, and his own son, Martin, Churchill's biographer. I can't pretend to rank with them, but I did win the school (BB le Tall) essay prize, a Bootham leaving scholarship, and a scholarship to Corpus Christi College, Oxford. Leslie, as I came to know him, was a man of enormous erudition who liked nothing more than to read himself along with his students new books and historical articles of interest and importance. He insisted that he learnt as much from his students' ideas as they from him – a practice that I sought to emulate when I began to teach.

I should not really leave my time at Bootham without mentioning some of my friends who had very distinguished connections which I came to know – not only my best friend, Michael Rowntree, but the two others I shared a study with. One was Franklin Braithwaite, the son of Jack Braithwaite, at that time the chairman of the London Stock Exchange, and of Netty, née Noel Baker, sister of the MP and Olympic runner, an old school friend of my father's and one time Vice-Principal of Ruskin College. I never really knew Noel Baker, but I used to stay with the Braithwaites in their big house in Hampstead at Christmas time, and go with them to the pantomime. Franklin became the chairman of a large manufacturing company in Northampton – another successful Quaker business.

The other friend sharing our study was Ted Branson, son of Sir George Branson, a High Court judge whose house in Frimley Green, Surrey I stayed in. It had large grounds with a lake, which we could boat on. Ted had a gun for shooting rabbits, which desecrated the herbaceous borders. I liked shooting at the range at the Dragon School and won a prize for my accuracy, but I didn't like killing rabbits or eating them. I had once kept a pet rabbit, and I knew their smell. One day, in error, I walked into Sir George's study mistaking two doors. I apologised for interrupting, but Sir George told me to come on in and sit down. He explained that he was very worried. I was amazed at being confided in – a mere 16-year-old boy – about a judge's worries. The next week, Sir George said, he had to put on the black cap – I knew what that meant – to condemn a man to death. It was his duty, but he did not like it, and had real doubts about capital punishment. I suggested that he should talk to my father who was coming to fetch me the next day. I told Sir George that my father had been in Pentonville Prison, as a conscientious objector in the First World War, when Sir Roger Casement was executed, and it was a terrible experience – all the prisoners banging on their doors at 6am so that they didn't hear the resounding bang as the trap door dropped. Sir George thanked me and, next day, had a long talk with my father.

There must have been some unusual ideas in the minds of Sir George and Lady Branson in sending one of their sons to a Quaker School. The elder son went to

Eton. Ted became a barrister himself and father of Sir Richard Branson, not quite the self-made man as he appears. I saw Ted again at his home outside Chichester just a year before his death. I met his mother Eve, then, who talked about her work helping the Berbers in Morocco. She was very pleased, she said, that she had got financial help through her Newsletter for her project of getting cashmere sheep for her Berbers.

In the term when I missed school recovering from polio, I saw much of the Murray and Gillett families. They were closely connected. Lady Mary Murray was a Howard, daughter of the Earl of Carlisle, and married to Professor Gilbert Murray, the translator of Greek drama. Lady Mary was a Quaker with left-wing views and a close friend of my parents. They lived in a large house with a big garden on Boars Hill just outside Oxford, to the south-west, called Yatscombe. The first time I saw the person who came to be my great friend, Robin Murray, was on my mother's knees, alongside Lady Mary, his grandmother. He was staying with her because his mother, Margaret Gillett, was ill. He had just stopped wailing, and I remember Lady Mary saying, 'It takes a Quaker to keep Robin quiet!' Gilbert Murray and the Gilletts had a great influence on my thinking, but in very different ways. Gilbert gave me copies of his humanist lectures to read, including *Five Stages of Greek Religion* and *From Stoic to Humanist*, and I added a distinctly Stoic edge to my Quakerism.

Gilbert probably did my father a great favour. In 1916, conscription was introduced, and some conscientious objectors were sent to France and, on further refusing military service, executed. My father's friend Rendal Whyatt was threatened with that fate, but survived and went on to be the head of Manchester University Department of Adult Education, where the sister of the Irish rebel, Constance Markievicz, taught one of those 'two fair ladies' (Gore-Booths) WB Yeats wrote a poem about. Gilbert Murray went with his brother in law, Geoffrey Howard, who was a Government Minister, to see Prime Minister Asquith. It was agreed that, thereafter, objectors should be charged in Britain and, if convicted, sent to prison in Britain. So that is what happened to my father. Lloyd George, who was Home Secretary, promised to give them 'a hell of a run for their money!' He introduced the 'cat and mouse treatment', originally used against the suffragettes. After a certain length of imprisonment, objectors would be released and then called up again, and charged, and if convicted given a further prison sentence. This is why my father was sent to four prisons, each for about six months, so that my poor mother never knew when he would be in or out. But my father was not sent to France and executed.

Gilbert Murray told us charming, and educative, stories. One I remember was about the way to catch camels in the desert. You need to choose a spot where the camels are feeding and take a number of large bodkins and place them in the ground among the camels. Then you need to persuade a member of the House of Rothschild to visit the site in an aeroplane, persuade him to walk about among the camels, and then fly off in his plane. When the camels see the rich man apparently ascending to heaven, they will rush to the bodkins, put their heads in the eyes of the needle, and they are caught. It would really hurt their necks, I feared, but Gilbert assured me that the bodkins would have a woollen bandage round the eyes.

The influence of the Gilletts could hardly have been more different from that of the Murrays. There were two Gillett families living near to each other in houses with large gardens in Oxford's Banbury Road, Arthur's the banker's family and Henry's, the doctor's. Several of the children of both families had become Communists, and made me think seriously about my socialism. There was an Oxford pub near the canal which they frequented, and where I met Philip Toynbee, whose father was Arnold Toynbee, the historian. Philip's daughter became Polly Toynbee of *The Guardian*. Philip's mother was a daughter of the Murrays, Rosalind, who became a Catholic, but Philip joined the Communists.

I remember once meeting Philip at the time of the succession of George VI, after the abdication of Edward VIII. We drank to the memory of Edward! Though we knew that he was a Nazi sympathiser, he had defended the Welsh miners' strike, and it seemed to us to be an appropriately dissident response to the Establishment. Edward's marriage was condemned by Prime Minister Baldwin and by the Archbishop of Canterbury.

A Quaker friend of my father's, the wife of James Meade, the economist, had a letter in *The Times* which simply read, 'Oh, Cosmo, what a cantaur!' (the Canterbury insignia sounding like 'cant you are'). The Archbishop was Cosmo Lang, brother of Andrew Lang, the head of the Scottish church at the time – both Scots. It is said that they tossed up to determine who should have which job. It is not said who won! I remember discussing this with Philip at the time, amid much merriment. I expect that I had drunk too much, and Philip was certainly drunk, as he often was. Jessica Mitford wrote a charming book about him, *Remembering Philip*. He, too, in the end, joined the Catholic Church. Philip's mother, Rosalind, claimed that she insisted on a Catholic priest going to her father, Gilbert, as he was dying, and claimed that Gilbert was received into the church. Robin's father and several members of the family denied it. Gilbert always described himself as a 'humanist', but he told me once that there was a great area in human life that we did not understand. Many years later, I went on a walk in Cumbria with Robin's brother Sandy, who was a Catholic, and I took the opportunity to ask what was the truth about this story. Sandy said that there was no doubt that the priest had given Gilbert absolution, but what Gilbert's response had been, if any, was unclear.

The Gilletts did something else for me. They provided a home for students who came to England from India and Africa, and through them I met my friend, Mohun Kumaramalgalam, and my sister's friend, Nontando Jubavu. We were immunised against any possible infection of colour prejudice.

I was quite happy to leave Bootham when I did because my relationship with the headmaster had deteriorated. I was a reeve deputy to Michael Rowntree as head reeve, but I had a serious row with Donald Gray. When John Peet left the school, he handed over to me the distribution of the leftwing schoolboy magazine, *Out of Bounds*, edited by the Romilly brothers, one of whom, Esmond, married Jessica Mitford. When I distributed my first copies, the headmaster called me into his study, and asked me to withdraw all copies. He objected to an article by a doctor explaining that there were no physical dangers likely to arise from masturbation. I told him that it would not be easy to get the copies back, and I did not see why I should, and I didn't. I met Desmond Romilly later and told him the story.

I also met John Peet much later, in Palestine in 1943. He was in some sort of secret service and checking up on the Stern Gang who blew up the King David Hotel in Jerusalem, housing many British soldiers, in 1946. I met him again in 1950 in Berlin, where I was at a Communist Party conference and he was the *Daily Worker* correspondent, a surprising career for the son of the editor of *The Friend!* At Bootham I had regarded him as something of a role model.

I had had a good time at Bootham, doing well not only academically and as an actor, but in other ways. I played the flute and piccolo in the School Orchestra until I got polio and could not use my mouth to blow. I was in the first Cricket Eleven and represented the school in high-board diving, to which I owe my severe deafness. Nobody told me to wear earplugs. I got into trouble with my highboard diving. When King Edward's school in Sheffield opened its swimming

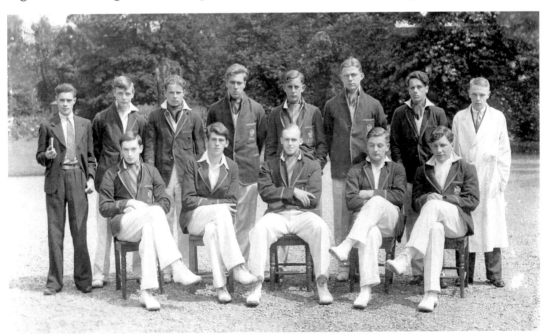

Michael in 1ˢᵗ cricket XI

pool, Bootham was invited to compete in swimming and diving. I went up to the ten metre spring board to do a double somersault. I took off and my feet touched the roof timbers. I said, 'Oh, fuck!' and fell out of control into the pool. As I got out of the water the headmaster screamed at me to get dressed and sit in the coach until we all left. I had disgraced the school, he said, by my outburst. My friends protested on my behalf that the board was dangerously near the roof. The headmaster was not to be assuaged, and repeated that I was a disgrace. I always looked carefully at swimming bath rooves from then on.

I also did woodwork and made a filing cabinet for my father, a radio set for my parents, and another set which I put under the floorboards by my bed, so that I could hear the music after 'lights out' in the dormitory. The school motto then was *Mens sana in corpore sano*, and I tried to achieve a healthy mind in a healthy body.

In 1937, when I was 19, in the Easter holiday, we went to stay at a farmhouse in North Wales, near Barmouth, looking across the estuary to Cader Idris. We went for wonderful walks, but the holiday was memorable for a special reason. My mother brought with her the recently published book by Bernard Shaw, *The Intelligent Woman's Guide to Socialism*, and persuaded me to read it. I could not put it down, and tried to understand the case for income equality, which Shaw was arguing. I can still recall the final sentence of the book, 'By such (income generosity) ladies and their sons can the human race be saved, and not otherwise'. One lady and her son never forgot the message and tried to live up to it; and I saw my mother in a quite new light.

Landschulheim, Holzminden

CHAPTER 4

Oxford University and The Next Five Years Group, London, Oxfordshire and Surrey, 1930s-40s

The period covered is from 1935 to 1940. The Next Five Years Group, which had been founded in the UK in 1935 as a democratic attempt at political and economic planning in response to Soviet Communist planning, received quite widespread British party support. World events, however, overtook this initiative. In 1936 Hitler entered the Rhineland and Mussolini occupied Ethiopia. In 1937 Hitler claimed the Sudetenland. Japan entered China. Meanwhile, King Edward VIII was deposed from the British throne because of his marriage to the divorced American, Mrs Simpson, and replaced by George VI, whose wife, Mary, was a Scottish Bowes-Lyon. Edward VIII was King for 325 days. All pillar-boxes in the UK have the name of the ruling king or queen on them when they were erected. The only box I know of which has Edward VIII on it is on the quayside in Tobermory on the Island of Mull.

The British response by Prime Minister Chamberlain was to reach, in 1938, the Munich Agreement with Hitler. In 1939, Stalin and Hitler agreed the Nazi-Soviet Pact. The UK stepped up its arms production programme and promised, with the French, to protect Poland. But Hitler invaded Poland and, in 1939, the Second World War began. Young people were called up for military service, and tribunals established to deal with conscientious objectors. The Friends Ambulance Unit (FAU) was re-formed, and I joined Michael Rowntree at the initial training camp. Michael went with an FAU ambulance convoy to the Soviet-Finnish war from which they were repatriated via Egypt. The 'phoney war' followed but, in 1940, the German army pushed the British and French forces back to Dunkirk, where only an amazing 'armada' of little boats evacuated the British troops to England, while Hitler entered Paris.

In 1934, my family moved from North Oxford to the Oxfordshire countryside, to The Malt House (yet another one!) in the village of South Stoke, near Goring-on-Thames. It was a pretty little village, with church and rectory, a Post Office, a pub and one shop. The house was old with a brick summer house, that had been the maltings. There was a long garden leading down to the river, where I had a canoe. A little used Methodist Chapel stood in the grounds, which you can see in the picture taken in 2007 with Annette, and the present owner in front of the house. From the living room and bedrooms there were fine views beyond the river to the Berkshire Downs. My father and I created a rose garden, tennis court, vegetable garden, and a grass path between the lines of elm trees. This came to

The Malt House – Front with Annette

be called 'the statesmen's walk', and certainly I can remember my father walking up and down it with Harold Macmillan and Sir Arthur Salter, the Oxford don. In the house my father installed William Morris wallpaper and curtains, willow pattern and roses, and took us each year to visit May Morris at Kelmscott. When Annette and I went to The Malt House in 2007, the elms had all died of elm disease, and a swimming pool has been built where our tennis court was until it was made into a potato patch during the war.

By the front door of the house we planted a wisteria, which still spreads its arms up the wall and over the door. In the first year it seemed to die, but we pruned it back. It recovered and my father commented, purposely misquoting Cowper, 'God moves in a wisterious way, his wonders to perform!' My friend Ann McKnight Kauffer loved that, when I told her, but then she was very emotional. I made her cry when I woke up one morning and told her that I had the following words in my head and sang them to her:

> *Early one morning, just as the sun was rising*
> *I heard a voice in the valley below, singing,*
> *'Oh, never leave me … Don't, please, deceive me …*
> *How could you treat a poor maiden so?'*

Where did I get this from? I don't know, but I can still remember it, and hear that Oxfordshire voice, lengthening all the 'eas' and 'eis'.

In the last year when we lived in Oxford, my father's old friend from the Independent Labour Party, Clifford Allen, by then Lord Allen of Hurtwood ('CA', as we called him), had come to see us with his beautiful wife, Joan (Margery), and daughter Polly (Conny), so-called because of CA's friendship with the Hon Constance (Conny) Annesley, better known as the actress Colette O'Neil. CA's daughter pronounced Conny as 'Polly'. CA brought exciting news. He planned to form a new political grouping, which came to be called 'The Next Five Years Group', with himself as Chairman, Harold Macmillan, the publisher and Conservative MP, as Treasurer, my father as Secretary, and Geoffrey Crowther, a Liberal, who later became editor of *The Economist,* as editor of a new journal. The need for a new political initiative was evident. The National Conservative Government in the UK was faltering, dictatorships were established in Japan, Italy and Germany, and the United States was in economic crisis.

War with Germany seemed imminent; father terrified us all by proposing to gather a number of Friends together to go to the Sudetenland, and lie down in front of the German tanks, if they invaded. He got his party together but, to our great relief, they were refused visas to enter Czechoslovakia. Instead, he felt that he had earlier responded to the situation by editing a large book, called *Great Democrats,* for which he had selected a number of authors to write on individual democrats in British history. Bertrand Russell wrote the entry on Tom Paine, GDH Cole on Cobbett, Dame Evelyn Sharp, later permanent secretary at the Treasury, on Mary Wollstonecraft, and the Countess of Warwick the one on the agricultural trade unionist, Joseph Arch. We visited the Countess when she offered Eaton Lodge to Ruskin College. My father turned down the offer because it had none of the library and other facilities of Oxford. My father had asked Francis Meynell to write on William Morris, but Francis had been too busy. I arranged for a new edition of *Great Democrats* to be published in 2013.

My wife Eleanor and I came to know Francis Meynell and his wife, Bay Kilroy, very well when they came to live in Suffolk. I have a copy of his autobiography with its reference to his political role in editing the *Daily Herald* and then, with Bay, in leading positions in the civil service. They lived in an old house on the river in Lavenham with its splendid 15th Century church. The house had a bridge to cross to enter the house, and on the bridge they had put a carving by Eric Gill. When we met them we talked mainly about poetry and theatre. Francis's first wife was the poet Alice Meynell. To do the entry on Morris in place of Francis, my father asked Oliver Baldwin to write. Oliver was a son of the Conservative Prime Minister, Stanley, but himself a Labour Party candidate. His aunt was married to the Pre-Raphaelite painter, Burne-Jones. Oliver lived near us, and we saw something of him during the writing of the book, but I don't remember discussing Burne-Jones.

In the same year, 1934, that *Great Democrats* appeared, Ivor Nicholson and

The Malt House – Father in the back garden

Watson published my father's London University Extension Lectures under the title of *The Machine and the Worker*. My father had been a lecturer in psychology at Birmingham University before going to Ruskin College, and these lectures comprised a comprehensive review of the psychological literature on human motivations and satisfactions in both physical and mental labour, illustrated by a remarkable number of confessions of their experiences from my father's working class students at Ruskin and from his tutorial and correspondence courses. My father took a very balanced view, neither despairing at the degree of stress often revealed by workers in mines and manufacturing, nor being over optimistic about the satisfactions in some forms of office work. He examined in detail the effects of fatigue, boredom and danger as well as the introductin of time and motion studies at work in a period of industrial conglomeration and rationalisation of mass production for avoiding waste (except, my father comments, waste of workers). This was a process which I found myself deeply involved in when I came to teaching steel workers in Sheffield thirty years later; and he argued the case for 'workers' control', using workers' unexplored knowledge and experience, with which I became closely concerned in later years. My father's lectures end with a profoundly felt appeal for governments to stop the scourge of unemployment, so desperate in the 1930s, and make provision of wider education to enrich all workers' 'leisure time', as Bertrand Russell argued so forcibly in proposing a four-hour work day. The message of the lectures could well be repeated today, especially perhaps the aphorisms he quotes, how under the curse of Midas the rule of capital creates the inequality of incomes both in advanced and developing countries, and with which he concludes:

> 'The fault is not in the machine but in ourselves that we are underlings ... The command of Nature has been put into man's hands before he knows how to command himself.'

My father was only too happy to take on the work of The Next Five Years Group, and my mother learnt to type to deal with all the correspondence that would ensue. The first task was to draw up a manifesto, 'For Liberty and Democratic Leadership', and seek signatures to support it. Several hundred were obtained, some in the Labour Party, including Bevin and Lansbury, several Liberals, and a few Conservatives, like Macmillan, and a large number of writers, including HG Wells, JB Priestley, Virginia and Leonard Woolf, and leading businessmen, especially Quakers such as the Rowntrees and Cadburys, but including Montague Burton, Alan Sainsbury and many scientists. These included Eddington, Gowland Hopkins, Lord Horder, Boyd Orr, Oliver Lodge, and also Lord Rutherford, who agreed to be the President, just before he died. There were also people of the arts such as Sybil Thorndike and David Low.

My mother told me that Rutherford was worried about some new bomb that Germany might possess which could destroy whole cities. Julian Huxley joined the Executive Committee, but when I asked him he knew nothing of this threat. The first manifesto with its hundreds of signatures created quite a sensation. It was followed by a detailed 'Programme of Priorities' which attracted even more signatures. This in the end became the basis of the Labour Party's 1945 Election Manifesto, edited by Michael Young, with its several proposals for the nationalisation of banks, railways, mines and industries, and health provision.

During all this activity, our family spent some time at CA's beautiful house on a hill by Hurtwood Common in Surrey. We came to know several local people. One was Bob Trevelyan, the poet brother of Sir George, the historian. Bob came on several holidays with us, and I well remember going out seine fishing with him in South Wales. He was used to communicating on the phone by asking the operator for the person he wished to speak to by name. I once heard him on holiday pick up the phone and say, 'I want to speak to Gordon Bottomley'. He was evidently asked for a number, for, he continued, 'No. Gordon Bottomley; he has a name not a number!' We once went for lunch to a rather smart hotel. Bob was in his usual corduroy trousers and enormous walking boots. The hotel manager asked him to take them off before going in, as he was not respectably dressed. CA pointed out that Bob came from one of the oldest aristocratic

The Malt House – Garden

families in England and should be allowed to wear what he wished. The manager withdrew, and the boots stayed on!

I got to know Frances Lloyd really well one summer at CA's. We visited Bob Trevelyan, and he gave us one of his long poems to read. We lay on the lawn and read passages of the poem out aloud to each other. It was a new translation of Lucretius's *De Rerum Natura*, and I will admit that, while we found it interesting, it was fairly heavy going. Some Cambridge dons were staying with Bob at the time, and we found their philosophical conversation well beyond us. But we greatly enjoyed our walks together around Leith Hill and Ewhurst, talking about our common interests in political questions.

Another local resident living near CA was Geoffrey Pyke, a crazy scientist who we called 'Popsky'. He lived by a farm in a little house at Elmhurst, which we visited. Later, he became one of the experts who planned with JD Bernal and other scientists the preparation for the D-Day landings in France. In Pyke's farm house he had a large table, with sheets of *The Times* newspaper laid out in temporal order to file important events. His divorced wife was the chair of the Women's Institute, and their son, David, became a great friend of my sister Deborah and a family planning doctor, who died at a tragically early age.

Many interesting people were attracted to visit CA when we were there. One was the American radio broadcaster, Raymond Gram Swing. We played an exciting hide and seek game, organised by CA, where one team hid in the woods and had to get to the home base without being caught. CA was not very strong, and ought not to have played this game, but Raymond and we children loved it. One regular visitor was Herbert Morrison. As a result, he took my father and me to look round the new buildings he had designed for the Greater London Council. I got to know them well when I worked there forty years later, in the 1980s.

We had important visitors also at our Malt House in South Stoke, walking up and down the statesmen's walk. Harold Macmillan came to visit us when I was about 17, and I well remember him asking me if I would care to read his address to the electors of Stockton. He suggested that I take it away with me, read it, and tell him what I thought of it the next day. I felt much honoured and very important. As I recall it, the address began roughly as follows, 'I am the National Conservative candidate. I believe in the nationalisation of the Bank of England and the Joint Stock Banks, the nationalisation of the coal mines and the railways and a National Health Service'.

When I saw Mr Macmillan the next day, and he asked what I thought of his address, I said rather cheekily, 'Well, sir, I have got the national bit but where is the conservative bit?' 'Ah, young man!' came the reply, 'That depends on what you intend to conserve?' I had to ask my father later, 'What had Harold meant?' and got the answer, 'the capitalist system!' I learnt from that that party political differences were less important than general agreement on the kind of society we lived in.

Harold Macmillan with his bust

I loved being up at Oxford, outside my College, Corpus Christi, Merton's cobbled street, the long High Street flanked by colleges right down to Magdalen Bridge, the Broad with Balliol, Brasenose and Trinity Colleges, Blackwell's bookshop, and the Sheldonian Theatre with its imposing line of statues, some being reconstructed with that lovely creamy sandstone. Many years later when I lived in Derbyshire, I could visit the quarries above Matlock where the stone was taken. While I was up at Oxford, a new building was going up next to Blackwell's, an extension of the Bodleian Library. It was greeted by Neville Coghill, author of the then current translation of Chaucer's *Canterbury Tales,* with the following lines of verse:

> *Hail! New Bodleian, nearly now complete,*
> *Raising your huge warts above the astonished street!*
> *At least, you show beyond dispute,*
> *The merits of the Indian Institute.*

The Institute was arguably the most ugly building in the street.

Then there was the broad thoroughfare of St Giles and the Martyrs' Memorial to Cranmer, Latimer and Ridley, executed by Bloody Mary (we called it the 'Magger's Memugger'), and beyond that the Parks, where I could watch cricket and cross the new bridge over the Cherwell, and bathe in the nude at Parson's Pleasure. Just to recall these names sends a shiver of delight through my old bones, as I respond also to the memory of Harold Macmillan.

My father had warned me to be very kind to Harold. 'He is a very sad man.' I didn't really see how a 17-year-old boy could behave 'kindly' to a famous publisher, writer and Member of Parliament, but my father would not be drawn. Only many years later did I read that Harold's wife, daughter of a Duke of Devonshire, was living with Bob Boothby, something my father must have known.

Sir Arthur Salter was a regular visitor – he became one of my tutors at Oxford, for whom I wrote an essay on a federal Europe. He was violently critical of Neville Chamberlain's concessions to Hitler – on 'Peace in our time!' I can still see him, his legs crossed, sitting by the fire in our living room. My father used to travel up to London by train with Salter, and told me that on one occasion they were both apparently reading *The Times* in their compartment when Salter dropped his paper and revealed that behind it he was reading the latest detective story by Dorothy Sayers. My father confessed that he was doing the same! In fact we had met Dorothy Sayers in Cornwall one summer, with our musician friend, Joseph Needham Cooper, and been amused by her elaborate bathing costume, and the notice in her lavatory warning users 'not to drop surplus matter into the bowl!' We had become enthusiastic followers of Lord Peter Wimsey in the Sayers novels.

I had several very good friends at Oxford. Michael Rowntree was at Queen's College, of whom more anon. Tom Maitland was at New College until he was called up. I had several Indian friends, some of whom I met much later in India, as we shall see. One of these Indians, John Khan, a prodigious rugby player, who died before the war began, was engaged to Monica Leaf from Ackworth School, who I found later was a great friend of Annette's, and whose son, Jeremy, has come with his wife, Vivien, from Canada to visit Annette in London every year. I had several pacifist friends. Richard Symonds was at Corpus with me, and joined the Friends Ambulance Unit with me, and I write more about him later.

Another pacifist who later changed his mind and joined up and was killed right at the end of the war was David Caulkin at New College, who married Annette. He and I decided to form an Oxford University Peace Council, and collect signatures of students recommending to the Vice-Chancellor that students' call-up for Military Service should be deferred to the end of the year, and preferably to the end of their course of study. It must be remembered that the Oxford Union – the debating society – had passed a resolution, in 1933, that they 'would not fight for King and Country', and at a later meeting, which David had attended, had confirmed their opposition to military solutions to international problems.

To form an Oxford-wide student body, David and I had to have a don as our president. I consulted my father about who to ask, and he suggested Donald McKinnon at Keble College. He was a Catholic, who believed in a 'just war', but did not think that this was such a one. David and I went to see him in his rooms at Keble. It was a very hot day for March, and McKinnon decided to shovel the coals out of the fire. He just threw them out of the window. Unfortunately, some of them fell on to the College bursar, who was passing by. We dashed downstairs to dust him off, and when we returned we hardly expected our mission to be successful. But McKinnon agreed to be our president, and we collected thousands of signatures. The Vice-Chancellor did do something to delay call up, and we felt pleased at having formed the first all-Oxford student body besides the Oxford Union.

Those of us who were pacifists used to meet in an Oxford café next door to the Randolph Hotel. Some time after the declaration of war in September 1939, we met together – I think, David Caulkin, Nathan Clark, Ralph Vaughan-Williams's nephew, and others and I – to discuss news that I had received from Michael Rowntree that the Friends Ambulance Unit (FAU) was being re-formed by his father, and Paul Cadbury and others. I decided with David to go to a preparatory FAU training camp in Birmingham. Frank Thomson burst in on us, slightly drunk. I had known him and his brother, Edward, since Dragon School days. Frank's message was that we were all hopelessly wrong. This was a war that had to be fought against fascism and to defend communism. He was joining up. When we pointed out that he was too young, he said that he would falsify his date of birth. I think he tried to. He joined the army anyway and fought with the Yugoslav partisans, and then with the Bulgarian resistance, and was executed, an appalling loss of a wonderfully brave and talented man. When my father died, by his bed there was a copy which I had sent him of Edward's tribute to Frank,

'There is a spirit in Europe', from which I wanted my father to understand my desertion of Quakerism for communism.

These years were not engaged for me solely with male friends. I had a succession of beautiful and rather distinguished girlfriends, through whom I met some fascinating people – first, my school friend Maureen Forsyth. I owe very much to Maureen. When I went back to school after missing a term with polio, we met again. I was terrified that she would be upset by my twisted mouth and an eye that did not close, and I said 'I am sorry about my face'. She said, 'You are still my lovely Barry' (as she called me), and gave me a huge kiss. It saved my life. A moment's hesitation, and I would not easily have recovered.

Maureen came to my 18th birthday party, and her brother Scott was up at the same time with me at Oxford, studying physics. He was at Exeter College, and I got a serious wound in my leg on the spikes, climbing out of his college rooms one night. Scott came to a Commemoration Ball with me and shocked every one by descending from an upstairs room on a fire escape and revealing that it was true that the Scots wore nothing under their kilts. Maureen and Scott's father owned a large drapery store in Glasgow, with a subsidiary in London's Regent Street. The Glasgow Park museum has, or had, a statue of him.

Maureen was followed by Jo Richardson, another girl from the Mount School, who came to the Balliol College Commem Ball with me. Without sleep, full of wine, we went swimming in the Thames at South Stoke afterwards. Jo trained to be an actress, and introduced me to her RADA friends. They sang the bawdiest of songs, rolling their Rs, hissing the sibilants and lengthening the As:

> *Rrip my sshimmy awaay! Awaayy! Rrip my shimmy awaay!*
> *I doant care what they doo to mee,*
> *So long as they play with my see-you-en-tee!*

In the holidays at South Stoke I met several charming people who came to stay at the old vicarage. Through them I met some lovely women with whom I danced in the village hall and they also introduced me to folk songs, two of which became my repertoire when I travelled and was expected to sing something. The first was a Cockney song, of which I can only remember the refrain:

> *She was poor but she was honest,*
> *Victim of a rich man's game.*
> *First he loved her, then he left her;*
> *And she lost her maiden name.*
> *It's the same the whole world over,*
> *It's the rich what gets the pleasure;*
> *It's the poor what gets the blame!*
> *Ain't it all a bleeding shame?*

The second was a very feminist American story of Frankie and Johnnie:

Frankie and Johnnie were lovers;
Oh Lordy how they did love!
Swore to be true to each other,
As long as the stars up above!
He was her man, but he done her wrong.
Now Frankie went down to the beer shop,
Just for a bucket of beer.
Frankie looked over the transom;
There to her great surprise;
There lay Johnnie making love to Nelly Bligh.
He was her man; he was doing her wrong.
Frankie drew back her kimono,
Drew out her little forty four,
Rooty toot, toot!, three times she shot,
Through that hard wood door
She shot her man, because he were doing her wrong
Though they had sworn to be true to each other,
And he was her man.
Bring out your rubber tyred coaches
Bring out your rubber tyred hacks
I'm taking my man to the graveyard
I ain't going to bring him back
He was my man and he done me wrong.
This story has no moral
This story has no end,
This story only goes to show,
That there ain't no good in men!
He was her man, and he done her wrong.

I have found that this has gone down well in many places, not just in Oxford, but in Australia and India, even in Spain, translated by Jose' Mari'a Tortosa, and in Peru, translated by Rebecah Morahan, when we visited a women's only co-operative in Cusco. I have never read it anywhere, but remember it from that singer in my University days. I can't really sing it any longer, but have not forgotten the words.

Then I found Ann McKnight-Kauffer. Her father was a painter, famous for his colourful posters on the London underground, a most loveable man, but separated from his wife. Mrs McKnight, as she called herself, was a concert pianist. Unfortunately for me she disapproved of me, not classy enough for her precious daughter. I used to drive in my little open MG up to London to see Ann, and she came to stay with us at the Malt House for my nineteenth birthday, along with Michael Rowntree. She confided, when we went to the local pub together, that she had never been in a pub before. I can still see her, long fair hair streaming behind her as we drove along the roads on a long visit to some friends at Bryanston School in Dorset. My father decided that, as I had a girlfriend in London and was driving there, I needed to go to a London driving school. So I stayed with a Quaker family and drove with an instructor in different parts of central London for six days, and the school taught me how to dismantle an internal combustion engine, decoke the cylinders and reassemble the whole thing so that it worked, something that you could never begin to do with a modern engine.

Ann and I went together to the funeral for CA in St. Martins-in-the-Fields Church. We both wept. Mrs McKnight put a stop to our affair, fearing that it would go too far. I was devastated, but my mother told me that Ann was 'too good' for me. I was amazed, as I thought mother held me in the highest regard, and I protested. 'Goody, goody, I mean', said my mother, and it is true that, for the next many years, Ann sent me religious poems she had written for my birthdays and Christmas.

Very fortunately, I found again my childhood friend Frances Lloyd, with whom I had grown up and had my first sexual experience, when our families had a holiday in Dylan Thomas's town, Laugharne, in South Wales. There were no contraceptive pills in those days, and I had no condoms, but Frances had fitted herself with a Dutch cap, which was smeared with VOLPAR (voluntary parenthood) gel. It is odd how we malign other nations in this matter, and the practice is mutual; 'French letters', as they are called in England, become '*capotes anglaises'* in France.

I remember telling Frances a sad story of an Englishman in Paris whose wife died. To go to the funeral he had to buy a black trilby hat. He went to a department store and asked for a '*chapeau Anglais noir'.* The lady serving him looked surprised and repeated '*chapeau Anglais?'* but added '*pourquoi noir?'* (why black?) He replied '*parce que ma femme est morte'* (my wife had died). 'Ah!' the lady said, '*quelle delicatesse!'* (what delicacy!)

Frances and I had a wonderful holiday in Laugharne, playing tennis, table tennis, sailing, reading history, acting in a pageant written by Joan Allen, where we were royal children, and listening each evening to CA reading a detective story, *Woman in White.* Sailing in the estuary with Frances's father, Ted, was almost fatal. In a sudden gust of wind, the boat capsized and Frances and I came up in the water under the sail. We just managed to rescue each other and clamber back onto the boat – a quite near thing to disaster, and a good thing we were together.

We met again when Frances came to St Hugh's College, Oxford, to study. It was at a play being performed in Worcester College Gardens, and we recalled the holidays we had enjoyed together, and especially the time when we had our first sexual experience together in Laugharne.

Michael and Frances married

After some further happy years together on other holidays and at Oxford, Frances became my wife. She was the daughter of old friends of my parents, Ted Lloyd, a distinguished civil servant at the Treasury and Margaret Russell, a cousin of Bertie's, and on her mother's side of Joachim the violinist. Our families expected us to get married, and Frances and I were married in 1940 at the Friends Meeting House in Jordans, near Chalfont St. Peter, and we had the reception afterwards in the Old Mayflower barn. Jimmy Mallon, Warden of Toynbee Hall, presided, and said that he felt 'a little godlike' bringing together the offspring of two of his oldest friends.

I had got to know Jimmy Mallon quite well. Toynbee Hall in Commercial Street was no distance from the London Hospital in Commercial Road, and we often found ourselves catching the same bus into the centre of London, sometimes *en route* for Political and Economic Planning (PEP) meetings. Jimmy had also founded a Stepney Rehousing Association, which met at Toynbee Hall, and I attended. Local residents gathered together to discuss the plans for rebuilding Stepney after the bomb damage. We prepared a questionnaire which was very widely circulated. One of the questions was about indoor and outdoor lavatories, and I was amazed to see how many families preferred their lavatories in the yard, outside the house. The overwhelming preference was for rebuilding the terraced houses. None of the town planners took any notice of that. Stepney was rebuilt with large blocks of apartments.

Frances and I honeymooned in the Lake District at Catharine Marshall's house on Lake Windermere, just opposite Keswick, where we shopped by boat. Catharine had been the Secretary of the No Conscription Fellowship. So, she knew both my father and Frances's mother. The photo shows Frances and me together just above the house, looking very happy.

I went up to Oxford in 1937, after a 'gap year' teaching English in a German *landschulheim*, and staying with the Krausers, a German family in Berlin. I went riding in the Grunewald with the *Herr Ritmeister* (Colonel) head of the family and

Michael and Frances on honeymoon in the Lake District

of the company *Max Krause Briefpapier*, and read Goethe with his lovely wife. She took me to Nazi parades, which she despised and laughed at the fat stomachs (*schmeerbauch*) of the SA men. We had a splendid canoeing holiday when I fell in love with their daughter, Fitti. She came to stay with us in England, and I met her again in Sydney, unhappily married to a drunken Australian.

At Corpus Christi College I leant to row, and became 'captain of boats' in my last year, when Corpus was still in the first division. We did not have to be so big then as now to row, but I am told today that my heart is greatly enlarged and I have heart problems because of my early rowing. At first, I had the bow oar, which I broke once by striking the bank, but later rowed at seven behind my friend William Cammock at stroke.

My first room at Corpus was in Merton Street, next door to the squash courts, where I liked to play, but in the second year I went in to college, in a beautiful big room in the 'Gentlemen Commoners' quad, looking out on to Merton

College and Christ Church meadows. It was big enough for me to hold meetings there for the Philosophical Society. I remember one meeting addressed by a Miss Fremlin on 'Hortatory Logic'. Her brother became a very radical philosophy professor. I made up a limerick at the time on Miss Fremlin:

> *There was a young woman called 'Fremlin',*
> *Who with hortatory logic was trem(b)lin.*
> *Until Stalin said 'she*
> *Should join the CP,*
> *And live with me in the Kremlin!'*

I am afraid that she did not think that was funny. Her brother enjoyed it, when I met him and told him of it.

My room was big enough also for supper parties which I gave with the pocket money my aunt Winnie supplied. As a result, my scout called me 'the last of my gentlemen'. I got to know the Dean of the College, Frank Geary, a considerable authority on Greek archaeology. I used to invite him to my parties, partly because he was very good company, partly because he had a key to the College gate, so that ladies at my parties did not have to leave by 10 o'clock, when the gates were shut. One of these ladies revealed that she had a huge key in her bag to get in to Somerville. Others had tried to climb over the spikes at Corpus with unfortunate results. Frank Geary became a University proctor – a sort of policeman, who had to dress up in 18th century costume and parade the streets of Oxford with an assistant called a 'buller' (bulldog) to catch any students wandering around after 10 o'clock. One day Frank tore a hole in the black stockings that were part of his costume just before he had to go out. He asked one of the larger serving maids if she could lend him hers. She agreed, and he told us, 'They were still warm, God bless her!'

Climbing into college at Corpus involved climbing up a creeper to the President's flat. On one occasion, I was behind a friend, and the President's wife opened a window. 'Lady Livingstone, I presume', my friend said, and we fell out of the creeper, laughing.

The rules about gates and forbidding us entrance to pubs were ridiculous. We had to go out of Oxford by car to find a pub to drink at. I used also to go to the Randolph Hotel to drink, and take a copy of the *Financial Times* and hide behind it, if a proctor or buller approached. I once had an evening meal at the Mitre Hotel with a heavily bearded and very tall student called Michael Marmorstein, who became an historical adviser to Ealing Film Studios, and was unlikely to be challenged by a proctor. I was then growing a small goatee. The evening I went with him to the Mitre, we were asked, as we were finishing our meal, if we could make way for two ladies to join us. We agreed and they sat down by us. The elder one introduced herself as 'Margot, Countess of Oxford and Asquith' and added,

'And this is my daughter Princess Bibesco'. Michael drew himself up to his full height and declared, 'And I am the Lord God, Almighty,' and, taking me by the shouders, added and 'this is my son, Jesus Christ, in whom I am well pleased'. We left the dining room in hysterical laughter. I have no idea what Margot and her daughter thought but she once, it is said, complained at the film star, Jean Harlow, calling her 'Margott' and finally said, 'The "t" is silent, as in Harlo(t!)w'. So she must have had a sense of humour.

One good friend at Corpus was Nigel Irvine, son of the Vice-Chancellor of St. Andrews University. He used to sing the *Ball of Kirriemuir*, and I can still remember all the verses, but they are much too rude to relay here. I can, however, safely reprint the refrain:

> *Ach, the ball, the ball, the ball of Kirriemuir,*
> *Some they came to dance the reel,*
> *And some they came to hoar.*
> *Singing this time, next time, last time!*
> *The man who did it last time cannot do it noo!*
> *Och! the ball, the ball, the ball of Kirriemuir,*
> *Some they came to dance the reel and some they came to hoar.*

Nigel died before the War broke out, just after he had married the sister of someone who became a very good friend of Eleanor's and mine, Jean Bannister. Jean had been a don at Somerville and had retired to a beautiful house on Loch Leven in Scotland. Eleanor had worked with Jean and Dennis Parsons, who became Jean's partner, in medical research in Oxford, and we saw them regularly when we visited Scotland. We only discovered the relationship of the two sisters by chance. Nigel's widow had become a missionary in Africa, whom we only saw once or twice. She was not at all the kind of person I would have expected Nigel to marry. We were very fond of Jean who was not only a distinguished scientist, but also an accomplished musician, a flautist. Her cousin was Roger, the first man to run the mile in under four minutes and later the Master of Pembroke College, Oxford. They are an interesting family, grandchildren of a British admiral, whose beautiful model ship graces Jean's living room.

At Corpus, I also became a good friend of the chaplain, Canon Sawyer, who had been the headmaster of Shrewsbury School. He was famous in the college for his loss of memory. His first letter to me asking me for breakfast was signed 'Michael Barratt Brown', and I had to ask my scout who could have written it, and he assured me that it would be the chaplain. The College porter told me one day that he had received a telegram from Sawyer, saying 'I am on Crewe station. Where am I going?' The porter had replied, 'Look at your ticket, sir!' And he went on his way. But by then he had written a Latin grammar, which we all used.

The canon asked me to read the lessons in chapel, to which I readily agreed. I liked doing it, but chapel attendance also counted as two roll calls at the dining hall in the total you had to complete each week. One Sunday I had been drinking the night before. My scout woke me, but I was a bit sleepy when I took my seat at 7 o'clock in the chapel. I found the place in the Bible, and began, 'Here beginneth the sixteenth verse of the first chapter of Saint Paul the Colossal to the Apostlians,' instead of 'Saint Paul the apostle to the Colossians'. I knew it was wrong, but could not then correct it. Instead of complaining, Sawyer met me afterwards and was delighted. 'Saint Paul was colossal, he was colossal!' he kept repeating.

I did take one piece of advice from the President, Livingstone, and went in the summer holiday with John Appleby, an old Dragon School friend, by rail and boat to Athens. John had an introduction to the Ambassador, Sir Charles Waterhouse. We called at the Embassy and met Lady Waterhouse. She expressed very left-wing views and we had a long political discussion, at the end of which she invited us to come out to a restaurant the next evening. We left for the coast in the embassy Rolls, registration Delta Sigma 1. Lady W. wanted to stop at one rather smart restaurant by the sea, but the French chauffeur said, 'Non, non, Madame, c'est trop chic pour vous!' And we went to one less 'chic', next door. Our knowledge of the Embassy phone number proved rather useful. We started our visits with Corinth, went into the vast basilica and arena, and stayed in the hotel. There we heard a news bulletin, which announced that the Italian navy had sailed round Crete and seemed likely to land an invading force. We were sufficiently frightened of a war developing that we rang the Embassy and were reassured by Waterhouse that the British navy was on hand and would scare the Italians off. We relayed this to our hosts and other guests at the hotel, and were served free drinks of retsina, and heard the manager say that his two young English guests had seen to it that Mussolini did not attack Greece.

We toured Athens, walked round the Acropolis, and followed the route to Marathon, only running part of the way. We cycled to Sunion, and slept under Byron's signature on the temple. We visited Delphi and even slept on the arena, and in southern Greece on the temple steps at Olympia. We walked over Taygetus to Sparta and bussed to Corinth. But the real excitement came on a visit to Crete. John had an introduction to Tsouderos, the Governor of the Bank of Greece, and he invited us to go with him to the island. At our first luncheon we made speeches of thanks in ancient Greek, and were not trusted after that to be present at their political discussion, but we were taken to Knossos and across the island to Phaistos. When I got back to England I went to report to Gilbert Murray, and suggested that in his reconstruction of Knossos Sir Arthur Evans had covered up the evidence of what was originally there. GM dashed out of the house with glee to see Sir Arthur up the road, and tell him what the students were saying about him!

My time at University introduced me to many interesting people. The

Knossos rebuilt

President of Corpus, who I had to call on in my scholar's gown, was Sir Richard Livingstone. He was a friend of my father's from his time in adult education. He tried to persuade me to return to the study of classics, but I did not feel that they would help me to understand the problems posed by the rise of Nazism. 'On the contrary!' Livingstone replied, 'Thucydides is your best guide!' Despite my 'decline', as he called it, from classics ('Greats') into PPE (Philosophy, Politics and Economics or 'Modern Greats'), Livingstone and I got on well.

Livingstone and I had one altercation. I had to take to him the news that the Junior Common Room had decided that the College-brewed beer was undrinkable, and beer should be brought in from outside. When Livingstone replied that 'Barrels of beer will be rolled into this College over my dead body!' I asked if he was proposing that as a solution, which I didn't think was a good one. We agreed in the end to bring in a trial barrel.

The most interesting of my several tutors was Dennis Brogan who set me history essays. His study was so full of books that it was hard to find anywhere to sit, and he continued reading while I read my essay, only interrupting to correct an error of fact. But his disquisition after I had finished was brilliant. He was knighted for his great historical work. He had a son who was called Vercingetorix ('Singey' for short!) but he changed that to 'Hugh' when he, too, became a well-known historian.

GDH Cole was not exactly a tutor of mine but a friend of my father's, whom I saw from time to time, and when I began writing my first book – on imperialism – he gave me much advice, and almost rewrote some of my chapters. I made a

GDH Cole

collection of his books, two of them in the Left Book Club series. I was impressed by his reconstruction of Rousseau's *Social Contract*, his enthusiasm for co-operatives, and the concept of guild socialism, which he advocated. I was particularly taken with the idea that there could be a 'general will' in mass elections, what Cole called 'the vital associative life' of the Guilds in face of the hugeness of the democratic vote, the State, and the private corporations. Later, I began to build on this in my lectures.

Apart from my tutors, who included, as I have mentioned, Sir Arthur Salter, my main inspiration came from a group of remarkable lecturers in Oxford at that time. The first for me was Roy Harrod, later Sir Roy, as the manager of the Queen's finances, but in my day the chief protagonist of Keynesian economic policies. I got to know Harrod personally when we both attended a London conference on a Commonwealth alternative to the European Union. He kindly recommended me for a chair, when I was then working as a senior lecturer in Sheffield University. Professor Joan Robinson, the doyenne of Economics at Cambridge, also attended this Conference and was another of my sponsors for a chair, together with my friend, Kenneth Alexander, then Professor of Economics at Strathclyde University. I did not get the chair!

My second inspiration came from AJ (Freddie) Ayer, who was introducing logical positivism to Oxford. He was regarded as second only to Bertrand Russell as a 20th Century philosopher. In his several marriages, he became stepfather to Nigella Lawson. I came to know him later, when he was meeting my friend Victor Kiernan's wife, Heather. Freddie was charming, but it was sometimes hard to follow the trend of his thought. I learnt from him to question all assumptions that were said to be 'given'.

Finally, and perhaps most influential, was my friendship with RG Collingwood, the Waynflete Professor of Metaphysics and a leading authority on Roman Britain. He lived near us in North Oxford, and I became friends with his children, and went on archaeological trips with them. After his divorce and marriage to his secretary, Kate, I came to know Kate, too, in Essex, and as his widow when she lived in Northumberland with my wife's great friend, Anne Clark. What Collingwood taught us was 'always observe!' 'When you see a hill, for example, ask yourself if it is natural or man-made. Either way, start thinking about what it was used for.' RG used to keep us permanently on the go with such questions. He insisted that observing was not just a matter of noticing, like a jelly fish that just let food float towards its mouth. You had to look out for your prey. He asked me one day why there was a windmill on the top of a hill. I impressed him greatly by guessing it was for an artesian well, which I had been reading about in a geography book.

I also attended William Beveridge's seminar on the social services. It was held in the rooms of Harold Wilson, who was a lecturer at Beveridge's college, University College. Wilson was a Liberal in those days, and I was amused to see on his bookshelves the lives of the British Prime Ministers in the Nineteenth Century. I did not get to see the famous Beveridge Report on the *Social Services* until I reached Cape Town, in 1942, on my way to Cairo. I read the first part on the train travelling from Cape Town to Durban, and was then able to give a lecture on it in Durban, and when I got to Cairo, to propose the adoption of its main measures by the Cairo 'Forces Parliament'.

I enjoyed my last year at Corpus. I worked hard and, as captain of boats, I rowed hard. We stayed in the first division in Torpids and in Eights, although we were bumped by Christ Church. We held off an attack from Jesus, our cox, Michael Pugh, shouting, 'Pull harder! It's bloody Jesus!' In the college pecking order, Jesus College, recruiting then largely from Wales, stood very low. Our coach used to tell us funny stories to relax us at the starting post. One I remember was about a recruit to the US Army, who was told to undress for a medical examination. He did so and the examining doctor pulled at his penis, and then wrote something in his record book. He did this several times, and finally the recruit said, 'Say, if this is for the honour and glory of the American Army, all well and good, but if it is for my own personal delectation, a little faster please!' Another story was of Mae West's reception of the Oxford eight, as 'Eight fine upstanding men welded into one glorious whole by their Cox' – the lines to be spoken aloud to reveal the *double entendre*.

As well as work and rowing, I saw a great deal of Frances. We had been together with our families in Cornwall in 1938, when the possibility of war with Germany seemed imminent. There was even some discussion of Frances and me staying on in Cornwall to be responsible for our brothers and sisters in the event of a German invasion or bombing of London. But Chamberlain made peace with Hitler, and the outbreak of war was delayed. When Frances came up to St

Hugh's, she and I met regularly and got to know each other really well. During Frances's first year, we met up in my room in Corpus, discussing economics and politics, and in the next year in my digs at the bottom of Headington Hill. Our landlady there was very accommodating and quite welcomed our being together. We were very happily in love. We had lovely times together and we decided to get engaged. Towards the end of my last term, we invited friends to an engagement party on the river Cherwell in hired punts. We drank Sangria. The only tutor in the party was my young philosophy tutor, who had become a real friend. He could not understand why I had done so badly in my philosophy finals. GDH Cole had told my father that I had done very well in politics and economics, but collapsed in philosophy, so that I only got a second class degree, not a first. I was not at all surprised. I did the philosophy paper while news was coming through of the British Army evacuation of Dunkirk. I could only think of what I would do if/when a German army invaded Britain. That is my excuse, anyway, and I had no thought then of an academic career, only of serving in the Friends Ambulance Unit.

CHAPTER 5

The Friends' Ambulance Unit
in London and the Middle East, 1940s

This chapter covers the period from 1940 to 1942. In 1940, Churchill had succeeded Chamberlain as British Prime Minister and had to face the Battle of Britain and the night bombing of London in the 1940-41 blitz. Britain was really alone against Germany and her allies, but the RAF prevented an invasion, and Hitler turned to invade Russia. Britain signed an Atlantic Charter with the USA in August 1941 to guarantee mutual support, and when in November the Japanese sank much of the US navy at Pearl Harbor, the USA was finally committed to joining forces to resist Hitler. But the Germans went on, in December 1941, to destroy much of the British navy. U-boats were torpedoing British convoys on their way to the East and Middle East and had sunk the boat in which my friend Tom Tanner was sailing. As I was travelling via Cape Town to replace him in Cairo, I narrowly escaped the same fate.

The German armies were held by the Russians outside Moscow, in 1942, but the war was not going so well elsewhere for Britain and her allies. Japan entered Singapore. The British army was in retreat in Libya, and a landing at Dieppe in France had been a failure. The Russians were demanding that Britain should open a 'second front' against Germany in Europe. Churchill went to Cairo and then Moscow to reassure Stalin, and by the time I reached Cairo, the British Eighth Army under General Montgomery had just held the Germans off at the battle of El Alamein. Churchill came to Cairo and met Chiang Kai Shek from China, and developed pneumonia. He would probably have died but for penicillin.

I joined the Friends' Ambulance Unit (FAU) in 1939, but left to return to Corpus for a last year, and rejoined in 1940. After my time at the Northfield Training Camp, I was sent to the London Hospital in Whitechapel to work in hospitals and then in taking food and medical aid to the people living in shelters in Docklands where the London blitz had begun. I had the use of a van with steel shuttering in place of glass windows and a small opening in the windscreen to see out of in the blacked-out roads. I was asked to take visitors around, as this was regarded as a safe vehicle. I had a ramp, and with a helper could take a piano where the shelters were in warehouses that had a lift. I took many interesting people on shelter rounds including Benjamin Britten and Kenneth Lindsay, but my most interesting companion was the American film producer, Sam Wanamaker. He wanted me to show him where Shakespeare's Globe Theatre had stood. I consulted drawings of the period and decided that it must have been just across the Thames, opposite St. Paul's Cathedral. I found a narrow lane going down to the river between two warehouses, at the right spot, and took Sam Wanamaker there. He was delighted.

His idea was to rebuild the Globe at the end of the War and put up some money for the project. He died before the project was launched, but his daughter carried it on. Sam especially liked the pub The Prospect of Whitby in Shadwell, to which I took him. The pianist there was playing with the back of his fingers, and had his girlfriend sitting on the floor by his side holding him between the legs to comfort him.

Apart from Freddie Temple, there were many people – men and women – whom I got to know in my time in the FAU, who were well known in important circles in Britain or became well known. First of all, I think of Tom Tanner, chair of the new FAU Executive, who became my closest friend. I shared a room at the London Hospital Students' Hostel with him. After studying at Oxford University, and playing rugger for Oxford, Tom went up the hard way in the family printing business. He became head of the subsidiary firm of Tanners in Glasgow, before joining the FAU. They used to print labels for Scottish whiskies, and had to dispose of any that weren't perfect. Somebody must have found where these were disposed of, because the labels turned up in Cairo, when I was there, on Bolinarchi whisky, so I was told.

Tom Tanner and I went together to lunchtime meetings of Political and Economic Planning, attended by Julian Huxley, then curator of the London Zoo, to which he took us one day, by Corder Catchpool, founder of the Youth Hostels Association, by my old friend Kenneth Lindsay, by Anthony West, the son of HG Wells and Rebecca West, by Michael Young, the founder of *Which*, author of *Meritocracy*, and many other books, by Jimmy Mallon, Warden of Toynbee Hall, and by several civil servants. These were fascinating meetings, and taught me much about the state of the British economy and British society.

Tom Tanner particularly encouraged me in my development of the FAU's relief work in cities suffering from German air raids. Tom made contact with the Ministry of Food to discover what they had in mind for emergency feeding in bombed cities, where the FAU could perhaps find a role. The idea of converting horse boxes into mobile soup kitchens emerged, and a fleet began to be prepared, for which the FAU would supply the drivers. We suggested that an information wagon should be included to distribute news about available accommodation for those bombed out of their homes and other advice, like a mobile Citizens' Advice Bureau.

The Minister of Food, Lord Woolton, informed Churchill of the proposed mobile soup kitchens. We went to 10 Downing Street to have Prime Ministerial support. In my excitement, I split the only smart trousers I had, and was forced to stand in front of Churchill holding my file describing the scheme behind my back to conceal the tear. Churchill's response to our proposal was that the vans should be called 'Queen's Messengers' and should be launched by the Queen with her blessing. This had to be organised, and seemed to me to be an almost impossible task.

A few weeks later, however, we had to drive the vans to Buckingham Palace for the blessing. I had to lead the convoy, and was seriously worried about getting the quite broad vans between the bollards on either side of the entrance to the Palace courtyard. Then we had to line up in two lines in front of the steps, which the Queen would come down to inspect us and give her blessing. Each van had a little flag-mast on the roof, with a string down to the driver's wheel which could be pulled, and the flag-mast would stand up with the Queen's Messengers flag flapping bravely. When the Queen appeared, I had to shout 'Company, attention!' My voice echoed round the courtyard in the most alarming manner. At that command all the flags shot up, except one – and there was one of the drivers desperately pulling his string to no effect. The Queen burst out laughing and walked to the poor man to apologise. She said how sorry she was, but she said it really was funny. As it turned out, the Queen looked closely at the van's equipment and this was the only driver she spoke to before she made her little speech commending the initiative of the Queen's Messengers and wishing us well in our important work. I then had the vans to lead back out between the bollards. The one blitzed city that I went to with the vans was Plymouth, where we certainly proved our usefulness.

I had another indication of Queen Elizabeth The Queen Mother's sense of humour. I was talking to a shelter warden friend of mine who had his shelter visited by her. She had asked a female shelterer with a very red-headed baby if the father had been red-haired. 'I dunno,' came the reply, "ee 'ad 'is 'at on!' The Queen laughed heartily.

There were three doctors at the London and at the Hackney hospital where I worked, who had a great influence on my life there. The first was the Quaker, Henry Wilson at the London, who arranged for the FAU to use the Students' Hostel, evacuated for the war, which became our London HQ. He was a remarkably concerned and caring friend. Among other things, he got Dr Medawar to conduct a whole series of tests on FAU personnel to discover the effect of different diets on our behaviour. I took part in one, where some of us were given large quantities of carrots to eat, and others were denied them. In the blacked out streets night vision was very valuable. The carrot eaters, of which I was one, did far better than the others. One of the doctors at the London seemed to me to be always somewhat drunk in the local pub we frequented. I had to have a minor operation one day on my polio-affected eye performed by him. I was terrified, but in fact he was most dexterous and successful.

The other doctor I got to know was at Hackney Hospital, where I was for a time a ward orderly. My job in the operating theatre was to put instruments into the steriliser. One day the surgeon asked me to get a screwdriver and take a screw out of the surgery door hinge, and he pointed to one. I did that and sterilised the screw, which the surgeon then used in putting two pieces of broken bone together. Another FAU member, Roger Pullbrook, worked with me. He was the

Annette Cooper, 1940

son of the chairman of Lloyds Insurance, which opened their basement for an air raid shelter manned by FAU members including my friend, Annette. Roger was himself a champion squash player, as I discovered when he offered to play squash with me. Tall and strong, as he was, he fainted at the sight of blood, which did not help me very much in the surgery. I spent some months at the Hackney Hospital, and was amazed at the long hours which both doctors and nurses put in, dealing with casualties of the blitz. I admired them, but I did not want to be a nurse. My strengths seemed to lie more in administration.

Tom Tanner did me one very good turn. Before I was due to go to the wedding of Annette Cooper and my Oxford friend, David Caulkin, both from the FAU, I had to go to the dentist to have a tooth extraction. I was given gas (laughing gas, as it was called). At the wedding I was served an alcoholic cocktail that was very powerful, and I left the party to take the tube back to the London Hospital. I didn't get to the station, but collapsed on the pavement in Piccadilly under the influence of the drink and the gas. I was picked up and taken to the local hospital and then to Marlborough Street police station. I stayed in a cell until about two in the morning, when they let me out, and told me to appear in court the next day on the charge of being drunk and disorderly. I managed to walk back to Whitechapel and the next day Tom Tanner took me to the court. He explained on my behalf that I was normally a sober and committed ambulance worker, but had alcohol added to dentist's gas. I was let off with a £50 fine, and I certainly had Tom to thank for looking after me. Annette and David went off happily for their honeymoon before he went to Sandhurst, as he had decided to leave the FAU and join up. Annette came back to the students' hotel, where I saw her from time to time.

Through Tom Tanner I met his brother-in-law, Oliver (later Lord) Franks, who was head of the Ministry of Supply, had been Master of Queen's College Oxford, later, Governor of Lloyd's Bank, and chief negotiator for Britain of Marshall Aid. Then among my friends there were Roger Wilson, Secretary of Friends War Victim Relief, Horace Alexander and Richard Symonds, who headed up the FAU Mission to India, Gerald Gardiner, who became Lord Chancellor in the first Wilson administration, Ralph Barlow, who was the head of the FAU Unit in Cairo and went on to be Secretary of the Bournville (Cadbury) Village Trust, Lewis Waddilove, who became chairman of the Rowntree Trust, Frank Blackaby, who became editor of *Social and Economic Research,* and Pat Barr, the actor. Of all these interesting people, some of whom reappear in this

Tom Tanner

memoir, I am inclined to add the most words about Oliver Franks.

Oliver Franks was a Quaker, married to a Quaker. Both regularly attended Quaker meetings, but Oliver was a particularly shrewd negotiator. The inter-war years were marked by a remarkable ascendancy of Quakers in British public and business life – Arnold and Seebohm Rowntree, Paul and Barrow Cadbury in cocoa and chocolate, Eva Reckitt and Allsops in pharmaceuticals, Barclays and Frys in banking, Truman, Hanbury and Buxton and Stopes' beers, Tanners in printing, Early (warm) blankets. But Oliver Franks was not mainly dealing with Quakers in the Ministry of Supply; they had withdrawn from all military activity.

I once asked Oliver how he dealt with big businessmen. 'I fix the meeting for 12 midday and have a sandwich and a drink at 11.45,' he said. 'I am generally beginning to win the argument by 1 o'clock, as my opponent gets hungry.' He adopted the practice of having phones in his car, not one but two so that he could say that he was on the other phone, if he wanted to stall. Despite the somewhat devious tricks, he was moved by deep emotions. At the conclusion of the Marshall Aid negotiations in France, he had something near to a breakdown. A friend took him to Chartres Cathedral, to sit in quiet for an hour or two. In his biography the cause is described as sheer exhaustion after long days and nights of negotiation, but I heard from his wife that it was at least in part conscience at the deliberate exclusion of the Soviet Union from Allied assistance. Molotov took a large Soviet delegation to Paris with their aid requirements, but when they found that it was not United Nations aid, and had capitalist conditions, they withdrew.

Other FAU members I got to know well included William Barnes, whom I had known at the Dragon School and who went with the FAU to China. William and I were sleeping in a dormitory of the London hospital when a bomb landed near to us. We dived under the bed and hit our heads – the only war wound we suffered! One of our number was in the lavatory, which stuck out from the rest of the building. He was a great humorist and replied to our inquiry as to his safety, that the bomb had fallen 'between two stools'.

William went with the FAU to China and after the War to do relief work in Europe. From his FAU days he remained a close friend of Annette Caulkin and her family. Later, he became secretary of the London Business School and a housing officer in Camden, where I met him when I came to live there. He became well known for his policy of mixing council house tenants with private owners in streets and on estates. He had become a Quaker by then, and I recalled his father, Bishop Barnes of Birmingham, who was a friend of my father. The bishop was married to a Quaker, who I met with William, and he held unusual views for an Anglican, doubting the stories of a Virgin birth or of a resurrection.

Richard Symonds had been a good friend of mine at Corpus Christi College in Oxford. He became secretary of the Oxford Union, when Ted Heath was the president. I made a speech in the Union, and was congratulated by Ted Heath when he had still not lost his East London accent. I admired Ted Heath, because he went to Spain and reported positively on the side of the Government against Franco. Richard Symonds and I spent much time together at our homes on the Thames. We had the same commitment to pacifism, and joined the Friends' Ambulance Unit and worked together in the FAU's response to the threat of the London air raids with his companion of those days, Angela de Renzy Martin. After serving the FAU in India with Horace Alexander, Richard went on to become a fellow at Sussex University Institute for Development Studies and, still later, a historian for Corpus Christi College, Oxford.

Angela later married Kenneth Sinclair Loutit, who became chief medical officer for United Nations Relief and Rehabilitation Administration (UNRRA) in Yugoslavia, when I was assistant to the chief of the UNRRA mission. Kenneth had served as a doctor with the government forces in the Spanish Civil War, and later became the head of the World Health Organization in Morocco, where he retired with a Moroccan wife and died. I inherited from Annette four long volumes of his typewritten autobiography, which have some fascinating stories – an interview with General de Gaulle and a description of the destruction of Shepheard's Hotel in Cairo by Egyptian dissidents. The recent revolts in Cairo's Tahrir Square are not a new phenomenon. But Kenneth's memoirs desperately need editing and shortening – a nice job for some young scholar.

Richard Wainwright was on the executive of the FAU, but I hardly knew him. He became a Liberal MP after the War, and with the moneys from the sale of his family surgical instrument firm in Yorkshire established a fund for helping young foreigners to study in England. One of his daughters managed the fund, and I got help from it for two Serbian friends of mine. His other daughter, Hilary, I worked with in the Greater London Council and have met since as the editor of *Red Pepper,* a really admirable journalist.

Richard Wainwright really deserves mention in this book because of a story told of him by Basil Davidson. Richard as an MP had taken an interest in the liberation of the Portuguese African colonies. Basil had been engaged directly with the liberating armies of Guinea Bissau. The Joseph Rowntree Reform Trust, of which Richard was a trustee, wanted to support this struggle and sent Richard and his wife Joyce to Guinea Bissau to investigate. Basil helped to organise and advise on their visit. They went taking two footballs, twenty-two pairs of football boots, jerseys and shorts and a set of Association Football rules. Guinea Bissau is now one of the leading lights in African football.

One other name I must add in my story of the FAU is that of Robin Whitworth. He was a bishop's son, who had worked for the BBC and became my London liaison officer when I was in Cairo planning FAU units to go into the Balkans for post-war relief work. All these friends were marked by extreme competence in their work, combined with a natural humility which I found very attractive. Robin had a delicious sense of humour. He once rang me when I was in bed reading a novel by Trollope. I explained this, to which he replied, 'If you are in bed and have a Trollope in one hand, you had better have a Hardy in the other!' Other FAU members whom I got to know in the Middle East deserve a separate chapter.

Some time after our marriage, Frances and I got the use of a house in Chester Place, opposite Regents Park, which belonged to David Astor. He let us have it rent-free because he depended on us as fire-watchers against incendiary bombs. I only rarely got there from hospital, but when I did I could run round the Park and take a skulling boat on the lake. Apparently, Sir Samuel Hoare, the Foreign Secretary, had stayed there, and on one occasion the phone rang and I answered it and heard a foreign voice say, 'Ici Laval, est ce que Monsieur Hoare est la bas?' I said, 'Non! Monsieur' and he rang off. But I could claim that I had spoken to one of the partners in the infamous Hoare-Laval Pact, which had agreed Mussolini's occupation of Abyssinia. Hoare was a member of the Quaker banking family and used to try to rehabilitate his reputation by referring to a common ancestor, Elizabeth Fry, whose portrait still adorns our £5 notes, shown along with the women prisoners in Newgate, whom she taught to read and write.

Before being posted to join the FAU in the Middle East, I was given a week's leave. I went with my wife Frances to Scotland to the large house on the Mull of

Kintyre of Dick and Naomi Mitchison. We had on several occasions been with them in their house on the Thames, watching the Oxford and Cambridge boat race, one time with Indira Gandhi. Dick and Naomi, in 1941, were in Scotland with several of their children and a young man who seemed to be a friend of Naomi's. At one point her eldest son appeared from a submarine in the bay. Frances spent most of her time with one of the Mitchison girls and I went out harvesting, shooting and fishing with Dick and with Naomi's friend. We had help with the cooking. But we all helped with washing up and clearing. The gardens and greenhouse were full of fruit and vegetables and Dick had a large store of wine.

I didn't much care for shooting birds for the table, and the fishing was a disaster. Dick showed me how to select a hook and fly and attach them to the line and then how to cast across the stream to a shady corner. I did what I was told, and the hook from my cast, as I threw it, caught on Dick's cheek. I was appalled and apologised profusely. 'No, nothing!' he said. 'All my fault. I stood too near behind you. I had no idea you would make such an excellent long cast!' We went to the doctor for the excision, and next day caught a three-pound salmon for our supper. I tried to spend more time with Frances. I was leaving her for God knows how long the next week.

The journey to the Middle East from London was surprising – to Edinburgh, round Scotland, through the Sound of Mull, which I knew so well, to join a convoy across the Atlantic to New York harbour. There we joined another convoy via Pernambuco to pick up fresh fruit, and back across the Atlantic, past the Canaries to the African coast, where we were torpedoed. Miraculously, while one boat was sunk, our boat was only shaved and one container could be sealed and we proceeded to Freetown with a list to starboard. In Freetown, Brandon Cadbury, with whom I was travelling, used his cocoa influence and saw the Colonial Secretary who tried to arrange for us to fly direct to Cairo. Unfortunately, a ship had been refused entry to the harbour and sunk, and the harbour commander was being repatriated in disgrace to Cairo, and needed our seats. So we spent a few delightful days in the Colonial Secretary's villa, reading the minutes of his Governor's meetings, and then struggled on with our starboard list along the African coast, via Takoradi, Luanda, and Walfish Bay to Cape Town.

In Cape Town, Brandon had an introduction to General Jan Smuts. He was in London, but we were received in his residence, and taken for a tour of the city, including a trip up the Table Mountain. I went to the Post Office to post a letter home, and was appalled to find that there were two entrances, one for whites and one for others. What would I do with my friends Kumara and Nontando? Brandon organised the next stage of our journey, to Durban across the Kalahari Desert. We arrived on a Sunday, and went to a Friends' Meeting and I gave a lecture on the Beveridge Report. Even at these meetings there were only white people present. From Durban we went by flying boat via Dar es Salaam,

Mombasa, Kampala and Lake Victoria, to Khartoum and finally Cairo. Flying by flying boat the whole length of Africa is the most wonderful way of seeing that vast continent. At a few hundred feet above land or sea, you can see everything, even monkeys playing in the trees. I gained my life-long love of Africa on that journey.

In Cairo, the Friends' Ambulance Unit wore Red Cross uniform and came under the nominal command of the Red Cross Commissioner. When I arrived, Mr Archibald, the Commissioner, was just leaving and was replaced by Annie Bryans, wife of an MP, and daughter of Lord Leathers, who was Minister of Transport in Churchill's National Government. She and I struck up a very good relationship. She took me everywhere in her smart staff car and introduced me to all her many connections – in the Minister of State's Office, in the Royal Army Medical Corps, and even among local exiled royalty, the King of Greece for one! Most important of all, she encouraged me to explore the possibilities of developing relief work for FAU members who were no longer needed, after the battle of El Alamein, for ambulance and other army medical services. Without her and her contacts in the RAMC, I should never have been able to launch the major relief programme for refugees in the Middle East or to have organised relief units to go into the Balkans, as the Germans left. When she and I left Cairo, she took over from Lady Limerick as head of the British Red Cross.

I only found recently reading a biography of Frank Thompson, that Frank had

Frank Thompson

Michael in Red Cross uniform, 1941

been at the Cairo Forces' Parliament in 1943. I didn't see him there but I did see his friend, Peter Wright (not the same as Peter Wright, the spy), also in SOE (the army's Special Operations Executive). I saw Peter many times after that – in Bari, Sarajevo, Belgrade, and then in London and Sheffield and, finally, in a home in Leicester. I watched the collapse of his love affair with the beautiful Helen Wright from Australia, and got to know his wife, who was the daughter of Alfred Sohn-Rethel. Robin Murray and I worked with Alfred in the Conference of Socialist Economists, and his widow came to live for some months with Eleanor and me. Peter Wright was a delightful companion, with a wonderful collection of funny stories to tell in one or other of his several languages, English, French, Russian, Serbo-Croatian, Spanish – almost as much a multi-linguist as Frank Thompson. Peter wrote poetry like Frank, and also painted. His last work was the result of living on Lake Titicaca in Mexico. Peter came to my 80th birthday party and is among the back row in the photograph on the front of this book, another Seeker …

One of Peter's favourite stories, told in French, was of a French schools inspector, who asked the boys the classic question posed in France to those who show excessive come-uppance – *qui est ce qui est cassé la Vase de Soissons* (who broke the Soissons Vase?) The answer is that a French soldier took a beautiful vase as his booty in war, but it was claimed by Clovis, the first king of a united France. When the soldier found he could not have the vase, he broke it, and Clovis sought him out and axed him down. Most of the boys in the class made a guess at the soldier's name but one little boy, perhaps knowing the story, said, *'ce n'etait pas moi, Monsieur!'* (it wasn't me, sir!).

The relief work in Bosnia made a good start. Writing in 2013, when a Coalition Government in the UK is planning to 'celebrate' the 1914-18 War, it seems more than ever necessary to recall the work of the medical and relief workers. I did not see anything of the First World War, but I saw much of the Second. Several of my companions in the Friends Ambulance Unit were killed by enemy action and I saw much suffering. One example of relief work is etched in my memory. Though it truly belongs in the next chapter, I will tell it here. In the late autumn of 1945 I went up into the mountains above Sarajevo to tell the village committees that I believed that emergency food supplies were on their way. From the first village I looked down on the winding road from the coast and there I saw the convoy of trucks crawling up the hills. They had decided to brave it out only a day or two after the roads had begun to be cleared of land mines. As they came past me they waved. I realised that we had done it; we had got the supplies in before the snow closed up the roads for the winter. I sat alone in my jeep and cried, and started on the drive back down into Sarajevo.

CHAPTER 6

MERRA and UNRRA
in the Middle East and Balkans, 1940s

This chapter covers the period from 1942 to 1945. In Cairo I was able to participate in the 'Forces' Parliament', and put forward some of the proposals made by Sir William Beveridge in his Report on the Social Services in a post-war Britain. The victory at Alamein had brought many soldiers back to Cairo, and also many FAU members, with nothing to do. Refugees from the German occupation of Europe were pouring into the Middle East. But the German army was defeated at Stalingrad in 1943. The Lend-Lease Agreement was signed between the US and UK, to share supplies. American forces landed in Algiers and entered Italy with the British and, in September 1943, Italy surrendered. Tito's Yugoslav Partisans, who had been holding the Germans at bay, took over Italian arms. At last, the Second Front landings by British, US and Canadian troops took place in France, with heavy bombing of Germany. But in the UK, London was bombed again, the worst losses took place from U-boat attacks, and food rationing was strengthened.

In the Middle East preparations were being made for British military occupation of the Balkans, with relief work to follow, organised by the Middle East Relief and Refugee Organisation (MERRA) in which the FAU established a role. 1944 saw the creation of a United Nations Relief and Rehabilitation Administration (UNRRA). The international Bretton Woods Agreement was signed on post-war recovery with an International Monetary Fund and World Bank, much modified from Maynard Keynes's original ideas. By 1945, the FAU moved with UNRRA into Italy, Greece and Yugoslavia. The UK bombing of Dresden took place in revenge for German bombing of British cities. Churchill and Roosevelt met Stalin at Yalta to agree on the post-war division of Europe. In May, victory in Europe was celebrated, followed in August by the US atom bombing of Hiroshima and Nagasaki in Japan, and by the Japanese surrender in September. In the first post-war British election in 1945, Labour won an overwhelming victory.

When I arrived in Cairo in 1943, a whole flood of refugees were arriving in the Middle East, driven out of their countries by the Germans – mainly Poles, Greeks and Yugoslavs. The first I met were Poles being cared for in a camp in Palestine by a Quaker couple by the name of Lock. They did not seem to want help, but in Palestine I found a Friends' Ambulance Unit under the command of Professor Gordon Cox from Cambridge, whom I had known in our FAU Training Camp in 1940. The unit were helping in a camp for Greek refugees at Nuseirat. Gordon was an Ancient Greek scholar, and I laughed at him screaming in perfect modern Greek at a refugee who had left a latrine tent door open. I got some extra FAU staff from Cairo to help Gordon.

The military authorities governing Egypt did not want Communists to come

Partisans in Bosnia, 1943

into the country, spreading seditious ideas among the Egyptians. When the next
flood of refugees arrived, they were also Communists, from the Adriatic islands
of Yugoslavia. They had to go to a camp established at El Shatt on the Sinai
Peninsular, far from mainland Egypt. We supplied several FAU members from
Cairo for this camp, and two new arrivals from England, Arnold Curtis and Keith
Linney, the Somerset cricketer, became leaders of a sub-camp where they
organised all sorts of activities – woodwork and music and many different sports.
One night when I was at the camp, a famous Croatian singer entered singing well-
known arias – almost unbelievable in the middle of the Sinai desert.

I had got to know in Cairo members of the Yugoslav branch of Special
Operations Executive (SOE), especially James Klugmann and Basil Davidson,

Basil Davidson

who became a life-long friend. They proposed that I should take a small mission from Tito's HQ to visit El Shatt. Gordon Fraser from SOE came with me to Sinai with General Velebit, one of Tito's closest allies, and we toured the camps. Velebit, who spoke perfect English, asked Keith Linney whether there were any unsolved problems that he might help with. Keith said that one was that he could not persuade the Yugoslav camp officials that it was important to close the latrine tent doors to keep the flies out. Velebit suggested an appeal to authority, and in his parting speech to the whole camp he said that the Prime Minister of England, Winston Churchill, had sent his only son Randolph, to fight with the partisans, and one of his orders was that all latrine tent doors must be kept closed. The appeal worked, but Keith's other problem was not so easily solved. The camp at El Shatt was surrounded by sand, and the weather was very hot. The women were used to a much cooler Mediterranean climate. Some, especially the elderly and a few who were pregnant, were suffering heat stroke.

The point was made when we got back to Cairo, and a new camp was established at Tolumbat near Alexandria and on the sea. I went to Tolumbat. It was there that I first met Dr Eleanor Singer, who was to be my second wife. At that time she was a doctor working with the Save the Children Fund and shared a tent with a nurse who turned out to be Larry Durrell's girlfriend. Eleanor had a jeep, and soon found that one of her off duty tasks was getting the girlfriend to regular assignations with Larry who was stationed in Alexandria. Larry along with Robin Fedden of the FAU became well known as the Alexandrine poets, as well as for his novels *The Alexandrian Quartet*. Annette, who was born in Alexandria, would often dip into Robin Fedden's book *Egypt*.

My main task in Cairo became the preparation of voluntary society relief units to go into the Balkans as the German armies withdrew. With the British Red Cross, we had formed a Council of Voluntary Societies in Cairo to work with the Council of British Societies for Relief Abroad (COBSRA) in London, on which Robin Whitworth represented the FAU. I was made the chair of the Personnel Committee of the Cairo body, and this Committee in fact came to do all the work of the Council. My contacts with the Yugoslav refugees had raised serious doubts in my mind about my pacifism. I hated war not only because of the human suffering but also because wars so obviously failed to make the human situation better. It was clear to me, however, that Tito's Partisans were creating a much better society. If I had been a Yugoslav, I would have fought alongside the Partisans.

I told my RAMC liaison officer that I had exemption from military service on condition of my membership of the FAU. As I was no longer a pacifist, I would have to leave the FAU and sign on in Cairo as a regular soldier. 'You will do nothing of the sort!' said my colonel friend. 'You are much too important doing what you are doing and can join MERRA, (the Middle East Relief and Refugee Administration), and continue our work.' It seemed an awfully easy way out but I accepted it, and bought two suits of civilian clothes. I also moved house from the FAU flat by Cairo's Bab el-Louk station to an army camp at Maadi. I was very grateful there for the silk sleeping bag which my mother had made for me because it kept out the bed bugs. From the camp at Maadi, I could walk down through the Acacia trees to Gezira Island, to swim before breakfast, eat in the NAAFI canteen, and be at work in the Minister of State's Office by 9am.

This change in my position was all the easier to accept because I had made friends with Cyril Pickard who was working with Sir William Matthews, the head of MERRA. Sir William had been one-time Chair of the Supplementary Benefits Commission in London. There could hardly have been two more different people than Cyril and Sir William. Cyril was quiet and scholarly and a brilliant negotiator. He became, as Sir Cyril, the Colonial High Commissioner in Cyprus, and later in Pakistan and Nigeria. Sir William had come up the hard way in the civil service, and was noisy and rather pompous. Cyril had a lovely wife who was a Baptist, and for her inauguration had to take total immersion in a special pool. She reminded me of Burne-Jones's model, Maria Zambaco. I attended this ceremony and noted the beautiful curve of her breasts under the clinging wet silk gown as she came out of the pool. Tragically, she died in childbirth. Cyril then married an old friend of mine in the FAU, Mary Cozens Hardy, who had just been divorced from our UNRRA Yugoslavia Finance Officer. As Lady Pickard, Mary continued, even after Cyril's death, to entertain a wide circle of friends in her Surrey home.

The first task facing Cyril and me in preparing for relief work in the Balkans was to persuade the military authorities planning entry into the Balkans, as the Germans withdrew, that a relief and refugee force would be required. The British Army had just established a head quarters in Caserta with 'Jumbo' Maitland Wilson as SACMED (Supreme Allied Commander of the Mediterranean Theatre). Cyril and I flew to Italy to see him, with the support of Commander Jackson, an Australian sailor, who had been given British responsibility for civilian affairs in liberated Eastern Europe. I knew of him because he was known to be in love with Barbara Ward, but could not divorce his wife to marry her since he was a Roman Catholic and needed some kind of Papal dispensation. I got to know and greatly respect 'Jacko', when at length we got into Yugoslavia. On our arrival at Caserta, I had to be listed as a Colonel, in order to be able to stay with Cyril and have access to SACMED. We did see him very briefly and got the message that everything would depend on our establishing good relations with those who took over power, most especially, with Tito. Here 'Jacko' helped greatly.

At this point in 1944, UNRRA (United Nations Relief and Rehabilitation Administration) took over the responsibilities of MERRA, and Cyril and I became UNRRA employees. Our first task was to set up an office in Italy, for a Yugoslav Mission – Yugoslavia was still under German rule. I was given this job, with the promise of an acting head of Mission being sent out from London. After a few weeks Alan Hall arrived, and I became his personal assistant. Leaving Cyril behind in Cairo was a great loss, but he joined us for some key negotiations with Tito's representatives. The flight to Bari was particularly hair-raising. My wife Frances had just arrived in Cairo to be with me, and I was being sent away to Italy, to be joined by her when she could get away. We met up again in Italy and had a lovely holiday together in Amalfi near Sorrento, where Christopher was conceived. Frances decided to return to England to have the baby, although I said I was sure there would be proper facilities in Yugoslavia.

I did not like the idea of a further separation from Frances, but I was assured that she would be able to join me in Yugoslavia after a quite short time, probably after I got to Sarajevo, where I was to establish the UNRRA mission for Bosnia and Herzegovina. Working in an organisation in a military situation, you did what you were told, and went where you were told, when they told you. The idea of a further long separation, after all the previous separations, was hateful, but that seemed to be the inevitable fate in war-time. I did, however, manage to get to London when the war ended for a visit in time for Christopher's birth, before our work in Bosnia was ended and we were ordered to Belgrade for new assignments. I was not allowed to be present at the delivery. I had to sit next door in the nursing home and wait. I went away full of joy. I had a son. He was named Christopher in memory of Christopher Cadogan, who was killed at Dunkirk in 1940 and had been married to Stella Zilliachus, then Frances's best friend.

Going back to my arrival in Italy, at the end of the flight from Cairo, as we dropped down to Bari, we were told to put on our gas masks because there had been an explosion in a ship with gas supplies in the harbour. I was not the only person who had used his gas mask case to stow away personal belongings and very few of us had a mask. Fortunately the gas cloud flew out to sea before we landed.

After a night or two in Bari's smart hotel, the Internationale, we were billeted in a large villa in San Spirito, on the coast just north of the town, but had our meetings in the town hall, the old government offices in Bari which still had murals celebrating Mussolini's regime with the fascist symbol much in evidence.

I managed to make contact with my SOE friends, James Klugmann and Basil Davidson, who had been moved from Cairo to form a military mission to Yugoslavia. Basil was shortly dropped by parachute into the Vojvodina with a radio operator to make contact with the Partisans there. James stayed behind in Bari, and could give me up-to-date information on what was happening in the fighting in Yugoslavia. There had evidently been major offensives by the Germans on Partisan forces, and Tito had been forced to move his HQ temporarily to the Island of Vis. He was able to move back inland in a few weeks. Randolph Churchill was a member of the military mission dropped into the Partisans. One day, I found James rather upset. They had dropped his supply of whisky to Randolph and it had come loose from the parachute and missed him.

When Alan Hall arrived he stayed with an American colleague in the smart Bari hotel, and our little party from Cairo MERRA was joined by some UNRRA recruits from the USA. Some of the FAU and other Voluntary Society units, which we had been planning to form Mobile Hygiene and First Aid Units (MHFAUs) for service in Yugoslavia, arrived. We then had to establish relations with the British military force (Allied Military Liaison or AML) that was planning to go into the country to complete the German withdrawal, and would be responsible for our movements into and in liberated Yugoslavia. I formed very good relations with the deputy commander of AML, who promised that 'After the inevitable balls-up of AML will follow the indescribable fuck-up of UNRRA!' We were all ready for action, but there were endless diplomatic delays.

A delegation from Tito's partisans arrived in Bari, and we began talks with them about the logistics of supply deliveries. We already had news of serious starvation on the Dalmatian coast. But Tito's HQ announced that they did not wish to hand the distribution of relief supplies to the British military and UNRRA. At the same time, UNRRA in Washington did not want anything to do with the military, and the Allied Military Supreme HQ in Washington did not want any supplies to go to Tito, supplies which had not the support of the Yugoslav Government in exile, stationed in London. This Government did have a representative in Bari, after Tito reached an agreement on a coalition with Dr. Šubašic, head of the exiled Government, but the question of equitable distribution of supplies remained.

In Bari I had made friends with a Yugoslav Colonel Neubauer, who was in charge of the care of the wounded partisan soldiers evacuated to hospitals in Italy. He tried to intervene with Tito's staff on behalf of our guarantee of fair distribution, but to no avail. I saw much of Robert Neubauer later over many years in Yugoslavia and in England, with his lovely wife, Nada Kraigher. Robert had been the head of the tuberculosis sanatorium at Golnik in Slovenia and became a top World Health Organisation consultant after the war. Nada, the sister of a leading member of Tito's post-war Government, took over the editing of a Party newspaper in Ljubljana. During one of our visits, she told us that she had

Kenneth Sinclair Loutit, Leslie Dow and Frances in Bari

been touring in the Soviet Union after Khrushchev's denunciation of Stalin, and in Georgia was surprised to find a statue of Stalin still standing. When she expressed her surprise, her guide said 'He was a Georgian, wasn't he?' Such is the power of nationalism! It reminded me of something an Oxford rowing friend of mine told me when I met up again with him in Cairo in 1942 and asked him about the evacuation of Tobruk. He was an officer in the Highland Light Infantry, and I asked him who they had helped to escape. 'The Scots, of course,' he said, 'but also the Geordies'. 'Why them?' I asked. 'They are our colony,' he replied.

Robert Neubauer did his best to help with the trouble over relief inspectors, but there was widespread suspicion, especially in the USA, that the Partisans would neglect the needs of those who had not fought along with them. The issue still depended on Tito's agreement to accepting large numbers of inspectors coming with the food supplies. Tito was adamant that he would not have them, and I overheard the officer representing SACMED at our talks, Air Vice Marshal Elliot, warning the Yugoslav delegates that the ship in Bari harbour full of supplies would go to Greece if they did not accept the inspectors. The ship went to Greece.

With no alternatives that we could see to this dilemma, Alan Hall and I decided that we had to fly to England to consult the head of UNRRA, Herbert H Lehman, ex-governor of New York State, who was then in London. We flew by Gibraltar and arrived in Poole from where I phoned to my parents to tell them, much to their surprise, that I was on my way to see them in South Stoke. From there I made contact with Margaret Lloyd, the mother of my wife, Frances. She was secretary of the Anglo-Yugoslav Friendship Association, and I told her the situation. She advised me to talk to Kingsley Martin at the *New Statesman* and immediately alert the editor of the *News Chronicle,* Aylmer Vallance, who I had got to know in the London air raids.

Thus, warned in the press, Governor Lehman received us at Claridges Hotel in his bedroom. He had fallen and had one leg in plaster. An advisor from the US State Department was there, who I subsequently believed was Richard Nixon. Alan Hall left the argument to me and I described the starvation conditions in Dalmatia, and the blame that was being put on UNRRA for denying Tito the food supplies he desperately needed, but for which he insisted on being responsible for their equitable distribution.

Nixon, if it was Nixon, warned me, after I had gone on for a bit, to stop. 'The Governor', he said, 'has got the message!' Next day Lehman saw General Velebit, who was representing Tito in London. Velebit proposed that a limit should be set to the number of inspectors, and responsibility for relief should be transferred at an early date from the army to UNRRA. When we returned to Bari, we got SACMED's agreement to UNRRA's role, and Tito agreed to up to a dozen inspectors going in to the country. The next problem was actually getting the supplies from the army and the vehicles for transporting them. When the vehicles came, half of them needed major repairs. Some had to be cannibalised, but fortunately we had some FAU drivers who knew what to do to make them serviceable.

In addition to a number of FAU drivers and vehicles and two mobile health and hygiene units, one from the Save the Children Fund, led by my wife-to-be, Dr. Eleanor Singer, we had a mobile pathology unit led by Dennis Greenwood. This unit had had a most distinguished career in the desert warfare in North Africa, and had added a remarkable final trip to Algeria in 1944. This had been to follow Churchill, who had pneumonia and was taken from Cairo to see his doctor, who had come out from England to Algiers. The doctor's story, as reported by his son, was that Churchill was cured by the use of sulpha drugs. Eleanor had never believed this, but preferred Dennis Greenwood's story that some penicillin had been flown out from England and had been administered by the doctor who headed Dennis's Unit. You can believe whichever story you prefer. Dennis was a strictly moral person, who could not tell a lie and continued to use sulpha drugs on many lesser illnesses than pneumonia.

The most important action I then took was persuading Basil Davidson, when he came out of Yugoslavia, to come and speak to all the UNRRA men and women and our voluntary society members about what to expect when we got into the country. Basil looked most impressive, well over six foot tall in a tailored battle dress and enormous boots. His message was that we should find extremely

FAU vehicles in Bosnia

well organised, democratically run local committees, representing the different ethnic groups, perfectly capable of distributing provisions efficiently and equitably. Several of our American members went home, realising that there was no job for them. Others relished the prospect of working with the different communities.

I was one such, and when at length we got into the country, I came to meet many local village and county committees, as well as members of the Government of Bosnia and Herzegovina in Sarajevo, where I was soon stationed, and was universally impressed by their competence and fairness, drawn as they were from each of the local ethnic groups – Orthodox Serbs, Catholic Croats and Muslims.

After a few weeks in Bosnia-Herzegovina, I was called to Belgrade to meet the new head of the UNRRA mission, Mikhail Sergeichic, a Russian from the USSR. I managed to establish an excellent working relationship with him through his interpreter and personal assistant, Vladimir Glouskin. Sergeichic had noted that, while most UNRRA personnel had had their travel permits temporarily withdrawn to allow the Yugoslav Government to check up on the numbers, I had managed to get my permit immediately extended. He invited me to go with him and Glouskin to Trieste.

The reason for the visit was that vehicles sent from the USA for UNRRA

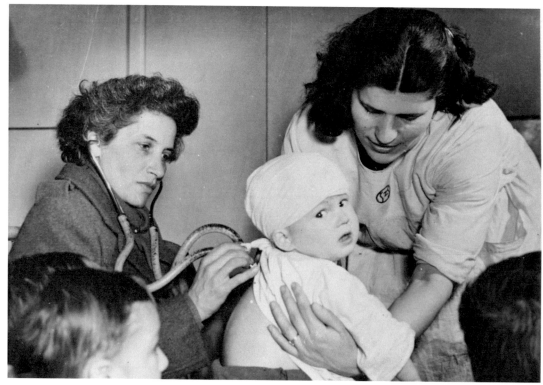

Dr. Eleanor Singer, Sarajevo clinic

Yugoslavia were being stolen in Trieste and sent back still in their packing cases. We were to see my old adversary 'Jumbo' Maitland-Wilson, and would be accompanied by Fiorello La Guardia, ex-Mayor of New York and currently head of UNRRA. With much Italian hand and arm waving, La Guardia made his protest. Sergeichic nodded from time to time, and Jumbo just smiled and said that he would issue an instruction about better security in the port. La Guardia was furious. It was summer time and Jumbo was wearing standard British Army shorts. Pointing at these La Guardia screamed 'I make my complaint about theft of United Nations property, and all I get is a "boy scout agreement". I will take the matter up with Allied Supreme Command in Washington.' In a further discussion, La Guardia told us that he had just been in Moscow and discovered that there were layers of dust on the top of the partitions in the lavatories at their beautiful metro. 'The world needed a taste of American efficiency!' he concluded.

The other major figure I met through UNRRA was Jo Grimond, who became leader of the British Liberal Party, but for a time headed up the London office of UNRRA. I had had an accident in a jeep in Bosnia and had to fly back to Britain for a cartilage operation on my right knee. This was performed in University College Hospital, and I recovered in time to be present at the birth, on Christmas Day 1945, of my son Christopher. Frances had returned to England to have the baby. When I was due to go back to Yugoslavia I had to have an exit visa, which

Grimond was to authorise. He questioned me at length about our work in Yugoslavia, and I got the impression of a very intelligent and well-informed politician, with a surprisingly sympathetic view of Tito. I met him many years later at a concert in Northumberland, when he had retired from the Liberal leadership, and enjoyed an hour or two recalling old times in UNRRA. He was the best of the post-war Liberal leaders, quite prepared for measures of public enterprise.

In Sarajevo and then in Belgrade I began to live with Eleanor Singer. We found each other perfect company. She was 15 years older than me, and, when I talked about living together permanently, she asked me what I would do when she was 80. We were driving along a road that had been cleared of land mines, but were told not to step out of the jeep onto the roadside. Only the day before, in front of us the typhus control team get out of their jeep to pee and we had seen them blown up by a mine. My answer to Eleanor was that the chance of our living another day was not very good, let alone into our eighties.

Eleanor was with me when we saw Tito at a reception in Belgrade. Eleanor had been given a *Titolik* medal for her work. She kept it underneath the lapel of her uniform jacket. Tito spotted this, and asked what she had been given it for. She told him and Tito smiled with those clear blue eyes. He said 'thank you very much' *(hvala ljepo!)* and turned to the next person in the queue. We saw Tito again when he came to visit the doctors at UNRRA, who had been performing cosmetic surgery on wounded Yugoslav soldiers, and that is what the photo shows, with Dr. Kenneth Sinclair Loutit looking in at the back.

Marshal Tito with UNRRA staff, 1946

UNRRA tractor, Bosnia, 1946

Frances came from England to join me in Belgrade when Eleanor had gone home on leave, and I did not know if I would see her again. When Frances rejoined me in Belgrade I told her about Eleanor. Frances became pregnant again. We went for long walks discussing what we should do. Belgrade was intolerably hot and baby Christopher was suffering. I arranged for Frances to go to Bled in the lakes and mountains of Slovenia, but then asked Eleanor to come back from England. She came and I realised that I could not live without her. She went to see Frances in Bled and told her. I was desperately busy with UNRRA work, but when I got some free time I fetched Frances from Bled, took her to Budapest and put her on a plane back to England. It is not a nice story, and I could have dealt with the situation very much more kindly, going back with Frances to England and facing the criticism of our parents.

I cannot easily justify my desertion of Frances with two little children, but I can explain it. In seven years of marriage we had had three separate weeks together and odd days and long absences. Having children together seemed to be a natural complement to our lives, especially when we re-met after a long absence. By contrast, though, it turned out that Eleanor and I adopted children. She and I had, in 1946, a close companionship, night and day, for six months of common endeavour in Yugoslavia. The contrast hardly needs to be explained, and almost inevitably led to our staying together. I managed the separation very badly, but the demands on me in UNRRA at that time were very pressing.

The last months which Eleanor and I had in Belgrade in 1947 were most enjoyable. We both had reports to write about our work for the official history of UNRRA in Yugoslavia, and there were a great number of good-bye parties. We gave several ourselves. We were regularly visited in our house in Dedinje on the outskirts of Belgrade by a peasant woman who had caught a hare, which she brought for us. We gave her a good meal, and for a party Eleanor would jug the hare with vegetables and plenty of red wine. It was especially enjoyed by our Russian interpreter, Vladimir Glouskin, and by Lore Sproule, who came back to join us in England and became a life-long friend.

When my time with UNRRA came to an end, in 1947, Eleanor and I went to Geneva, believing that we might be employed by the UN there, but most of us were not accepted. Our friend, David Leacock, from UNRRA, son of Stephen Leacock, and father of Phil, the film maker, was accepted, and we spent a very pleasant time in his flat in Geneva. Some years later, we stayed on his farm in the south of France and on his estate in Grand Canary. He had been expelled from Spain because of his support for the resistance to Franco, but returned on Franco's death. He was a committed democrat, and I dedicated my first book on *Imperialism* to him. His wife was one of the Wills tobacco family, and their daughter spent much time with us before her marriage to one of the Jacobs chocolate heirs.

UNRRA port operations, Trieste, 1946

CHAPTER 7

Film Industry, Workers' Education, the Communist Party, the New Left and CND in London and Essex, 1940s-50s

This chapter covers the years 1946 to 1957. The Labour Government was elected in 1945 on a programme that included the nationalisation of the Bank of England, of the mines and railways, and the creation of a National Health Service (NHS). Welfare state contributions from full employment were to pay for pensions and social benefits. In 1946, the NHS was established and, in 1947, the National Coal Board. After a fuel and convertibility crisis, gas and electricity were also brought into public ownership. In 1947, the Marshall Plan for US aid to Europe was introduced and its funds were used by the UK to finance British imperial obligations. In 1947, India won its independence under the leadership of Pandit Nehru. Britain's African colonies benefited from the high price of their raw material exports, but the Middle East was unsettled. The first war between Israel and a British-controlled Egypt took place in 1948, with other Arab forces involved. The US withdrew its support for UK finances and, in 1949, the pound was devalued from $4.03 to $2.80. In 1949, the Communists gained power in China under Mao Tse Tung. In 1950-51 the war between South Korea and North Korea broke out, the North supported by China and the South by the USA and UK. The result was a stalemate, in which the UK suffered serious losses. In Vietnam, Ho Chi Minh came to power with Chinese support and was regarded as a major threat by the USA.

Labour just survived the 1950 UK election, but was defeated by the Tories in a re-run, in 1951. In 1952, the US tested the first hydrogen bomb, followed the next year by the Russians. Kwame Nkrumah became the first African government President, but the Mau Mau rising in Kenya was brutally put down, and guerrillas in Malaya suppressed. In 1953, Stalin died. European discussions began about a European Common Market to follow the European Coal and Steel Community, formed in 1950. The idea of an alternative for Britain of a stronger Commonwealth organisation was mooted in London conferences in 1954. Labour was again defeated by the Tories.

Stalin's successor, Nikita Khrushchev, made his famous speech, in February 1956, to the 20th Congress of the Soviet Communist Party, denouncing Stalin, and the world was changed. Khrushchev's speech was released later in 1956 and in the same year Soviet forces put down a Hungarian revolt. This and the implications of Khrushchev's revelations were too much for many Communists, and everywhere they left the Party. Colonel Nasser seized the Suez Canal for Egypt and a Franco-British force failed to move him. Macmillan became British Prime Minister in place of Anthony Eden. In 1957, the Campaign for Nuclear Disarmament (CND) was founded, and Ghana won its independence.

The Second World War ended in Europe with a Labour Government in power committed to a welfare state in the UK, full employment, a national health service and compulsory school education for every child. That was good, but I was chiefly interested in the international situation. Ernie Bevin was the new Foreign Secretary, and I knew that he had been a supporter of Keynes's ideas in the 1930s. Would he support them now? Keynes had proposed the establishment of a World Bank and International Monetary Fund to help poorer countries and to stimulate world-wide economic growth, and these proposals had been discussed at the meetings at Bretton Woods in 1946. But the US, while agreeing to set up the international organisations, had seen to it that they were brought under US control. Bevin went along with this because he was anxious for Britain to get its share of US aid under the US Marshall Plan which, as we noted earlier in writing about Oliver Franks, excluded the Soviet Union.

There is a nice story about Bevin's time in the USA to consider these matters. The US authorities were very anxious that he should be well looked after, and at one meeting during a recess he was asked if he would like something to eat. 'Yes,' he said, 'a couple of chops and,' they understood him to say, 'some newts'. They considered what ponds they could search to find newts, but decided to ask an English journalist what the Foreign Secretary had in mind. The journalist told them that Bevin would be referring to the French red wine *Nuits Saint Georges*, which was duly found for him with the lamb chops.

Eleanor and I found ourselves back in England in 1947 after a complicated journey by car from Yugoslavia through Italy, Switzerland and France. The car had broken down in Rijeka and only through the kind intervention of General Velebit on the border did we get to Trieste for repairs and proceed via Switzerland to France. On that border we had trouble declaring our supplies of petrol (gas stations in 1947 were few and far between) but they let us through and we made our way to Cassis to stay with the Wrights, Eleanor's Bloomsbury friends. The Wrights proved in fact to be the parents of a boy I had known at the Dragon School and the mother, Bertha, was a Quaker, sister of Nettie, the mother of my Bootham friend, Franklin Braithwaite. I felt greatly relieved that the new world I was entering with Eleanor would not be so alien after all.

The Wrights in Cassis lived near Vanessa Bell (née Stephens), Virginia Woolf's sister. Eleanor's connection with the Bloomsbury set had started with her friendship with Yvonne Kapp, divorced wife of Kapp the cartoonist. Through her, Eleanor had met Quentin Bell, brother of my friend Julian, son of Clive and Vanessa Bell. Eleanor had considered marrying Quentin, and kept up with him over the years when he lived and worked in Newcastle. Very much later we met Angelica Garnett, née Bell, in fact not Clive's daughter, but the daughter of Vanessa's lover, Duncan Grant, whose boyfriend was David 'Bunny' Garnett, who married Angelica; all very complicated. For long Angelica believed that her father was Clive, and when she learnt the truth she wrote that sad story, *Deceived with Kindness*, about her upbringing.

Eleanor drawn by Tom Poulton

Angelica became a distinguished artist, many of her paintings being shown in an exhibition of 'Bloomsbury Artists' at the Tate some years ago, which we went to see.

Eleanor and I met Angelica by chance. We were staying with our friend Vicky Bawtree in Forcalquier in Haute Provence. We had met Vicky in 1965 at a Gramsci Institute conference in Rome, when she was working with Danilo Dolci and a human rights group studying the Sicilian Mafia. After that we often met her in Rome where she worked for the Food and Agriculture Organization, editing their *Freedom from Hunger* magazine. From Italy she retired to France. One time when we were visiting her there, we went for a walk up to the citadel above Forcalquier and passed a door labelled 'Angelica Garnett'. We announced ourselves and Eleanor's friendship with Quentin and thereafter visited Angelica each time we stayed with Vicky, going once with her to an exhibition of the photographs of Cartier-Bresson, another local resident.

But this is all a diversion from the journey which Eleanor and I made back to England from Yugoslavia in 1947. We saw the Davidsons in Paris, with their new son, Nicholas, and proceeded to our next border crossing. At Calais we had to declare our bottles of plum brandy. This created a problem until we shared some with the customs officers, who seemed delighted and let us through. Our troubles were still not over. When we got to Tunbridge Wells on our way to London, the car broke down again. We slept in sleeping bags on the village green until we could phone a friend in London and get a lift with all our belongings back to Eleanor's flat. I never trusted Riley cars again.

In London Eleanor and I stayed for a time in the flat in Lloyd's Square, which she shared with her dearest friend, Diana Poulton, and where the Communist MP, Bill Gallagher, and Eleanor's brother-in-law, Paul Terry, stayed. Bill was out most of the time at the House of Commons, and Paul at Simpson's, the Piccadilly tailors, or at the *Daily Worker*, where he was their Air Correspondent – a funny situation! Because he had been in the RAF he could get anywhere on RAF bases. His old friends just laughed when he said he represented the *Daily Worker*. But I got to know Diana. She had been working in the war as an editor at the

Communist Party publisher, Lawrence and Wishart. She was really a musician, who taught the lute at the Royal College of Music, and was researching and writing the standard work on Dowland. She was a friend of all the great in her musical world, Dolmetsch, Julian Herbage, Peter Warlock. She had been married to an artist, Tom Poulton, who drew the beautiful picture of Eleanor shown here, and illustrated the five volume Nonesuch edition of *Plutarch's Lives,* with Eleanor as the model, as shown in the cover to the book. During the war Tom was employed on aircraft design and in his spare time created the most lovely drawings of naked bodies in positions that would now be called pornographic. Thanks to my discovery of them, they were subsequently collected together in three volumes. We saw Diana several times in Derbyshire and again just before her death in her daughter's home in Sussex – a truly remarkable lady.

Frances and I divorced in 1948, and Eleanor and I got married. I had left Frances in the worst possible way, with two baby children. She changed the name of our two boys from Barratt Brown to Ronald, and bore two more children and brought them all up to be successful professional people. But that does not excuse the way I left her and our two boys. We had had such good times together, but the long separations, even after I saw Frances and Christopher at his birth, proved fatal. I was allowed to see the two boys on days at regular intervals and tried always to keep in touch with them after our divorce. Eleanor contributed to a Lloyd Barratt Brown trust fund to help with their finances.

Meanwhile, my father died in 1947 from a heart attack, before Eleanor and I on our return to England could see him. He was barely 60, much too young to die. He had been not just a father but a wise friend who had guided me in my thinking about society and how it might be improved, especially in relations between rich and poor and between different peoples, always working from below, not from on top.

My father had not been able to go back to Ruskin College, which had been closed and turned into a maternity home during the war. It always was a 'Labour Ward', my father quipped. A new Principal was appointed. At Ernest Bevin's request, my father had become a Ministry of Labour welfare officer in the Southern Region. He had to drive all over the region where the D-Day landings were being prepared, and see to the care and family accommodation of thousands of women who had been recruited for work in munitions' factories. As he smoked his pipe all the time sitting in his car, it took a heavy toll on his health.

My father told an interesting story about welfare officers' meetings with Bevin. One such was called to meet at the Russell Hotel in London's Bedford Square. One of the welfare officers was the West Indian cricketer, Learie Constantine. The manager of the Russell Hotel refused to admit him on account of his colour. My father and others decided to move the meeting elsewhere. At the same time, my father pointed out to the manager that the Indian prince, the Nawab of Pataudi, was sitting in the hotel lounge. 'How was that?' he asked. 'Oh! But he's a gentleman!', the manager replied. So it was a question of class as well as colour. My father got to know Learie quite well, and asked him one day to what he, a West Indian, attributed his success in his work. 'Ah! Yer see, Ah'm a Lancasher lad!', Learie replied. He played cricket in the Lancashire League. Learie took the hotel to court and won. Later, he became a life peer.

My father's influence on me was profound. I often wondered why I was so regularly made the chairman or secretary of meetings, and decided that it was something that I learnt from my father. I once asked him how he came to write such excellent minutes of Quaker meetings so soon after the end of the meeting where he was the clerk. He told me that he prepared the minute *before* the meeting and then adjusted it to follow the discussion. I adopted the same practice, and it proved popular! When I gave this explanation to one good friend he said that this was nonsense. It was my 'Oxford accent' that did it. I suppose that I got that also from my father, but why was my accent associated with Oxford? It is supposed to be 'ruling class'; hence my chairmanships etc. But is it 'home counties' English? It is not the way the Queen speaks, as exaggerated by Steve Bell in his cartoons, where 'badgers' become 'bedgers' and 'catching' becomes 'cetching'. Nor is it what is now called 'Estuary English' in which 'showers and bright intervals' become 'shars' and 'brart' intervals. Perhaps, someone will give me the answer.

In his *Intelligent Woman's Guide to Socialism*, 2012 edition, with a Foreword by Polly Toynbee, Bernard Shaw offers a most profound discussion of this question on pages 302-3. Shaw argues that no one resents 'beneficially and tactfully exercised authority'. This is not just 'mental illness', but the common acceptance of 'creeds and codes' that make for a certain 'tutelage'. Shaw, however, admits that this is often a matter of class. Some people may resent authority because it comes from some assumed class superiority. I suppose that I always worked with middle class people or working class people who accepted my authority. Maybe the key word is 'tactfully'. That means being sensitive to my collaborators' condition. I hope that I have always been that. Shaw gives the examples of Napoleon and Nelson, but these two quite extraordinarily charismatic characters tell us nothing about ordinary people. It was what I had learnt from my father and from Leslie Gilbert that we were all, teacher and students alike, equally learners, 'seekers', following the old Quaker usage of the word, which I have taken for the title of this memoir, after the truth.

When my father died, he had been visiting miners' educational settlements in South Wales in his new job with the Educational Settlements Association. My mother and my sister Deb left me to go to the crematorium in Cardiff, and bring back the ashes to be buried in the rose garden at the Headington crematorium. We had a service of remembrance at the new Oxford Friends Meeting House in Saint Giles. Then I got appendicitis, and had to stay in bed for some weeks before the operation. I went back to my old economics books, to prepare for the future. I thought that I should do something to carry on my father's work in adult education, but I was still enthralled by the idea of international work.

My father told a friend who was with him at his death one extraordinary story of his last meeting in South Wales. My father had to attend the funeral of a coal miner who had been a student, and had been killed in a mining accident. My father was very struck by the appearance of a young man with red hair who was sitting in the front row of seats and did not move throughout the service. After it was over, my father asked his friends who were with him, who that might be. They looked deeply shocked. 'That was the young man who had died,' they said. Every one there would be thinking of him, but my father had never known him.

In London, I used my old connection with Sir Arthur Salter to explore the possibility of going into the Foreign Office, and took the necessary exams and attended the interview but my enthusiasm for Tito disbarred me. I settled for a life in education. We bought a house in Essex where Eleanor had found a job as an Assistant County Medical Officer. The house was called 'The Live and Let Live' because it had been a pub that catered for Huguenot immigrants as well as locals. It had a long garden running down to a fifty-acre field, still ploughed by shire horses. There was a bowling alley by the side of the house, which we converted into a double garage for two small cars, and a study called 'Sans Souci' for me. When our children, Daniel and Deborah, grew to need separate rooms, we added two bedrooms and a new sun room/dining parlour and a second bathroom. The house was on the edge of the beautiful village of in the Constable country on the Essex-Suffolk border, with good

Dedham Mill by Constable

Dan and Michael in my old car

walking places in all directions.

Our friend Henry Grant, the photographer boasted that he could make a picture as good as a Constable painting of the Stour Valley. He made many attempts, but had to admit defeat because Constable had imagined what was a typical cloud formation above the sea at the mouth of the Stour estuary and Henry could never quite get it. His photographs were still very beautiful, and I have used some of the pictures of me in this book.

When Daniel was about four he was already very keen on motor cars and had a little model run-about car that he could drive on the paving round the outside of the house. He especially liked to take the keys of our two cars in the garage, open the doors and switch the indicators on at either side, to see how they worked. He said to me one day, rather excitedly, the following phrases: 'Dadn-dee, Dadn-dar (Daddy's key fits Daddy's car); Muman-dee, Muman-dar (Mummy's key fits Mummy's car). Dadn-dee ner Muman-dar' (Daddy's key does not fit Mummy's car); Muman-dee ner Dadn-dar (Mummy's key does not fit Daddy's car). I was just at that time reading Noam Chomsky's book on language, and realised how right he was. Neither Eleanor nor I had ever said these words to Daniel. He wasn't imitating, but constructing thought from his own analysis, which is what Chomsky saw as a built-in capacity of the human brain. Fascinating!

I offered my services to the Workers' Educational Association (WEA) for evening classes in Essex, and started teaching after my appendix had been removed. I then decided to travel up to London every day to make an economist's contribution to a documentary film unit in Soho, with which I had worked in Yugoslavia. This unit, which had been founded by Paul Rotha, was called 'DATA Films'. I learnt the whole business of film making and got to know many famous film makers – Raymond Asquith, Humphrey Jennings, Max Anderson, Harry Watt, Wolfgang Suschitzky – partly from my work and partly though introductions from Arthur Calder Marshall.

I had met Arthur when I had helped in making *The Bridge*, a story of rebuilding a bridge over the Drina River in Bosnia. Arthur became my friendly guide to all the pubs in Soho and elsewhere in London that the art world frequented. One surprising sighting was of Marilyn Monroe standing by a bar with Arthur Miller, to whom Arthur introduced me. I was overwhelmed. I had seen some of her films, but I had no idea how plump she was, if that is the right way to describe her voluptuous breasts, when she briefly held my hand.

We made our films at DATA for the Crown Film Unit, including a whole series on the coal mining industry, called *Mining Review*, and a number of other documentaries on educational subjects. I worked with a good friend, Jack Chambers, and greatly enjoyed the work. But the defeat of the Labour Government in 1951 led to the closure of funds for our Unit. Harold Wilson, when he was Prime Minister in 1967, seeking to revive the British film industry, founded the National Film Finance Corporation (NFFC), for which Annette Caulkin, née Cooper, whom I had known at the FAU and who married my Oxford friend David, and was the partner of my last years, worked for some time, and was awarded the MBE for her work. Their offices were near where ours had been in Soho Square, but we never met at that time.

While film-making in London I continued lecturing in the evenings on economics for the Workers' Educational Association (WEA). When my film work in London ended, I increased my lecturing, adding courses in the local Essex technical colleges and for the Cambridge University Extramural Delegacy.

I found that I could work part-time in the days teaching young workers who were released from work for one day each week and I could combine that with my evening WEA classes. Then I could continue my caring for Daniel and Deborah. These day-release classes took place in towns where there were factories employing young people. In Essex, not only Colchester, but also Braintree, Manningtree, Halstead, Thaxted, to all of which I went at different times. We had to meet in church halls and similar accommodation, and find a playing field somewhere nearby for games. Some classes had only boys, some only girls, and a few were mixed, with ages ranging from 16 to 20. Very few of the students had any grammar school education beyond school leaving age, or wanted to study, apart from some technical instruction for their work. My teaching was called 'General Studies', and I could choose to teach what I liked. That gave me freedom to find out what would interest the students, but I was subject to the supervisory advice of one of Her Majesty's Inspectors of Education. Several became very good friends, most especially David Hopkinson

My idea of what to teach may seem peculiar. I had been reading Darwin and I decided to introduce the students to *The Origin of Species*. Somewhat to my surprise, I found that they were fascinated by tracing their evolution over millions of years, from single cells and the emergence of our ancestors after the destruction of the dinosaurs. That gave me the chance for a lesson on meteors and meteorites. There were some amusing incidents in these classes. One day a student asked if he could tear out from his notebook all that I had talked about two weeks earlier. I asked what that was, but I guessed that it was the story of Piltdown man, which had been shown to be a fake. I was very impressed that the student had read about this in some paper. On another occasion I found on my desk when I arrived a human skull and some crossed bones and a page torn from a notebook with HOMO SAPPY written on it. There was a graveyard by our schoolroom and grave diggers had been clearing a site for a new burial and dug up an old skeleton. While the gravedigger was away, my student had nicked the skull and two bones to shock me. He didn't get the Latin spelling quite right, but I was most amused. What I didn't know was what to do with them for fear of getting my student body snatcher or myself into trouble. So I wrapped them up in a hand towel and took them home to keep in our airing cupboard. When we moved house, they got thrown away with other rubbish, but I often wondered what the grave digger thought had happened to the skull.

In my Thaxted and Manningtree classes there were mixed students – boys and girls. I had some difficulty keeping order and finding games that both could play, but in the summer term there was running and jumping and hurdling on nearby playing fields. I actually had two jobs in Manningtree. In 1956, petrol rationing was introduced and I was told I must only go by car to the nearest educational centre to my house. This was Manningtree. Access to the other centres was closed to me and I was sent to teach at Manningtree Secondary Modern School. As I drove into the school gates, the first time, I was greeted by a large notice: SLOW SCHOOL CHILDREN HERE. It was true; they were slow. I had to do an English class and I decided that we should act a play, copies of which I had found. We started the first act of the play and made so much noise that the headmaster came in to shut us up. He came in again on several days when we continued the play. I also had a maths class. In this class I got the boys measuring motorcar cylinders and deciding on the horse-power. The girls had to work out the numbers of moves in the rows of the jumpers they were knitting. I ran a gardening class for growing vegetables, but boys and girls kept disappearing behind some bushes, to give or take a kiss. I got them to look out the Latin names for the seeds they were planting, and the school librarian was astonished at students actually coming to her to ask for her help.

I took one big risk at Manningtree Secondary Modern. I asked my class in the afternoon games period to plan a way of getting the whole class across the River Stour, which ran just by the school, with only one student getting wet. It was the summer term with lovely weather, and I had found that all the pupils could swim. I chose one boy, who said that he was a strong swimmer, to swim across the river and gave him a long piece or rope, which I had in my car for towing. He saw that he had to attach this firmly to a willow tree on the near side, take it across to a tree on the far side, fasten it at two places one about four feet above the other and bring both ends back to the near side tree. He then showed the class how they could one by one hoist themselves across the river, standing on one rope and holding onto the upper rope. Then, when they were all over, to get themselves back. I am sure that I broke all the rules of health and safety in schools, but the whole class enjoyed the exercise, and I shared in the crossing. The strong swimmer came back with my rope, which he had untied from the further tree. Many years later, I used this double rope trick to get Sarah and Claire, my grandchildren, between the trees I had planted 20 years earlier above the garden at our house in Derbyshire, to get them to a tree house I had built for them.

My big idea at both Thaxted and Manningtree day release classes was to make a film with my class. I had the experience in my documentary film unit, and I bought a 16mm. film camera and a projector and loud speaker, so that I could hire films from the British Film Institute (BFI) and show what we had hired. But I could also make films and discuss what and how to cut. In Thaxted I got permission from Jack Putterill, the vicar, for the students to use the church to act out in film part of TS Eliot's *Murder in the Cathedral,* the story of the assassination of Thomas à Becket. So that all the girls as well as boys had parts to play, we invented some girls' parts. Through Jack Putterill I go to know Joseph Needham, but that is another story. In Manningtree we made a film of the maltings and the lugger that still carried the malt by sea to the breweries in London from the River Stour and the barley fields along its side. There were jobs in our films for all the students as well as for those who acted in them, and lessons that had seemed to them to be a bit of a bore turned out to be really exciting. They certainly were for me, and I learnt much that became of value for me in future adult education work. I got money for making the films from the Essex County Council, and had to give the Council the films, when I left their employment, so that, regretfully, I don't have copies.

In my evening WEA classes I added Film Appreciation and showed films for review and discussion, scene by scene. I could show them to Eleanor and any one staying with us the night before my class. At the same time I founded a Colchester Film Society and then, when we moved, a Chesterfield Film Society. This was in the days before we had television, and we had audiences of several hundreds for our Film Societies. When we showed some Chaplin films, I wrote to Chaplin, then staying in London, to ask him to speak about them to us. He declined but wrote me a charming letter, which I seem to have lost. The Film Societies came to an end when television became widespread, but I continued making my own films with my film camera of the children growing up and of our holidays and travels in Europe and in Australia and India, and I have had these converted to video. My son Daniel has them.

I got to know Noel Annan, Master of King's College, who presided over our Cambridge Extra-mural Delegacy conferences. I started to go to King's College choir services, which I can still watch on television, the last of the light coming through those tall Henry VIII windows and picking out Rubens' wonderful 'Adoration of the Magi' above the High Altar. I heard Noel Annan, a confirmed atheist, reading the lesson, 'his voice positively shaking with insincerity', in the rather unkind words of one of his fellows, CP Snow. I once found myself sitting next to

Annan at King's high table and asked him why he had got the Italian communist painter, Renato Guttuso, to paint his College portrait. His answer was that he had to frighten his unruly set of dons, and most of the possible portraits were too bland; 'only Guttuso,' Annan said, 'had discovered the element of awe that was needed'. Annan went on to become a Lord and Vice Chancellor of London University, when I had a correspondence with him about an honour for Joseph Needham.

As mentioned, I founded a local Film Society, using my own 16mm projector and speaker, and added film appreciation to my lectures. Well-established in Essex, I got to know Jack Putterill, successor to Conrad Noel, the 'Red Vicar' of Thaxted. Through him I met his friend, Joseph Needham, the author of the several volumes of *Science and Society in China* and one of Britain's greatest scholars. This led me to include Chinese history in my lectures.

Eleanor had been in the US at Berkeley University at the same time as Needham and his Quaker wife, and got to know them well. They were among the few members of the staff at Berkeley who cycled across the campus to work. When I went there fifty years later, no one was cycling. We invited Needham to the Peace Council, which we helped to found in Colchester. He had been in China during the Korean War, and told us that the US forces had used chemical weapons. What he said was made public and officially denied. It has since been queried. But in a recent (2013) BBC film about North Korea, a North Korean complained that the Americans had employed chemical weapons from which some of his military friends had suffered. For many years, Needham, though he became the President of Gonville and Caius College, Cambridge, was not granted any state honour. My friend, Ken Coates, took up the issue with an Archbishop of Canterbury, who promised to intervene, and in the end Needham received his Companion of Honour.

Needham drew my attention to Proust's discussion of time. There is still time – so we reassure ourselves, but time lost. What about that? Proust's immense novel, only a part of which I have ever read even in English translation, is called *À la Recherche du Temps Perdu* (literally *In Search of Lost Time*) and at the end in *Le Temps Retrouvé* (*Time Found Again*) we are told that only art can recover time. I am not an artist, and I have found in writing about my life that I am not able to recover time as I would wish, but in the search I have found something about myself that has interested me and may interest others. It is this sense of lost time, not only personal but also for all humanity, which haunts me.

I was much inspired in my youth by W.H. Auden's great 1937 poem on Spain. In it there is a phrase which Needham took as the title for a collection of his 1930s essays: *Time the Refreshing River*.

> …'Our day is our loss, O show us
> History the operator, the
> Organiser, Time the refreshing river.'

The reason for the title is Needham's view of evolution as a progress over time from the less organised to the more organised forms of life, from the inorganic to the organic and thus to the social, and different levels of social organisation on to the ultimate Kingdom of God on Earth. In this process 'History' is 'the operator, the organiser'. And when Auden, whom Needham quotes at length, came to exalt love as the essential, central social cement in life's organisation, he returned to the same metaphor:

> *O beggar, bigwig, mugwump, none but have*
> *Some vision of that holy Centre*
> *Where all time's occasions are refreshed;*

Auden was the poet of my twenties, and in my thirties Needham came to have a great influence on my thinking. His ideas reinforced my innate belief in human progress, while recognising with Needham that progress is not continuous. For, after quoting T.S. Eliot's *East Coker*

> *There is only the fight to recover what has been lost*
> *And found again and again: and now, under conditions*
> *That seem unpropitious. But perhaps neither gain nor loss.*
> *For us there is only the trying.*

Needham then wrote again of 'time, the refreshing river'. Of these words of Eliot's, he said:

'Again that is too individualist. Time is for all men a refreshing river; not merely a perpetual recurrence of opportunities for individual souls to scale the heights of mystical experience or to produce great artistic achievement or to break free from the wheel of things, or to obtain perfect non-activity or whatever metaphor of individual perfection you happen to like. The historical process is the organiser of the City of God and those who work on its building are (in the ancient language) the ministers of the Most High. Of course, there have been set-backs innumerable, but the curve of development of human society pursues its way across the graph of history with statistical certainty, heeding neither the many points which fall beneath it, nor those many more hopeful ones which lie above its average sweep.'

I have long lost Needham's faith in a God that sustains our lives, but I shared for a long time something of the wonderfully robust optimism of Needham's belief in human progress, with its grand religious metaphor of the City of God, Christ's Kingdom on Earth, and the epigraph for his book that Needham takes from the 12th Century Bernard of Cluny's *Rhythm, Hora Novissima* ('Latest Times')

> *Oh Zion! Oh City of Peace!*
> *The beauty that is thine overwhelms every heart,*
> *City beyond time!* (MBB's translation from the Latin)

I seemed always to be building a 'city beyond time'. I was a practical person, doing practical jobs, and trying to make a success of them. But I had a haunting sense of time passing, indeed time lost that could not be retrieved, and yet the city was there to be built, through all my endeavours. Far greater men and women than I had undertaken the task and dreamed of success. Being in Cambridge with Needham and his friends only confirmed my faith that I could do something useful.

Needham the scientist finds in this Christian faith the same hope for the future as he sees in science. The concept of scientific progress, of man – and it was first thought of as 'man' – mastering nature, goes back to the Renaissance. But what was reborn in the 16th Century in Europe draws on the learning of Egypt and Greece and India developed by the Arabs, especially in astronomy and mathematics and irrigation works, most spectacularly brought together in Cordoba and Andalusia in what we call the 'Middle Ages'.

I saw more of Needham at a conference in Cambridge on 'Marx's Asiatic Mode of Production', organised by Ken Coates and Greg Blue, in part to celebrate Needham's 100th birthday. I had the pleasant task of showing Ahmed Ben Bella, one time liberator and president of Algeria, round Cambridge, and was fascinated to learn from him that our famous 16th Century scientist, Francis Bacon, whose statue in Trinity College we were looking at, had sent his sons to Fez in Morocco to learn their mathematics from the Arab scholars.

Ahmed Ben Bella in Cambridge with Deborah Coates

I was to see much more of Ben Bella. When he was deposed in Algeria, he was exiled to a remote village in the desert. Ken Coates and Stuart Holland, who was then an MP, decided to get a message to him inviting him to address the House of Commons. They got past the police to the village and delivered the message. Ben Bella eventually came to London, but was not allowed to return to Algeria, and settled in Switzerland. Later, Ben Bella was allowed to return to Algeria, and invited Ken and Tamara Coates, Stuart Holland, Glyn Ford MEP, and me to travel by boat along with other returning refugees, and a number of journalists from different countries. We ate with Ben Bella, and slept on the boat, and were woken up by the hooting of steamers in Algiers harbour, welcoming Ben Bella and the other refugees back home.

We disembarked and walked up towards the central square of Algiers, which was full of people and crowds pouring in along the roads leading to it. Ben Bella spoke, and we were told to return to the boat to collect our belongings and join Ben Bella at the hotel where he was staying. But when we tried to go to the hotel, there were guards on the boat who prevented us from getting off, and we were told we would be sailing back to Marseilles. Ken tried to protest, especially on behalf of those journalists who did not have visas for France, but to no avail. Apparently, Algeria's new Minister of the Interior had not agreed with the policy of the Foreign Minister, about our presence with Ben Bella. We were accompanied on our return voyage by a member of Ben Bella's family, to make sure that we were well looked after. We were soon back in France, greeted by our friends from Longo Mai at Forcalquier, who had picked up the news on their radio station.

Ben Bella was expelled again from Algeria, this time for his support for the Palestinians. I had kept in touch with him, and had arranged to take some Palestinian olive oil from a co-operative which Ben Bella was supporting. I wanted it for sale by the Fair Trade company which I had founded in London. Unfortunately, the Israelis had left the oil in the sun at the airport, and it had gone off. We could only sell it for cooking oil at a very low price, and no further consignments were received. Ben Bella had not only been a very brave soldier in the liberation of Algeria from French rule, but he also believed profoundly in democratic co-operation. He was criticised for his Marxist opinions and inadequate regard for Muslim susceptibilities. He was a real comrade, and I am proud to have known him.

In 2002, Ken invited him to an international human rights conference in Cordoba, where we met again. In 2012, he died after a long illness.

Among others besides Joseph Needham who spoke to our Colchester Peace Council was Canon Charles Raven, the Master of Christ's College, Cambridge. He stayed with us, and I travelled up to London with him and took the opportunity to explore his convictions as a 'consistent pacifist'. I had no religious base for my lingering pacifism, but I found his belief in pacifism as the necessary base for building any sort of decent society very persuasive. After some more serious discussion, I reminded him that he had spoken on behalf of Hugh Russell at the same conscientious objectors' tribunal that I had attended with my father. Russell was asked what he intended to do when others of his contemporaries had gone to fight. He said that he would continue his studies. 'So,' said the judge, 'You hope to steal a march on them while they are away!' Raven interrupted to say that he did not think that the son of the Duke of Bedford would be moved by such pecuniary considerations. That silenced the judge. In fact, Russell joined the FAU and came out to the Middle East with me.

My brother Hilary went to Christ's under Raven, but abandoned his family pacifism, and went into the navy. He was seriously wounded, but recovered to return to Cambridge to study law and agriculture. He became for a time an embassy agricultural attaché and then for some years worked in New York for the World Federation of United Nations Associations, married and had two children. When that marriage broke up, he married an exceedingly wealthy woman and bought the farm in Mallorca. With his inherited wealth, among other gifts he made, he funded a bursary for poor students at Christ's College, and was given what he called 'Darwin's telescope'. His daughter and I laugh at this, as a figment of Hilary's vivid imagination. The telescope is still in the living room at the farm, and just maybe it was that of Darwin, who certainly was a student at Christ's.

In Essex in the 1950s, I took a correspondence course in statistics and obtained a certificate. But I eschewed the abstractions of mathematical economics, 'abstract' meaning taken away from the real world. Then, when I went to London, I obtained a ticket for membership of the British Library to read up on several historical books which I needed for my studies of imperialism. I was amazed that when I went the second time to the Library, the janitor recognised me and did not require me to show my ticket. I also discovered that I could leave for a week or two on my desk the books I was reading for my studies. No chance of doing that now!

In my work on imperialism I got much help from Charles Feinstein who had married Ruth Loshak, the daughter of our next-door neighbours in Dedham. We went to their wedding. The ring, which he had to stamp on in a Jewish wedding, ran away across the floor – a bad omen, they say, and the marriage did not last. Charles was teaching at Cambridge and I went to stay with them there and later in York where he became a professor and remarried. Charles had a major influence on my thinking and writing and I kept in touch with him when he became a Fellow of All Souls College, Oxford, and I saw Ruth again many years later in Derbyshire. Their son is a well-known economist. I shall always think of Ruth as a model of a fond mother who did serious academic work. She was a librarian at the main Cambridge library.

Among our very closest friends in Essex were Bill (Frederick) Le Gros Clarke and Alan Nunn May, the famous (or infamous, if you will) nuclear spy, and his wife Dr Hilde Broder. Eleanor's husband had been the secretary to Bill Clarke, but was killed by a bomb in 1940.

Thomas Hodgkin's 80th birthday with Alan Nunn May, Hilde Broder and all

Eleanor told an extraordinary story about her husband Sid's death. She was staying with Jack (Sir John) Drummond with whom she was working on vitamins. One night she dreamt that Sid was dead. She asked Jack to go and see. He found that a bomb had fallen on the warden's post where Sid was stationed and all in the post were killed. Jack was the author with his wife, Ann Wilbrahams, of *The Englishman's Food*. He and Ann and their daughter were all killed on a camping holiday in France just after the war by a French farmer on whose land they had camped. The reason for this murder has never been made clear, but it is suggested that Jack had connections with the *Maquis* (the French Resistance). Bill lived nearby in Finsbury. He was blinded towards the end of the First World War. He was a nutritionist, who had worked for a time in the Agricultural Institute in Harpenden, with two other friends of Eleanor's, Bill and Antoinette Pirie.

Bill Clarke advised the Government on food issues and wrote several books. He had remarried and we saw him and his wife while we were in Essex. She died and he moved to Cambridge. Bill and I used to go long walks together in Essex and then in Derbyshire, holding my arm in one hand, when we talked endlessly about politics. Bill was not a Communist, but we agreed about most political questions. When he was dying, I went to see him in Cambridge. I felt very sad at the loss of a real friend. He left his papers to me, and I placed them in the archive of the Northern College library, and circulated information about where they were.

Hilde Broder was an old medical friend of my wife Eleanor, and Alan Nunn May had been arrested outside Eleanor's flat, where he had been staying. When Alan finished his 10-year prison sentence, he went to join Hilde who was working as a doctor in Cambridge. They announced their engagement at our house in Dedham, and after marriage in Cambridge came to us, to escape the press interest in their relationship. Eleanor helped to arrange the adoption of a son, Johnny, and our two families had several happy holidays together, including a long stay one summer in Dorset, where I taught my son Dan to read and write.

Alan was an excellent pianist, as well as a distinguished nuclear physicist. After his jail sentence, no one would give him work in the UK, but President Nkrumah of Ghana arranged for him to be made a professor of physics in Accra. Hilde got a job as a doctor there, and they stayed in Ghana until their retirement. Alan was a quiet, scholarly character who had become involved in the preparation of a nuclear bomb, greatly regretted this, and believed it to be essential for world peace that the USA should not have a monopoly of this devastating weapon, but should share possession with the Soviet Union. So, he had passed on some key information to a Russian.

While we were in Essex, we spent much time with my friends from Cairo days, Basil and Marion Davidson, when they came to live in Essex with their three boys. Basil, after writing for *The Times,* had continued to work as a journalist, ending up as a leader writer on the *Daily Mirror.* But he also travelled a great deal in China and elsewhere in Asia, and began his studies of African history, for which he became famous. Through Basil, I established a friendship with Tom Driberg, then on the *New Statesman,* who lived with his wife near to us both, and I helped him in his election to Parliament.

Basil also introduced me to Eddie Penning-Rowsell, when he was a Communist 'fellow traveller', secretary of the Swindon Trades Council, who became a publisher of left-wing books. Eleanor and I stayed with him in his Oxfordshire house, which had a stream by it full of watercress. He revealed that he was a wine connoisseur, who had written a book on Bordeaux wines. He was on the Committee of the Wine Society, a co-operative founded in 1851 from the stocks of wine imported for the Great Exhibition. When we were in Essex, Eddie persuaded us and all his other Communist friends to join the Wine Society – Eleanor was already a member – and to vote for him as the Society's Chairman. We did and he was duly elected. Then we left the Communist Party, and I chanced to meet Eddie on Waterloo station. He upbraided me for deserting the cause, though he had never joined the Party himself, and said that he did not wish to see me again. Some years later, we met again and renewed our friendship. Eddie recalled that we had disagreed about the Soviet invasion of Hungary, but should forget that. This meeting happened at a Wine Society tasting in Buxton, which each year preceded a performance at the Opera House. This became an annual event – to sit at Eddie's table for the Wine Society tasting and go on to the opera, until Eddie retired from the chairmanship in 1987. He still wrote articles on wine for the *Financial Times*, received a French honour, and always spoke of himself as 'a man of the Left'.

We had splendid holidays with the Davidsons, not only in Dedham, but twice with our families in Norfolk, on the Broads and on the coast, boating and bathing. It became a regular ritual, when they moved first to Hereford and then to Shropshire and Somerset, for Eleanor and me to stay with them for a week or two in August. We went for long walks from their houses, and on several occasions went to a bird sanctuary by a lake. I became a keen bird watcher when we moved to Derbyshire. Our house there was just below the wooded edge to the hills and we were woken every morning by the dawn chorus, and spotted more than thirty different species of birds on our bird tables. Feeding them became especially important in the long frost of 1963. In that year also, we read Rachel Carson's *Silent Spring*, her careful scientific study of the fatal effects of spraying pesticides on crops and trees against insects. She gave the book its title from the haunting lines in Keats' 'La Belle Dame Sans Merci': 'The sedge has withered by the lake, and no birds sing'. After reading Rachel Carson, we destroyed our stock of DDT, the worst culprit, and stopped spraying our lawns and apple trees with chlordane. Losing our birds would have seemed to us to be the end of the world. I miss the birds desperately, living now in a London flat with no garden, and am so grateful to Basil for arousing my interest in them. But I also came to learn so much about Africa from Basil's experiences there, which I was able to draw on, when I came myself to write about Africa and Fair Trade.

All this time we were active members of the Communist Party, and I got to know some leading members such as Johnny Gollan, Margot Heinemann and Sam Aaronovich, but most especially, Maurice Dobb, the Cambridge don at King's College. Maurice and Sam were strong supporters of the Conference of Socialist Economists (CSE). The May Day Manifesto Conference in 1968 had brought together a number of economists, including Robin Murray, Bob Rowthorn, Sean Gervasi and Hugo Radice. At the Workers' Control Conference in Sheffield, in April 1969, a group including Bob, Ernest Mandel and Hugo Radice discussed holding a conference, with a view to setting up a permanent body to undertake economic research for the Labour Movement. Robin, Sam, Bob and Hugo organised the first CSE Conference in London in January 1970, which I attended, when Maurice gave one of the papers. The following year we all met up with Alfred Sohn Rethel, Joan Robinson and others in Cambridge when Paul Sweezy from the USA gave the Marshall Lecture on monopoly capitalism. The Conference of Socialist Economists not only organised conferences, and still does, but also published pamphlets and books.

Raymond Williams was one of the most distinguished of all those people who I got to know in the 1960s and 70s. I had met him in Oxford in the 1950s, and afterwards was gripped by his political and cultural studies, *Culture and Society* and

The Long Revolution, which I shall write about later. The idea of culture being ordinary and not just for the élite, and the belief in human capacity to co-operate as well as compete, was just what I wanted at that time in my adult education work.

My Communist friends at that time were mainly members of the Communist historians' group, Eric Hobsbawm, Victor Kiernan, Ivor Montagu, John Saville, Edward Thompson who, with his brother Frank, I had been friends at the Dragon School. Many years, perhaps fifty years, later, I discovered a strange connection between Ivor and Victor. Victor had married Heather Massey, (Raymond Massey, Massey Harris and all that in Canada) and I met her at a historians' conference in UCLA, Los Angeles, where I gave a paper in 1980. I discovered that her mother was Ivor Montagu's sister, and Heather had a cache of letters, exchanged between Ivor and Charlie Chaplin when Ivor was working as a film producer in Ealing Studios. I don't know where the letters are now. Ivor, who had become Lord Swaythling, was chiefly known for his introduction of Chinese table tennis players to competitions in Europe. I wonder if the Chinese players in the Olympics know that?

Along with many others I left the Communist Party in 1956, after the Khrushchev revelations and the Soviet invasion of Hungary. Maurice Dobb and I and some others tried to persuade the Party leadership to end the centralised control of Party policy and organisation, but without success. So we left. I saw my old friend Edward Thompson who, with John Saville, had founded a new journal, *The New Reasoner.* I joined the editorial board with Malcolm McEwan, John Rex, Doris Lessing and Iris Murdoch among others, and we met in Malcolm's house in Hampstead. Malcolm was an architect and a friend of the town planning expert, Buchanan, about whom he told a good story. Ernest Marples was a Minister for Transport in a Tory Government, and very proud of his two innovations in London, the Hammersmith fly-over and the Hyde Park underpass. Marples invited Buchanan to a meeting to consider traffic overcrowding in London, and Buchanan proposed closing down the flyover and stuffing it up the underpass. Marples was not amused.

From one of our meetings we sent Iris Murdoch to join a complaint being made to RA Butler, the Home Secretary, about the vicious treatment by the Metropolitan Police Force of political protesters and demanding the removal of the Commissioner. Iris came back with Butler's answer that the alternative candidate for Commissioner she would find even less acceptable! Many years later, I felt very close to Iris while reading John Bayley's account of the progress of Iris's Alzheimer's disease, so much like that of my own love, Annette.

When Malcolm and his wife moved to Devon, we still saw them and heard much of Malcolm's experiences on the local planning board for Dartmoor. Malcolm introduced us to the chairman of our local planning board in the Peak Park of Derbyshire. This was then Michael Dawes. His mother was a Trevelyan, and his wife was a Quaker. We became good friends, and Michael invited me to several planning conferences where the big issue of local against national planning was discussed. Michael went on to be an important national planning officer, but I remember him best for his enthusiastic leaping into our swimming pool. We met him again one year at the Trevelyans' family home in Northumberland.

At the same time that I joined the *New Reasoner* board, I was invited on to the board of *Universities and Left Review,* which had been founded in Oxford among others by Ralph Samuel and Charles Taylor, later a party leader in Canada. We decided to amalgamate the two journals and form *New Left Review (NLR).* As a member of both boards, I was made the chairman of the meeting, and I shall not forget the complaints from Ralph Samuel, that he could not take any more 'Quaker compromises'. We launched *New Left Review* with a grand meeting organised by my friend Peter Gracey, who then went to work in Australia, where we visited him many times in his home outside Sydney. Stuart Hall was appointed editor, and we began a long and very productive relationship when he became an Open University professor. The *Review* established a whole series of New Left Clubs throughout the UK, and I found myself called upon to speak to several of them, not only on Yugoslavia, but more often on an article I had written, based on research into the ownership of British industries and the effect of its concentration on the condition of the British economy.

My first task after the *New Left Review* was launched was to travel to Yugoslavia, to report for the new journal on what had been happening there under Tito. After a brief visit to Belgrade, I visited my old haunts in Bosnia and then met up with my dear friends from Slovenia, Robert Neubauer and Nada Kraigher. Robert had been working for the World Health Organization (WHO) in Sri Lanka. I wrote two articles on Yugoslavia for *New Left Review*, and made many subsequent visits to our friends there and took our family there for holidays.

I remained on the editorial board of *NLR* with Stuart Hall and Edward Thompson and enjoyed the regular meetings at the club in Soho run by Ralph Samuel. Among others I would see my friend Ken Alexander from Scotland, who was later knighted when he became chairman of the Highland and Islands Development Board, John Hughes, principal of Ruskin College, and Ralph Miliband, by then a professor at Leeds University, father of David and Ed. I well remember seeing Ralph in Leeds with David and Ed. David said 'hello, Michael!', and Ed hid under the table. Does that tell us something about their future careers? Their mother, Marion, looked on with enthusiasm at Ralph's Marxist political analysis. It was a good gathering, and I missed it when the whole project failed and *New Left Review* was taken over by Perry Anderson.

During all this time, Eleanor and I were involved in marching and demonstrating against the spread of nuclear weapons of war with CND, the Campaign for Nuclear Disarmament. I was present with Eleanor at a historic meeting in the house in Camden on the bank of the canal of Clive Jenkins, leader of the Association of Scientific, Technical and Managerial Staffs (ASTMS). AJP Taylor, the historian, was there and Ralph Samuel from Ruskin College and others. Eleanor, with a doctor's eye, was worried that Clive quite certainly had mumps. Ralph proposed, as I remember it, the adoption of the semaphore signals for the letters, C, N and D, formed into a sign, which became the CND logo.

The support of well-known figures such as AJP Taylor, JB Priestley, Michael Foot and Canon Collins was undoubtedly important for the CND movement, but the devoted work of people like Clive and Ralph and ourselves was essential. We took our children on two of the marches, one the last mile of the Aldermaston to Trafalgar Square march and the other a local march in Essex. I spoke in a public place in Colchester, a garrison town, against the Korean War, and was heartily laughed at by a group of soldiers. Eleanor and I joined a protest in London and had to face a charge of mounted police. I just got Eleanor into a doorway and away from their hoofs in time. We did not stop the spread of nuclear weapons, but at least they weren't used again, thanks probably to Bertrand Russell, as we shall see.

One good friend we made in the Communist Party was Henry Collins, an Oxford University extra-mural lecturer in economics. We shared common friends, the Loshaks in Dedham, the village in Essex where we were living. Henry wrote a brilliant book on trade union history, which I used in my classes. What was more, it was he who introduced me to an extra-mural colleague of his, Raymond Williams. I had much enjoyed Raymond's novel about Wales, *Border Country.* But I began to read his other books, and especially his *Culture and Society 1780-1950,* published in 1958 and revised in 1963. This really overwhelmed me – the scholarship revealed as he reviewed the great writers of the two centuries, and his fascination with the meaning of words, fully developed in his little book *Key Words.* What I got from *Culture and Society,* however, was my first understanding of Rousseau's 'General Will' and of GDH Cole's promotion of 'Guild Socialism'. Faced by the huge scale of the national electorate, of the giant corporations and of the nation state, one could only begin to build on what Cole called 'the vital associative life' of small self-governing communities. This idea of building from below in this way, not at all the Communist way, was to influence the whole direction of my life's work – in schools and colleges and trade unions and in the international exchanges of small co-operative farmers and the co-operative consumer societies.

Alongside our concern about the threat of nuclear war, there remained the reappearance of unemployment and the consequent increase in the degree of inequality, not only between the developed and developing countries, but in the developed countries themselves, not least in the UK, although some families, in Macmillan's words, 'never had it so good'. I could only begin to work on this problem where I was, having moved to Derbyshire, and that was in a coal-mining area.

CHAPTER 8

Sheffield University, the Society of Industrial Tutors and the Institute for Workers' Control in Yorkshire and Derbyshire, 1960s

This chapter covers the years 1958 to 1968. 1958 began with a great Campaign for Nuclear Disarmament (CND) rally in Central Hall, London. There were protests at the Prime Minister's house in London's Downing Street about nuclear arms and police actions against the protesters. In 1958, a Direct Action Committee organised a march to the nuclear research centre at Aldermaston in Berkshire. The march was supported by leading political figures in Britain such as Michael Foot and JB Priestley, and by religious leaders like Canon Collins, and followed by annual marches from Aldermaston to London. But Labour was defeated in the General Election, in 1959, and Macmillan returned as Prime Minister with his claim that 'You have never had it so good'. A Labour Party conference at Scarborough adopted a policy of unilateral nuclear disarmament, but revoked it the next year. In 1960, Bertrand Russell resigned as President of CND and inaugurated a 'Committee of 100'. In 1961, he was arrested and jailed with his wife and many others for sitting down in a public place in protest against the exercise of nuclear arms. The next year, he corresponded with Khrushchev and US President Kennedy to persuade them to hold back from confrontation in the crisis caused by the Soviet threat to use nuclear missiles to protect Cuba from US invasion.

In 1963, President John F. Kennedy was assassinated and succeeded by Lyndon Johnson. In 1964, a group of 77 developing countries was formed to try to defend their earnings from the falling price of their commodities for export. War broke out between India and China. In the UK, Labour under Harold Wilson's leadership was re-elected to government in 1964 by a small margin, which was increased in 1966. Steel was nationalised in Britain in 1966 and, in 1968, the Institute for Workers' Control was founded following a series of earlier conferences.

In 1963, the Bertrand Russell Peace Foundation was founded. One of the main tasks of its early years was to set up a Russell Tribunal to examine war crimes in Vietnam. By 1966, when Russell inaugurated the Tribunal, there were massive protests against the Vietnam War, especially by students in the USA. Martin Luther King, the African-American civil rights leader, was killed in 1968. The second Egypt-Israel war occurred in 1967; this time, Egypt was under Colonel Nasser's rule, and Israel occupied the West Bank.

1966 and 1967 saw important international developments. A United Nations Trade and Development organisation (UNCTAD) was formed in Geneva. A meeting of 'Non-Aligned' powers was held at Bandung in Indonesia; elsewhere, an Organisation of African Unity was founded. The USA continued its war in Vietnam.

In 1968, student protests against government power took place in Paris, and in Prague there was a major revolt which was suppressed by the Soviet Union. There was even some unease in British universities. 1968 ended with Rhodesia's declaration of independence.

In 1958 our family moved from Essex to Sheffield, and I took up my new job as a lecturer in Sheffield University's Extra-mural Department for which Royden Harrison, whom I had met at a trade union conference in Sheffield, had groomed me.

My first impression of Sheffield had not been good. Before the Clean Air Act required smokeless fuel to be burned in built-up areas, Sheffield seemed to be enveloped in smog. Sir George Sitwell, writing from Renishaw, just south of Sheffield, commented that, as he looked across to the Derbyshire moors, there was no one between him and the Hely-Hutchinsons in Grindleford. In fact, there was the whole population of Sheffield, but they were covered by a pall of smoke. By the time Annette and I were invited to visit the Sitwells at Renishaw in 2007, we could see all Sheffield and beyond them the hills of Derbyshire. The smog certainly lifted soon after Eleanor and I came to Sheffield. I stayed with Royden for a time after my appointment, before Eleanor and the children moved north, and I was present at the birth of Pauline Harrison's second daughter. When we did move north to a crescent house in Rutland Park, Sheffield, we found a splendid lady, Mrs Rutherford, to clean for us, and she followed us when we moved into the country. We also found that our next-door neighbour was a Jewish tailor who, thereafter, with his son, made all my suits, which I still wear. We used to play some classical music each morning before breakfast, and one day the tailor asked, very politely, if we could open the window a little wider so that he could hear the music better!

Royden and I had to establish our authority with Maurice Bruce, the University extra-mural department's director. He had the chair behind his desk raised up on wooden blocks, so that he looked down on you as you stood in front of him. Royden decided to scare him by banging on his door very loudly before entering, and speaking very loudly and clearly to a prepared script. We planned very carefully our schemes in advance for the developments which we wished to encourage, and what we were determined to do was to expand the work of the Department with new staff and new courses for trade unionists.

At the University I found Kenneth Alexander who had started day release classes for coal miners from Yorkshire and Derbyshire released from work one day each week. Kenneth left Sheffield to become a professor at Strathclyde University, and later chairman of the Highlands and Islands Development Board. We remained good friends, and saw each other regularly when I bought a holiday home in Scotland.

After a couple of years, we moved from a house in Sheffield to a farm in Derbyshire, near a village called Baslow that had a church and chapel and post office, five public houses, and a street full of shops – grocer, butcher, vegetable and fruit shop, ironmonger and hairdresser. All such shops are now gone, except a clothes shop and a flower shop. We had bought a ruined farmhouse on the edge of the moors, which looked across to Chatsworth Park, and we took a year and a half having it done up and extended. I spent my weekends and holidays building walls, shaping terraces, planting trees and bushes, and making a kitchen garden. There was a spring at the top of the hectare of land, and this could be channelled to flow into a swimming pool, which I built. When the children grew up and went away it was turned into a fish pond, where we bred trout and carp, until the local heron spotted them. And, when grandchildren arrived, it went back to its original use. Robin Hood Farm was a perfect place for a family with outhouses for horses and with trees to climb, and I could go straight out onto the moors for my morning run. When Sarah and Claire, my grandchildren, came to live there, I loved the games we played in the garden and felt my life was fulfilled. In the winter, I could ski down the fields above us, and the house was cut off from the road.

In the photograph of Robin Hood Farm as it was when we bought it in 1958, there is a Union Jack flying from the roof, reflecting the right-wing views of the previous owner. He little knew that a fascist would be followed by a communist. At the corner of the house you can see the edge of the piggery and the stone 'beebow' – a beehive built into the stone wall, which attracted visits from enthusiastic apiarists. These relics and the stone troughs, together with the tool

Robin Hood Farm, 1959

grinder who came each year on his grinding bicycle to sharpen our knives and garden tools, were all that remained of farming practices at Robin Hood Farm.

Living right across from Chatsworth Park did not mean that we saw anything much of the Devonshires. I did once speak to the old duchess. We were both walking in the field we called 'the hare field' between our house and her mansion. She asked where I had come from, and I pointed to our house which could be seen in the distance. 'Oh, so you are the red professor!' she said. I could have replied that I liked the writings of her 'red sister'. Two of the Mitford sisters were fascists, one in love with Hitler, and one married to Oswald Mosley, but the youngest one, Jessica, had been married to Esmond Romilly, whom I had known, and then married an American Communist lawyer who defended the students who refused to fight in Vietnam. Jessica wrote a book I loved, *Remembering Philip*, about my friend Philip Toynbee. The Chatsworth House bookshop has all the books by the Mitford sisters except Jessica's, which tells you something. What I actually discussed with the duchess was the mowing of the grass in the 'hare field' in place of cattle grazing. The mower was driving the rabbits, shrews and hares out of their burrows, killing some and scattering others. It was a tragic loss of wildlife. The duchess said that she would talk to the farm manager and for the next few years there was no mowing and hares returned.

I never saw the duke in the Chatsworth fields, but one of my coalminer students came upon him on horseback, when my student was wandering through fields not open to the public. The duke asked him if he knew that he was trespassing on his land. The student asked how it came to be his land and was

Robin Hood Farm, 2012

Robin Hood Farm, 2012

told that it had been Cavendish land for many generations. 'How did the first Cavendish get the land?' asked my student. 'He fought for it,' replied the duke. 'Right!' said the miner, 'I am ready to fight!' But just then the duke's companions came up and they chased the miner off.

I saw more of the old duke myself when I was for many years a governor of Lady Manners School in Bakewell. The Manners were the other large landowning Derbyshire family, dukes of Rutland at Haddon Hall and Belvoir. The duke of Devonshire came to the school prize giving ceremony each year and made a funny speech about the head mistress, always separating the two words to give it a somewhat salacious meaning. During those years the duke confessed to the House of Lords that his butler was planning to leak to the *Daily Mirror* the story that he was responsible for finding ladies for the duke's bed, if the duke did not come up with a large bribe. Instead of paying up the duke told the Lords that it was only too true. From then on the 'duke's favourite cheese cake' in the very popular Chatsworth Farm Shop was given a new name! 'Cheese cake' in our day was a word for a prostitute, as well as for what it sounds like.

Princess Margaret, the Queen's sister, was a regular visitor at Chatsworth and brought her husband Viscount Snowden for the pheasant shooting. He was a particularly good shot, and when he came, the roads around Chatsworth were strewn with dead birds. Eleanor used to go out in her car and pick up a couple, take them home, hang them for a week or so, pluck them and cook them – a very tasty dish, but labour intensive. I did meet Princess Margaret when she came to

Michael teaching

open some new school buildings, which included a new room dedicated to me that I had asked for to house the 'statemented' children who had serious learning difficulties. Princess Margaret was much smaller than I had expected and was escorted by two simply enormous policemen. I always liked the story of her taking off her shoes at a party and being ticked off by the Queen, to which Margaret responded, 'you look after your empire and I will look after my feet'.

Being in Derbyshire meant learning about the coal industry. I was taken on a visit down a mine and was astonished to find ponies pulling coal on wagons and men hacking at the coalface with pickaxes, under the pit props. Mechanisation was only just being introduced. The centre of the coal mining seemed to be Clay Cross. Eleanor had a baby clinic there, and thinking of the famous book about Eboli, said that 'Christ stopped at Clay Cross'. The Skinner family ruled Clay Cross. Dennis was the MP for Bolsover, one brother was a County Councillor, one a district councillor, another a union branch secretary. I once gave a lift to a miner who was hitchhiking to Clay Cross – in those days you could safely hitchhike. I asked him if he knew the Skinners. He said, 'of course, but I don't approve of feudalism'.

The MP for North East Derbyshire was an ex miner, who was well known for his large family. He had 9 children, several of whom had followed him into the pits. One day, a lady from the BBC came to interview the MP's wife. The interviewer congratulated them on their contribution to the country's mining force, and added, 'Your husband ought to get a knighthood for that!' 'He has got one,' the wife replied, 'but the trouble is that he never puts it on,' (assuming no 'k' in knight).

When we settled in Derbyshire, I soon became a good friend of Bert Wynn, the secretary of the Derbyshire miners, who had helped Kenneth Alexander on starting the day release classes. I worked with him on planning the courses which I taught, and it was with him that we considered the establishment of a Northern College, to take students on to university, a northern Ruskin. Sadly, Bert died before that idea could be realised. At Easter every year, Bert organised a school at the miners' convalescent home in Skegness, with lectures from distinguished political, economic and cultural authorities. I attended several of these schools and got to know, among others, the playwright Arnold Wesker, the then chairman of the British Council, Roy Shaw, and the BBC film maker, Christopher Morahan. It was a great experience to hear our mining students really putting these experts through their paces.

The day release classes for coalminers ran for three years of three terms, and anyone could apply. We had many more applications than places to offer. So, each year, we had a selection meeting over a weekend at a hotel in Buxton. We were not looking for academic skills, but for serious commitment to studying. The test was whether they would stay the course. Drop-outs were a serious waste of resources. In fact we had very few, until pits began to be closed. The first year of study combined study methods of reading and writing with examination of the Coal Board and individual mine organisational structure and the place of the miners' representative in industrial relations.

In the second and third years of study, essays had to be written, and an introduction was given to economic, political and sociological theories, and their application to the current political, economic situation. My method of teaching I had already learnt in WEA classes, but it was refined by what I learnt from Royden Harrison. It was to give a short introduction to the subject, and then start asking questions about it to each one of the group of students in turn. If my back was turned writing on the blackboard, students would change places so as not to be the next to be asked! [See photo of MBB teaching.] When I used this technique with internal university students, those in their teens would complain that it was not a proper lecture that they were getting. Only the mature students liked it.

Royden Harrison

As well as teaching miners to help them to improve their life's chances, I began collecting the statistics on the distribution of income between different workers and different regions in the coal industry, and their relation to earnings in other industries in the UK. This study of the early 1960s was published in 1967 in the *Bulletin* of the Oxford University Institute of Economics and Statistics. I concluded that skilled workers had advanced their position in the industry, and that miners' wages on average had done well in relation to other industries, but in regions where employment was growing with higher wages, miners were being attracted to leave mining because their earnings were not keeping up with those outside. Incoming Japanese car companies in the 1980s, in particular, were picking up highly skilled mining technicians and placing their factories in old mining areas to attract them. My paper was recognised as an important piece of work, and got me a University Senior Lectureship.

With Royden Harrison's support at the extra-mural department, we extended the day release courses from miners to workers in the nationalised steel industry in Sheffield, Rotherham and Scunthorpe, and then into engineering works in Sheffield and Doncaster, and finally into the glass works and British Rail. Many members of the Sheffield extra-mural department helped in this development, but most especially John Halstead, who joined us from the Civil Service and became a life-long friend. We applied the same principles of selection and organisation as we had pioneered with the miners, but in some cases the course had to be somewhat shorter.

Royden left the Department to become professor of politics at Sheffield, and then professor of history at Warwick University, following upon Edward Thompson. He continued to spend his weekends and holidays at his home in Sheffield, where I could see him regularly. He became seriously ill, but not before he completed the first volume of his *Life and Times of Sidney and Beatrice Webb*. To celebrate its launching, we had a meeting at the London School of Economics, followed by a meal in the House of Commons, at the invitation of David Blunkett, who was by then the Secretary of State for Education. I had to wheel Royden in his wheelchair miles as it seemed through the Parliament buildings to get to our dining room, the Churchill Room. There, Royden's chair was much too low for him to eat at the table. So I asked a flunky for a cushion. As he seemed doubtful, I added jokingly, 'I am not asking for the Woolsack!' 'I should think not,' he replied rather angrily, and in the end brought a small cushion. At the meal, David Blunkett's first question to me was, 'Well, Michael, what have I done wrong in this job?' I replied that I didn't want to talk about what he had done wrong, but about what he could do right. 'What is that?' he asked, and I told him to find some more funding for the Northern College, which he had earlier helped me to found. 'Done!' he said, and he was as good as his word.

Among the most interesting people I met in this extra-mural work was Peter Parker, chairman of Rockware Glass in Doncaster, who went on to be the chairman of British Rail. He was an enthusiast for involving workers' representatives in management and explained to me that when he took on the railway job, he travelled incognito all over the country by rail, to get a feel of the job. When I asked him how the various concessions on cheap fares were determined, he said that he and others he had consulted hadn't a clue.

Another interesting person I met in this work was Lord Melchett, chair of British Steel. He had consulted my good friend Kenneth Alexander about bringing two or three leading steel workers on to the British Steel board. Kenneth asked me to see Melchett with a list of my best trade union students in steel. I saw him in his posh offices in Grosvenor Crescent. He thanked me very courteously and said that he would consult the unions. Two of my students were appointed, an engineer and a steel maker. I saw both of them some time later, and they said that board meetings were a farce. All important matters had been decided previously by the chairman and managing director. The board was simply a rubber stamp.

Side by side with my work in the extra-mural department, I became involved in founding and chairing a Society of Industrial Tutors. This was not a trade union but a think-tank, preparing materials and organising conferences of tutors from universities, trade unions, the WEA and technical colleges, all engaged in industrial studies courses. I had strong support from my deputy, Geoffrey Stuttard of London University. Geoffrey had, as I discovered rather surprisingly, been on the other side in Yugoslavia, supporting the Chetniks against Tito, but we worked well together. We even saw Michael Foot, the minister responsible, to persuade him to extend more widely shop stewards' day release for industrial studies. Michael had given a very generous review to a book which I had written called, rather hopefully, *From Labourism to Socialism.* The book was full of warnings about the concentration of capital in the hands of a few giant transnational companies, a fact which Michael recognised as of great importance. The response to this development by Labour at the top was not clear. We had to begin from below.

A further extension of my work with the industrial tutors was my involvement in discussions, led by Ken Coates of Nottingham University extra-mural department, on workers' control in industry. We had a first meeting in Nottingham with a number of trade union officials and several industrial tutors including Tony Topham of Hull University. Ken and Tony went on to write the major two-volume history of the Transport and General Workers' Union (TGWU). The Nottingham meeting initiated a long and close personal friendship between Ken and me, which ended only with Ken's death in 2010.

We formed an Institute for Workers' Control and organised a series of conferences with the support of leading trade unionists, in particular, Jack Jones of the Transport and General Workers' Union and Hugh Scanlon of the Amalgamated Engineering Union (AEU). Several thousand men and women attended our conferences in different cities, and we had the support of Tony Benn at the Department of Industry. He came to some of our conferences and took the concept of workers' control into actual practice in several industrial experiments. The involvement of Tony in our work led to the development of a very close relationship between him and Ken Coates, in which I had a very minor share. The Institute published a regular Bulletin, three Annual *Trade Union Registers*, and a good number of pamphlets and books on particular industries.

The climax came with the public ownership under workers' control of the Upper Clyde Shipyard. Three of my friends were involved in different ways with me representing the Institute. Tony Benn gave industrial ministerial support. Robin Murray wrote up the story in a little book for the Institute, and Ken Alexander was appointed chairman of the company that took over the whole operation of the yard. One source of constant support was Michael Meacher MP, who became a minister for the environment in a later Labour Government.

Founding these organisations – industrial day release classes, an Industrial Tutors' Society, an Institute for Workers' Control – might just seem to be making space where one could talk and write together with agreeable comrades, and forget that the aim was to help them to lay the foundations for building a better society for working people. When in the next chapter we look at the founding of the Northern College and in the last chapter at the founding of a fair trade movement in the UK, the same question has to be asked about the long-term aim. It was never for me a top-downward exercise, but always an attempt to support the building of solidarity and co-operative activity from below.

While I was at Sheffield University I was kept heading in the right direction by my new friendship with Teodor Shanin. He came to Sheffield in the 1960s. Having fled with his father from Russia, fought and studied in Israel, he had come to the sociology department via Oxford. He asked me to lecture to his students on my book *After Imperialism*. There was a ferment at that time among the students, starting in Paris and in the USA and spreading widely. Teodor and I discussed what we could do in Sheffield, and decided to call on senior lecturers in several departments to meet and discuss what we should be doing. We expected two or three to turn up, but to our surprise two dozen came to our first meeting. We took the latest 'in word' of new 'models' of scholarly thought to describe our search. Every fortnight someone prepared and delivered a paper on their ideas for their teaching. I presented my paper on Marxism as a 'Newtonian Model'. Teodor collected a year's papers, added some inside and some outside comments, and had them published under the title *The Rules of the Game*.

The book was much ahead of its time, but it started me thinking about different political economies. Teodor moved to Manchester to take the chair of sociology there. With his senior lecturer, Hamsa Alavi, he began a series of studies of 'developing economies' and asked me to contribute. I did, and began to lecture and write about the inequalities of international trade, which became the basis for my three economics texts published by Penguin Books. These writings coincided with my teaching at Northern College, which is the subject of the next chapter.

But Teodor's influence on me was not finished. He was a continuous inspiration.

When Gorbachev succeeded to the Soviet presidency, Teodor saw the opportunity to return to Russia and establish a British School of Social and Economic Studies. A major supporter was Abel Aganbegyan, Gorbachev's chief economic adviser. One of Teodor's friends, Pauline Tiffen, was given the job of translating Aganbegyan's book on his plans, and Teodor asked me to work with her in using the appropriate economic terms. Thus began a most valuable period for me, of co-operation with Pauline in the founding of fair trade. But I saw something myself of Aganbegyan. He came to visit the UK and Teodor arranged for me to show him around Manchester University. He is a vast man, and seated in the front of my little car, his thighs were so big that I could not get the gear lever into the two lower gears! He had been very impressed, he told me, by his visit to Cambridge, discovering that Francis Bacon, Milton, Wordsworth and Bertrand Russell had all studied there. He was going next to Oxford and asked if he would find that such people had studied there, too. I mentioned several Prime Ministers, but he wasn't interested until I mentioned William Harvey and Oscar Wilde.

Teodor also sent two lecturers in accountancy from his Moscow school for me to introduce to the Manchester professor of accountancy. I met them and duly made the introduction. They discussed syllabuses for some time and then I took them out to lunch. We talked about Teodor as a quite special person, and I emphasised his knowledge of the peasantry, what he called 'the awkward class'. I jokingly added that I sometimes wondered if Teodor knew one end of a potato from the other. 'What is the difference?' they asked. They obviously did not cook and serve the most popular vegetable in Russia. I guess that, in fact, Teodor does know that one end has the sprouts, but the accountants, apparently, didn't.

One story about Teodor has to be told. He flew to Philadelphia to give a lecture and was stopped at the airport terminal by immigration control officials to ask why he had earlier been refused a visa. Jokingly, and stupidly, he said that perhaps it was because he had tried, but failed, to blow up the White House. He was detained for some hours until the professor who had invited him came to his rescue. When he returned to the UK, he saw his doctor who wanted to know what had happened at the airport. She said that she had been rung up by the US Embassy in London to ask if her patient, Professor Shanin, was quite sane. She had replied that he was probably the sanest man she knew, but he did have a sense of humour that might not be understood in the US. I last saw Teodor two years ago, on his 70th birthday, retired from his work in Russia, in great form, absolutely sane, dividing his time between London and Cambridge. Bless him! Now that we both live in London, I must see him.

Various proposals were made once more at this time to give me a University chair, without success. But I had not abandoned the idea of founding a 'Ruskin of the North' and the big opportunity occurred with the appointment by Mrs Thatcher, as Secretary of State for Education in the early 1970s, of a committee to review the provision of adult education in the country. The chairman was Sir John Russell, one time director of education in Birmingham, and the secretary was HMI Christopher Rowland, with whom I had worked for some years on the body which allocated state scholarships to mature students seeking university education. With a friend I had made in the Sheffield education department, Bill Carter, we were able to suggest the inclusion of a recommendation for the establishment of one more adult residential college, to be in the North of England. Only Jack Straw, representing the National Union of Students, and later to serve as a Labour Home Secretary, voted against, so we were told.

Scotland did have one such college, Newbattle, near Dalkeith. I applied for the job of principal there but was unsuccessful, although my father had persuaded Lord Lothian to give his Newbattle home for a residential adult education college. I had thought that a period there would be a good qualification for appointment to a new Ruskin of the North, but there was more work to do before it was established.

As a representative of the adult residential colleges, I went to Shap Fell hotel in Northumberland in 1960, to a conference called by Jennie Lee, a Labour Government Minister for Education, to discuss the foundation of a 'University of

Dan and Bobby married

the Air', using broadcasting for those unable to attend lectures on full-time courses, but able to work at home. Shap Fell is pretty bleak, and it was very windy and pouring with rain, while we were there. I suggested, jokingly, that the new university should be called 'the Open Air University!' The word 'Open' stuck, and it became the 'Open University'.

During all this time our little family at Robin Hood Farm were growing up. Daniel left Abbotsholme boarding school and studied hair-dressing, becoming a teacher, first in Cardiff and then in Chesterfield. He then took up car sales – Land Rovers and Range Rovers! After travelling to Sweden with a Finnish girlfriend, he met Bobby Brown, and after some years they got married. When their children, Sarah and Claire, were born, they came to live with us at Robin Hood Farm. Debbie after school went to London to study art and met her first husband there. When that marriage broke up, she found Bjorn Brensdal on holiday in Spain. They were married and lived for a time in Norway. Daniel's children found Robin Hood Farm a wonderful place for playing, climbing trees and swimming. When they began to grow up, the family left for their own house in nearby Calver.

One great pleasure of having Robin Hood Farm was that we could keep horses there for the children to ride on. Daniel and Deborah had learnt to ride in Essex along with Randolph Churchill's children going to Miss Champness's riding school. At Robin Hood Farm we had a stable and meadow for one horse, and we built a second stable in the meadow of our next-door neighbour's farm. Daniel was a very good rider, taking his grey 'Patchy' over jumps. Debbie entered gymkhanas and won several medals for dressage. I took her one evening to an election meeting in Matlock where a group of Young Conservatives were heckling the Labour candidate. Debbie recognized one of them as a girl who had fallen off her horse in a trial and shouted, 'you can shut up! You can't even sit a horse'. That shut them up! One day, Debbie's horse 'Clanty' jumped over a fence into the main road and was struck by a passing car. She was so badly hurt that she had to be put down. I had to do the worst job I have ever known, holding her head, completely trusted by her, while our friend the farmer next door shot her. We got Debbie another horse, 'Melody', much larger, a thoroughbred with a long pedigree. We had her covered by another pedigree horse, and we brought up the foal. In the end, we sold the mare and foal to a Dutchman, and Daniel went to work for him in Holland for a time.

I have also tried to keep in touch with my other family, of Frances's two boys, Christopher and Richard. Frances changed their names to their stepfather's, Ronald, and I was allowed to see them once a month, but never overnight. Frances consulted me about their education, and we agreed to send Richard to Bootham, where I visited him. When they were old enough to make their own decisions, both boys came to stay with Eleanor and me and brought their girlfriends. Both became involved in good professional jobs, Chris working for the UN Development Programme successively in Botswana, Madagascar, Afghanistan, India and New York, finally retiring there to teach Scottish dancing all over the world. Richard studied as an architect. We saw much of each other when he came to build a house on Mull, where his marriage took place. For that I was joined by my sister Deb, her husband Howard, and my brother Hilary. It was a family reunion, except that Frances had not invited Eleanor.

Richard became a member of the Building Design Partnership and then worked for a Regional Housing Assocation. He has always had a keen interest in social housing, and in a voluntary capacity has helped to develop youth sports facilities. I went to the weddings of all my grandchildren – in New York, Edinburgh, Bolton Abbey, and Hemel Hempstead. To my delight, I regularly see three of these grandchildren who live in London.

Frances died in 1991 and, during her final illness, Richard phoned to ask me if I had a message for her. I did, indeed, and I wanted her to know that I was thinking of all the happy and interesting times we had together before our separation and divorce. She was a lady of great courage, resolution and personal warmth, who had achieved considerable intellectual success, as a lecturer in sociology, at Garnett College. She maintained her interest in Yugoslavia, making many visits there with her family, and gave up much time to progressive causes such as nuclear disarmament but, most particularly, reviving the Friends of the Earth organisation in Hampstead. She made little of the fact, but she was an accomplished musician. She played the oboe in the Oxford City Orchestra, and for some time considered a professional career in music. Her musical ability she passed on to Christopher and his daughter.

Fiona MacCarthy

In Derbyshire, Eleanor and I made very good friends, particularly Helen Ullathorne, who worked in my old Sheffield University extra-mural department and with whom I went on many country walks and learnt much local archaeology. One other particular friend was Fiona MacCarthy, whose book on William Morris first led me to contact her in Grindleford. I had happy meetings with Fiona and her husband, David Mellor, the cutler and designer, at the Round Building in Hathersage, until his tragic death. Fiona and I enjoyed discussing her subsequent biographies – on Byron and on Eric Gill. I was able to tell Fiona a good story about Eric Gill, which I had from Arthur Calder Marshall. Fiona ended her book on Gill with an oblique reference to his promiscuity. 'Gill shot across the art world like a comet', she wrote, 'and a comet has a tail'. Arthur's story was that when Gill's sculpture of Prospero and Ariel was installed above the entrance to the new Broadcasting House, Lord Reith was lifted up to inspect it and decided that Ariel's penis was too long. Gill explained that from the ground, in perspective, it would appear proportional. Reith said that he was thinking of the people looking out of the windows of the Langham Hotel opposite and on the same level. Dr. Alington, the headmaster of Eton, was called in for his advice, and declared that 'the young man was uncommonly well hung'. Gill had to chip off a couple of inches!

Since leaving Derbyshire I have missed discussing Fiona's latest life of Burne-Jones, but I did spend a whole day at the Tate with David Browning seeing the Pre-Raphaelites exhibition, and enjoying particularly, I have to admit, the originals of the several paintings of Burne-Jones' model and lover, Maria Zambaco. One couple I have kept up with from Derbyshire are Peter and Liz Jackson, whom I have seen both with Liz's son in Australia and in London. Peter was a member of the Peak Park Planning Board and as an MP introduced the bill that led to the ending of capital punishment in the UK – one huge advance in our society, which would have greatly pleased my father after his experience in Pentonville.

We went to our cottage in Ardnamurchan in the Highlands of Scotland for forty years, from 1969 to 2009; Eleanor and I, until her death, and the last three times with Annette. Before that, always with Eleanor, sharing the boating even in the year when she died. At first the roads were windy and the ferries irregular, but they became straightened and well organised. We generally went in the spring and summer, and my main pleasure was not so much the jogging as sailing and fishing in my little boat with my good friend, Alastair MacColl. When I could no longer make that long journey from Derbyshire, I gave Alastair my boat. It was clinker built and every two or three years had to be sanded down and re-varnished. In the first twenty years we could drop a line down in the right place

Peter Jackson and Liz

and catch any fish we wanted – cod, haddock, pollock, herring, but as the sea got over-fished there was only mackerel in August and the occasional tasteless saithe (rock salmon). Whenever we set out on the rolling Atlantic waves, I had Pascal's little prayer on my lips:

> *Protegez-moi, mon Seigneur,*
> *Ma barque est si petite,*
> *Et votre mer est si grand.*

Despite sudden storms and upsets, we survived. On one occasion, when I was out in the boat, the engine failed, and I drifted towards the rocky end of the little island in our bay. I failed to keep the boat off the rocks with an oar and had to land up on the island, but the boat was holed. I collected up all my tackle and the engine and dumped it on the non-rocky side of the island. I started waving at passing boats, but no one recognised that I was in trouble. I had, however, agreed

with Eleanor that, if I ever failed to turn up after two hours, she would alert a friend, John Alec, who had a large boat. He spotted where I was and soon appeared and in his quiet Scottish voice said, 'Were you needing some help?' We loaded my engine and tackle onto his boat and towed my boat back to the shore, where Eleanor was waiting for us. The boat had to be towed again on the trailer to a boat builder in Oban, and I did not get her back until the next year, when I bought a new engine. All is well that ends well, and many years later the engine still runs well, according to my friend Alastair MacColl.

Alastair MacColl

CHAPTER 9

The Northern College
and the Defence of Adult Education
in the 1970s-80s

This chapter covers the years 1969 to 1987. Labour was in government in 1969, and I thought I should get down to writing. We took the whole summer off in Scotland and I wrote my book, What Economics Is About. *As relaxation, we went fishing in my new boat with Alastair MacColl, who became a life-long friend. With my book out of the way I began, with Basil Davidson, to think about Africa again. The Biafran war was on, and the tribal and religious differences were disturbing African unity. In 1970, Labour was defeated and Ted Heath succeeded Harold Wilson. Bertrand Russell died in February, in his 98th year. In 1971, the Yorkshire miners, led by Arthur Scargill, had a remarkably successful strike for improved wages, followed the next year by a national coal strike. By 1974, coal supplies to the power stations were so limited that offices and factories were reduced to working a three-day week, and lights went out. The Heath Government fell and Wilson came back as PM.*

In the meantime there had been major changes worldwide. Indira Gandhi served three consecutive terms as Prime Minister of India. I saw her in 1972 when I got a sabbatical year to teach in India and Australia. In that year President Nixon went to China, to make peace. Concorde began to make supersonic crossings of the Atlantic, and my brother Hilary would fly by no other, slower, plane.

In 1972, on 'Bloody Sunday', the British Army shot 13 Catholic residents of Derry in Northern Ireland. In 1973, the UK entered the European Union and membership was confirmed by a referendum in 1975. The US left the gold standard, the pound floated, and oil prices rose sharply. But from the North Sea rigs oil and gas began to flow. The US at last pulled its forces out of Vietnam, in 1973, after fearsome casualties, but in the same year the third Israel-Arab war erupted with more of Palestine occupied by Israel. Mao Tse-Tung died in 1976, and Tito in 1980. 1978-9 was the 'winter of discontent' in the UK. Dustmen were refused pay increases, such as had been granted to engineering workers, and stopped work. The Labour Government of James Callaghan, who had succeeded Wilson, fell, and in 1979 Mrs. Thatcher became the UK's first woman Prime Minister. In 1981, the Greater London Council was won for Labour under Ken Livingstone, but in the same year the 'Gang of Four' left the Labour Party to become 'Social Democrats'. In 1982, Thatcher fought the Falklands War and, in 1983, was returned to power with a larger majority over a divided Labour movement. Domestically, it was not a good time for a new Northern College, with obvious Labour and trade union connections, to survive, but we did. The miners' strike in 1984-5 was defeated by heavy police action, which is still being debated. Unemployment rose to three million. The stock exchange crashed but Mrs Thatcher won her third election victory against Labour in 1987. China invaded Vietnam in 1979, and the Soviet Union was embroiled in Afghanistan, but these seemed to be very distant problems, which still made for interesting classroom discussion.

My big moment in the 1970s was when the Russell Committee recommended the establishment of one new residential adult education college, to be in the North of England. Thereafter, a long battle began, to create the circumstances in which the recommendation could be realised. Fortunately, the reorganisation of local government had created a number of larger authorities in Yorkshire, on which several of my mining students had key positions and could be mobilised in support of a 'Northern' college in South Yorkshire. They had fairly radical views, and walked around with badges declaring their membership of 'The Socialist Republic of South Yorkshire'.

At the same time, I found an important ally among the Sheffield University senate in Harry Armytage, professor of education, who had supported my original application for the Sheffield job, and whom I had got to know well. Instead of choosing cathedral cities for all the new universities then being established by the Lionel Robbins Committee, Harry had proposed Scunthorpe. This was rejected, but a Northern College seemed to fit the bill. A number of teacher training colleges were then being closed, and Harry told me to go to Wentworth Castle to see what I thought of it as a possible site.

Northern College, Stainborough, Barnsley

John Halstead and I drove straight away to Stainsborough, near Barnsley, to see the Castle. It was perfect – a magnificent Palladian building with a great dining hall, having a ceiling painted by Angelica Kauffman, shown in the picture,

Wentworth Castle ceiling (by Angelica Kauffman)

Mo Mowlem and three Northern College Principals

with outhouses, set in formal gardens, and just the right size, large enough for 200 students and staff, but not so big that we would have to share it with another institution. All the other sites on offer – in Sheffield, Doncaster and Rotherham – had spare buildings, very large in the case of Sheffield, and magnificent, Wentworth Woodhouse, in Rotherham, but the Northern College would then have been part of another establishment.

I then organised a supper with trout from our pool, cooked by Eleanor, for Bill Carter from Sheffield City Education Department, Roy Bailey from Sheffield Technical College, and Ray Fisher, secretary of the local WEA. We became a kind of steering committee for promoting the College. Bill Carter had himself been a student at Ruskin College, and I have to say that without his wisdom and wide contacts we would not have got far. He and I attended every possible adult education conference and seminar and local government and Parliamentary Committee to spread the message. I received special encouragement from David Hopkinson, the HMI, who had inspected my teaching in Essex and became a particular friend.

Eleanor had met David Hopkinson's wife, Diana, in Germany before the War and before Hitler came to power, when she went to visit her sister, Barbara, in Berlin. Barbara and her husband Coen were studying the violin under Max Rostal, and had met up with Adam Von Trott, an ex-Oxford, German Rhodes scholar, who had a wide circle of English and American friends. One of them was Diana, who later married David. Adam was a very tall man, and Eleanor described going to a party and dancing with him, her toes never touching the ground throughout the dance.

A very brave man, Adam was hanged for his part in a failed plot to kill Hitler at Berchtesgarden, in 1944. Coincidentally, another of Adam's lady friends was Miriam Dyer-Bennett, a bosom pal of Eleanor's from her Berkeley days in California. Miriam did not want to meet Diana, but while we lived in Essex, she came every year from the United States to London for the Proms, and always stayed with us for some days. Miriam was a great talker, and told us once that she had attended a gathering in the Houses of Parliament to celebrate the life of Lawrence of Arabia. She had asked the main speaker a very direct question: 'what had the Arab commander, working with the Turks, done to Lawrence when he was captured, tortured, and then released? Because,' she added, 'the story was that the commander was homosexual.' Miriam told us that she did not get a reply. No surprise there!

With help from one or two local MPs and strong support from David Blunkett, then leader of the Sheffield City Labour Group, a Northern College was established, and I was appointed its first principal. Building on my knowledge of Ruskin, I was determined to have courses for men and women with no previous education beyond school leaving level, to run short courses as well as the standard two or three years, and to ensure equal numbers of women and men students and that there would be the necessary accommodation for families, and a nursery, for which I got funding from the Rowntree Trust. It was a tall order and in my second year, when the whole future of the college was in doubt, we

David Browning at sea, Ardnamurchan

appointed Jean McCrindle as a lecturer in history with responsibility for women's studies and David Browning to lecture on community studies and take responsibility for developing the short courses. The only short courses I had started were quite medium length courses for mineworkers. Without the work of Jean and David, the college could hardly have survived the fall of the Labour Government and the arrival of Mrs Thatcher as Prime Minister.

The three-year course was still the centre of the college's provision, and students could choose one of several courses, literature, history, political economy, trade unionism, and we added women's studies. But in the first year everyone had to take the common core course. The aim was to unite the disciplines of learning and see the development of human societies as that of one species facing common problems of survival from the earliest emergence of hominids, but inevitably in our case in an English literary tradition. The course was evolved from my earlier experience of teaching day release courses and the combination which I had developed of a history of the English language, prose and poetry, with a potted history of mankind, the political-economic institutions and technology which have emerged world wide. It seemed an absurdly ambitious project, but the whole staff, as we assembled before the first term began, sat down together to draw up a syllabus. I had the strong support of our literature tutor in drawing on Gordon Childe, RG Collingwood, Chaucer, Shakespeare, Milton, Blake, William Morris, TS Eliot, and John Berger for short excerpts to study, and to this we added elements of a history of working class organisation and of the international struggle for universal suffrage in the great revolutions in Britain, the United States, France and China. No kings and queens or world wars. We provided a continuum of selected readings with essay questions that I would recommend to those who are today re-examining the school curriculum. Our course went down well and, in somewhat modified form, was continued for many years. The preparation for writing an essay was given special attention and greatly appreciated by students when they went on to study at universities.

One innovation, which I was particularly happy to introduce to the College, was the appointment each year of a resident artist. We had painters, musicians, producers and film-makers. Roy Bailey, who was not only a professor at Sheffield Hallam University and one of the College's founders, but a well-known concert folk singer, became a regular resident, and Barry Hines, the author of the book made into the film *Kes*, was one of our most popular residents.

I kept in touch with Roy Bailey for many years and went with Natasha Gomperts and Peter Parker to Roy's last concert at King's Place, London in 2013. Roy was accompanied as ever by another old friend, Tony Benn, who often sang with Roy. After the concert, I had a long talk with Roy and ordered the CD of the concert. Roy sang to his guitar with his usual gusto the songs of working people over the ages and called on the audience to join in the refrains:

All along, down along, out along, lee
For I want to go to Widdicombe Fair
... wi' Uncle Tom Cobleigh and all

Till we have built Jerusalem
In England's green and pleasant land

and many others. It was a great evening.

On top of this, I persuaded a number of quite famous people to give lectures at the College where they sometimes announced startling new discoveries. One such lecturer was a friend of Eleanor's, Professor Richard Doll, who announced that he had definite evidence of the connection of smoking with lung cancer. Eleanor and I stopped smoking except for an occasional cigar. On a walk Richard and I took together later from our home in Derbyshire, he told me further how worried he was at his discovery of a correlation between some forms of contraception and cancer. The danger from death in childbirth was still greater, but how was he to present the discovery without creating unnecessary anxiety?

Another revelation came from my friend Basil Davidson about the impressively high levels of civilisation achieved in Africa, and not only in Egypt, long before the Europeans arrived. Great Zimbabwe, with its long high wall, built in the 13th century, was but one example. Another was the carved heads of Benin. And how come that one of our coins still in use not long ago was called the 'golden guinea' if it did not come from Guinea? And how could Regius Professor Trevor-Roper describe African history as 'nothing more than a succession of barbaric wars'?

Hugh Trevor-Roper, Lord Dacre, was not necessarily accepting this description of African history, but he was failing to recognise the work of Basil Davidson, Christopher Fyfe or Terry Ranger in establishing an African history of powerful empires, south of the Sahara, long before the Europeans arrived. This absence has been subsequently corrected by a BBC series of programmes on 'The Lost Kingdoms of Africa', introduced by Gus Casely-Hayford, in 2010.

The achievement of the Northern College, however, was not to be measured by the visitors it attracted, but by the students' successes both in gaining places at universities and being elected to leading trade union positions. Considering the low level of education from which students started, the results were remarkable, and fully justified the hopes of its founders, particularly in the successful transition for many students from short, even weekend, courses, to long courses. Two or three students I particularly remember were dyslexic, but with gentle personal tuition largely overcame their incapacity. More remarkable were students who came to us from prison. They had committed quite violent crimes. Serious learning proved to be a wonderful corrective.

I handed over the job of Principal to Bob Fryer in 1983, but continued to lecture at the College for another ten years. David Browning left Northern College in 1985, to be Director of Manchester Open College Federation, then, the first Open College Network (OCN) establishing credit awards for units of study at four levels – from learning to read and write, through to entry to university. When adult education funding was threatened by the Department for Innovation, Universities and Skills (DIUS), David and I submitted a paper on our Northern College and Open College experiences directly to John Denham, the DIUS Secretary of State. We were very graciously received by a DIUS representative, and we agreed to prepare a further document detailing 100 adult students' experiences and achievements in community, college, trade union and university education. We achieved that through our networks across the UK.

Follow-up work building on these case studies is still ongoing. Northern College principal Jill Westerman agreed to provide access to ten academic years of students' records, both long and short courses, records of their achievements, awards, qualifications and dates and contact details. Dr Steve Wisher, managing director of Information by Design, a social research company based in the business park at Hull University with a strong community-based research track record, agreed to work with us to analyse the issues and benefits for mature students on both short and long-term courses, and the ways in which the national Open College Network (OCN) credits enabled progression. Professor Jill Brunt, then CEO of the Open College Network in Sheffield, provided a grant for the research costs, and we donated the fee we received from DIUS for the case studies. Analysis on the outcomes continues, with the tantalising prospect of being able to establish whether and how parents as mature students affect the educational achievements of children in their family.

Currently, David and I do what we can through our own and past adult education and Open College Network contacts to keep the argument running against a tide of cuts in financial resources and raising of fees imposed by the Coalition Government. In the 1990s, at least half of all undergraduate students at University were mature students. That proportion has now greatly diminished.

It is a tragedy not only for the people involved, deprived of education, but also for the country in the loss of educated men and women. Recently, I went to a Gaudy at Corpus Christi in Oxford, and was seated next to the President of the College. He had been professor of history at Sheffield University, and was telling me that some of his best students had come from Northern College, with little previous education before going there. That is a major tribute. When I asked him how he thought that came about, he said he thought it was probably because these students could set the place and time of the period of their particular historical studies in the wider context of world events – shades of our college common core course.

CHAPTER 10

'Jogging Round the World'

Derbyshire, Scotland, Europe, Japan, India, China, Cuba, Australia, Papua New Guinea, Canada, Peru and the USA in the second half of the Twentieth Century

This chapter covers a long period, really from the 1940s to the 1990s when I was travelling round the world year by year. The background to my travels was inevitably the changing situations in the various countries I visited.

I started in England and then in Scotland, which was still part of the United Kingdom, though a nationalist movement and party was obviously growing. In the UK, Mrs Thatcher in government sought first to reduce the power of the coalminers by using every form of police power against the strikers. In Europe, she cut Britain's financial contribution and sought to reduce the impact of European legislation, but signed the Maastricht Treaty on European Union. Soon, she was able through her close relationship with President Ronald Reagan to enforce the 'Washington consensus', which aimed to free international financial movements from national control and leave them to free market operation. My friends in Europe were not happy about this.

When I started my travels in Asia and Australasia, there were all the signs of new socialist, but not communist, government initiatives in India. Mrs Gandhi had formed a government with two of my Oxford friends among her ministers, and received the delegates to our Peace Conference as true friends. But within a year she declared a state of national emergency and withdrew her more radical proposals. I arrived in China after Mao's death and the disastrous Chinese famine of the 1970s, when the 'Gang of Four' had been replaced, and the country was trying to recover some economic momentum. Small-scale industrialisation was spreading everywhere, but without much co-ordination. Australia and Papua New Guinea were rapidly expanding exports, some to China, of their raw materials, especially iron, coal and copper. Cuba, which I visited next, was suffering from the US embargo, but still selling its sugar to the Soviet Union, in exchange for manufactured goods. These exchanges were ended soon after we left and Cuba experienced a serious recession. In Canada I found a generally successful economy based on worldwide sales of grain and other commodities, but an economy increasingly dominated by the United States. What I hadn't expected was the enormous growth of the Californian wine industry, equalling the similar growth in Australian wine production.

After retiring from Northern College in 1983, I was given honorary degrees at three universities. The first came from the Open University and I went to the ceremony at Leeds with Eleanor and our friend from Cairo days, Bertha Gaster. I had seen her since then, as a foreign correspondent for the *News Chronicle* in Rome and in Budapest, and then with her friend JD (Sage) Bernal in Essex. She had recently completed work on the *Oxford Dictionary of Quotations.* The honorary degree I received from Sheffield University involved an amusing incident. I went to the ceremony with Eleanor and Royden Harrison, by then in a wheel chair, and David Donnison, then a professor at Glasgow University. The ceremony was presided over by the Yorkshire Lord Lieutenant, Lord Lumley, in full regalia. Eleanor was seated next to him, and I heard her admiring his uniform and asking how the Salvation Army was faring these days. I did not hear his answer, but happened to meet Lord Lumley (Earl of Scarborough) at another university do some weeks later, and I apologised on behalf of my wife for the gaffe. 'Not at all!' Lumley replied, 'I loved it. I have been dining out on that story ever since!'

When I was given my honorary degree at Sheffield Hallam University, this was presented at the same time as Sebastian Coe received his award after his competitive running records. The public orator mentioned my jogging and also the many countries where I had lectured. Seb asked me over lunch where I had found to run in all those places, and I said that I had kept diaries and could let him know. 'Jogging round the world', Seb said. 'That would be a good title for a book!' I agreed and he said he would write a Foreword. I kept in touch with him while writing, and had some drawings made of me running to illustrate the book and sent him a copy.

Bill Owen, Sebastian Coe and Michael at Sheffield Hallam

I submitted the manuscript to several publishers. All said that they did not know how to market the book. It wasn't autobiography or a travel book or a sporting manual exactly or a story about Coe. I had to tell Seb that the book had failed. At one point I asked him what he was thinking about in that last hundred yards of his run as he raced ahead. His answer was: 'The playing fields that our kids don't have, but need to run on, and my winning might get them'. It was a politician's answer, and Seb had soon become an MP and then a Lord, and in charge of the 2012 London Olympics. His advocacy is evidently still required, as more and more playing fields have been sold for housebuilding, and the overwhelming majority of British 2012 Olympics competitors are said to have come from private schools providing education for just 6 per cent of the population.

My jogging began as an exercise every morning in Derbyshire and led me to complain to the Peak Park Planning Board at their cutting down of trees. They said that the shepherd could not see the sheep for the trees. I answered that he now had some new glasses. My friend at the Board laughed, but when I wrote to the *Derbyshire Times* with my complaint, the board desisted, and henceforth always consulted me about tree cutting on the edges.

My other main running ground was along the sands by our house in Scotland. There, for many years, my running companion was Don Sproule. He was a physicist who had developed forms of radar which would travel through water and through metals. He was regarded as so important to the war effort that, in 1939, he and his wife were sent for safety to the US. When, in 1942, it was thought safe for him to return to England, the boat on which they were travelling was torpedoed. His wife was drowned, but Don survived. He then married a friend of Eleanor's and had three children, finally marrying our friend Lore, and they had a daughter, Vivien. Lore has died, but Vivien, now a consultant psychiatrist, remains a very dear friend.

Don's little laboratory, in the basement of their house in Notting Hill, was where he continued his research. It was once visited by the head of research at Rolls Royce to whom Don had made some proposals for discovering faults in aero engines. The man from Rolls Royce could not believe that such important work was going on in a tiny basement. Don got little or no pay for this work, but was kept going with funds from his brother's rich contracts in the Canadian oil industry.

On the sands of Sanna Bay in Ardnamurchan in the Scottish Highlands, where I ran, the author of *Night Falls on Ardnamurchan*, Alistair MacLean, used to hide away when I appeared on the beach, but Denis Healey, then Chancellor of the Exchequer, who was holidaying there, asked my friend Kenneth Alexander who I was. On being told, Healey said he had read some of my books, and he thought that they made a lot of sense. Kenneth commented that they hardly seemed to influence government policies. 'I can't listen to that sort of sense in making

View from our Scottish house

Sanna Bay, Ardnamurchan

policy,' Healey snapped. Denis Healey was not soon forgotten in the local shop in Kilchoan. He went in to buy some cigarettes, but forgot to take any money, and asked to be trusted to pay later. The lady who was serving in the shop refused. Healey explained that he was the Chancellor of the Exchequer. 'That is another reason why you should go back to your hotel and get your purse!' was Morag's response.

On the way to Scotland we regularly stopped with the Alexanders at Callander (Tannochbrae in the TV series), and also with my sister, Deb, first at Jedburgh and then at Darnick near Melrose, all places with beautiful hills to run on, especially the Eildon Hills above Melrose.

Kenneth Alexander

Jogging outside Britain sometimes raised problems of where to go. Staying with our friend David Leacock on his farm in the south of France or on Lake Geneva or in the Canary Isles presented no problem, nor did any other of our visits in Belgium, Germany or Italy, where there were parks near to where we were staying. In Spain, staying with our friend, Jose Maria Tortosa of the University of Alicante, I could run round the beautiful garden surrounding the block of houses

Deb in her garden, Darnick, Melrose

Our house in Callosa d'Ensarria, Spain

where he lived, and our own house in Callosa de Ensarria had direct access to the orchards and vineyards above our village. I could call on my trade union friend Jim Mortimer, one-time Labour Party General Secretary, who regularly visited Benidorm, and run on the sandy beach there, preferably early in the morning before the crowds descended.

Holidays at Callosa d'Ensarria in the Costa Blanca became a regular feature. We made the house a pleasure to live in, and I could go surfing from the local beaches and running each morning in the hills above our house. But by the end of the century the Costa Blanca became terribly overcrowded and we left.

On our way to Spain we made regular visits to Portugal to see Eleanor's Seruya relatives. I could run round Lisbon, Coimbra and parts of the

Michael wind surfing

Algarve. The family owned a large department store in Lisbon, and one of the family was a famous flamenco singer. My book *After Imperialism* was translated into Portuguese, not so much for readers in Salazar's Portugal but for those in Brazil.

One other happy running ground in Europe was in France, when we visited our friend Vicky Bawtree at Forcalquier, which I have already described. But I visited Forcalquier several times also to attend conferences at the nearby farm and conference centre, Longo Mai, and could run round the hills there where an 'Alternative Information Network' had been established among others for Yugoslavs unable to publish in their own country. They operated strict rules of behaviour at Longo Mai. Breaking one of the rules might see you thrown into the fish pool fully dressed. I watched this happen. It was not so deep that you would drown, but unpleasant.

Teodor Shanin was one of their advisers at Longo Mai and over the years he and I became good friends with one of the organisers, Nick Bell, and established a long-lasting friendship with Milica Pesic from Belgrade. She came to work in England with a very little help from me, and founded in London and still runs a most successful Media Diversity Institute. This institute helps excluded peoples like the Roma to have a public voice in the media, an invaluable service.

The main opportunity I found for jogging was at my brother Hilary's farm in Mallorca. From the house and courtyard there was a zig-zag road up to his Atalaya (one-time look-out) and further hair pin bends up to a large open area of

Pedruxella, Mallorca

ploughland, where I could scramble through the bracken to the mountain from which I could look over to the sea – heavy going all the way. From below the house there were twenty more hairpin bends through the olive trees down to the valley. My brother wanted to be as isolated as possible.

I visited Mallorca two or three times a year. Once or twice I went in September for the olive picking. We shook the branches which had olives onto nets on the ground, gathered them up and took them to the garages, where they were laid out on mats to dry. Then I went several times for the olive pressing at the end of November. Hilary had rebuilt an original medieval olive press, driven by a mule. At one olive pressing my niece had told me to behave well because we were going to be joined by an earl. I found a very tall man and introduced myself as Liz's uncle. 'That sounds very important,' he said, and I asked him his name. 'Suffolk!' he said, and I said, 'Oh, you are a Howard'. 'How did you know that?' he replied. 'I do know some history!' I said, at which point his wife came up taking the rings off her fingers, thousands of dollars worth, and asking Suffolk to keep them because she wanted to help collecting the ground olive mush that had to be put in baskets with boiling hot water for pressing. 'Where shall I put them?' he asked. 'In your pocket, silly!' she said. He wrapped them up in his handkerchief and put them away.

I once asked Hilary why it was called 'virgin' olive oil. 'Oh, Michael!' he said,

In Mallorca with Deb and Annette

'the first pressing, of course!' 'And 'extra virgin?' I asked, 'extramarital?' 'No!' he said, 'just the very first pressing'. There is a splendid book called *Extra Virginity: The Sublime and Scandalous World of Olive Oil,* which argues the case for olive oil in place of animal fats and quotes the 'Cretan diet', with no animal fats. In Crete there is no Alzheimer's disease and very little heart disease. This book also warns that much so-called 'olive oil' is not from olives. So follow Popeye, the sailor man, whose girlfriend was Olive Oil!

Hilary had inherited the farm with its thousands of ancient olive trees through his marriage to a member of the Houghton family, owners of the US company Corning Glass. He had worked for many years in New York for the World Federation of United Nations Associations. On his new marriage he had left that work and become a Vice-President of the Corning Foundation. This involved travelling all over the world to oversee the grants made by the Foundation to charitable and other causes. One such was providing funds for the excavation of the thousands of clay soldiers in China. Another involved preserving forest land in Costa Rica. A third made him Treasurer of the Save Venice Fund, for which he was awarded an Italian honour. He was an honorary Vice-President of the World Wide Fund for Nature, based in Geneva. Between trips he and his wife Patricia would return to Mallorca for peace and rest.

Hilary used to phone me roughly every month, and my first question was always 'Hilary, where are you?' It could be Park Lane in New York, Eleuthera Island in the Bahamas, Venice or Geneva, all places where he had an apartment. When Eleanor and I went to Venice we stopped outside at the booking office for accommodation. When I gave my name, they assumed that I was Hilary and directed us to a splendid apartment on a small canal leading into the Grand Canal. It was a bit costly but well worth the extra money. We found a plaque on one church that had been restored recording the help given by Hilary for its restoration.

When Hilary died, his daughter Liz took over the farm in Mallorca, and I continued to visit twice or three times a year, running every morning before breakfast and bathing in the pool which my brother had built. I still visit, but cannot run. My niece is a most distinguished person, an advocate of the

Liz and kids

Natural Resources Council of America, stationed in Washington. She has been involved in several major acts of environmental protection. For her work in resisting the depredations of the loggers on Vancouver Island she was paddled ashore in a celebratory dug-out canoe by the Kwakiutl tribe, the only woman ever to be thus honoured.

'When in Rome do as the Romans do,' they say, according to the proverbs of Ambrose. Driving a car in Rome was a tricky business, but I found that my open Alvis was given amused respect if I just drove it around as if I owned the place. Running in Rome was much easier, when we stayed with our friend Vicky Bawtree in Trastevere. I could go up into the hills above the Vatican. I could not go into St Peters, dressed in shorts, but I could run in the gardens above. There I came across the statue depicting Anita Garibaldi on a horse, donated by the women of Argentina. She is holding a baby and wielding a gun. On a plaque below her Garibaldi and the ten thousand are shown, and are about a tenth of the size of Anita. I met Anita Roddick, founder of the Body Shop, when we were establishing our fair trade chocolate company, and asked her if she had ever seen this representation of the lady after whom she was named. She had not, and was delighted to know of it. Some months later, I saw Anita again and she told me that she had been in Rome, and had found her namesake, for the information about whom she was most grateful. Whether that cemented our relations with the Body Shop I would not claim, but it may have helped.

My first major move out of Europe after the Second World War was to India. I was given a sabbatical for two terms by my university, with some financial support from the British Council. I had been invited by an old Oxford University friend who was professor of history at the University of Aligarh to teach there for a term. By the time I got there, however, he had been made Minister of Education for All India in Mrs Gandhi's Government. Before getting to Aligarh I had attended a conference of historians in Delhi. We had been received by Mrs Gandhi, and I could remind her that my wife, Frances, had shared a study with her at Oxford, and we had also met at the Mitchisons.

I gave my lectures at Aligarh and we visited the Taj Mahal at nearby Agra. The lectures went well, but I had to give some tutorials – no problems with the men, but Aligarh was a Muslim university, and women students came to tutorials with their faces fully veiled. I had no idea how they were responding to my comments on their essays. Several seemed to me to be quietly giggling. I didn't like the experience, but the playing fields at the university were spacious and I could get my run in every day. There was one problem. A bell was rung each morning to get the students up. I responded to it by going running. On Sundays, however, it was rung an hour later. I went out as usual, following the bell, and found that it was unusually hot, and I needed my doctor wife's attentions to cool me down.

When I returned from Aligarh to Delhi and saw the Minister, I found that he wanted me to visit several universities and report on their extra-mural work. I also called on my old school friend Mohan Kumaramangalam, who had been made Mrs Gandhi's Minister of Industry. He wanted me to study educational provision for shop stewards in the steel industry. So I had a programme of study visits all over India. I was determined to keep my jogging exercise going – no problem in university playing fields, but more difficult in the big cities. However, many had surrounding countryside and local parks, where I could run.

The most pleasant venue was in Kerala, where I could run along the beach. I went to Trivandrum to visit an old Oxford friend, Professor Raj, who had been Vice Chancellor of Delhi University and had moved to direct the work at the Institute of Development Studies in Kerala. He met us at the airport, and Eleanor said 'How wonderful in India to see healthy looking children!' 'Don't speak so loudly, please!' Raj replied. 'We get a huge subsidy from the Central Government, because of the report we submit of dire poverty in Kerala, and we can't have people questioning this!' Raj gave us a comprehensive tour of institutions in Kerala, and we were much impressed by the effect of a part Christian, part Communist establishment. One agricultural plant that the Institute was developing was the cashew nut, so that its branches did not start growing near the ground, where snakes liked to hide. I was therefore delighted, many years later, to find that the fair trade nut company, which I had helped to found – Liberation Nuts, sold by Sainsbury's – was getting its cashews from Kerala.

I decided to go to Srinagar in Kashmir to write up my report. In this Himalayan mountain region the country was beautiful, but at several thousand feet above sea level I was soon out of breath if I ran. I was quite happy to return to the lowlands of Delhi's public spaces and hand in my reports. Before I did that, however, we had several days resting on a houseboat on Lake Dal. Luckily, at this time, the running war over Kashmir between India and Pakistan had temporarily abated, and we enjoyed the peace. I handed in my reports in Delhi. They were received very graciously, but I have no idea what happened to any of my recommendations for greater expenditure on adult education. The next year, Mrs Gandhi declared a state of emergency, and many of her more radical proposals were dropped.

Going to crowded Japan for the first time in 1970 was another matter. I had a map of Tokyo and other Japanese cities from my friend, Hideo Yamada of Hitotsubashi University, Tokyo. He had come to see me in Sheffield and on seeing the red brick buildings of the University, had commented, 'Oh! Led blick, not metafolical?' On the basis of my writing on *Imperialism*, he invited me to lecture in Japan. When we arrived in Tokyo, we soon found that Hideo knew everyone of importance in the academic world and had organised a lecture tour for me in several universities in each of the three main islands where he had contacts. He was an authority on African history, but his friends as we met them had wide political and economic interests in line with mine.

We stayed with Hideo and his wife in their house in Tokyo, and discovered that Japanese baths are vertical, to occupy less space, so that you stand up in them.

More seriously, when Eleanor asked about Hideo's wife's friends, she was told that they were the wives of Hideo's friends, so powerful is the patriarchal influence in Japan – and Hideo's wife was the daughter of an ambassador who had been to the US and could sing English songs. Her favourite was 'Lavender Blue'! She explained to Eleanor that she did not want to challenge what she believed was her fate, and, though highly educated, she seemed to hold quite mystical views of what determined her life.

This experience of Eleanor's typified two characteristics of Japanese inter-personal relations, as we saw them in the 1970s. The first was the low status of women. When I told Hideo that I would like to meet a Japanese woman lecturer whom my nephew, David Donnison, had taught at the London School of Economics, Hideo told me not to waste my time. Then, the mystical influence on Japanese behaviour can be seen on the trees of any holy place. They were covered with little slips of paper with writing on them. When I asked what the writing said, I was told that on them all was a prayer from someone that they would be happily married or pass their next exams or avoid infections.

I did find, with difficulty, somewhere to jog in Tokyo. On the map there were large green areas denoting big parks, but all belonging to the Emperor and closed most of the time to the public. There were other green spaces, which turned out to be cemeteries, where in the end I had to run among the tombstones. In other Japanese cities there were public parks around temples and museums, where I could run. Running in Nagasaki, where I met several active members of anti-nuclear organisations, with which the Bertrand Russell Peace Foundation has maintained contact, was terrifying because the main space had been cleared by the atomic bomb. By far the best facilities for my jogging were in Sapporo, on the northern island of Hokkaido. But when we were there the roads were covered with snow and access to the parks was difficult.

After Japan, visits to China and then to Cuba were organised in 1978 and 1981, respectively, for parties of medical personnel and health activists. I was included as a spouse. Nancy Worcester was the deputy leader. She was a nutritionist, lecturing at Richmond Adult College, while her husband was a physicist working in Grenoble. Originally from the USA, after some years in England she returned there with her friend, Mariamne, to teach on Women's Studies in the University of Madison, Wisconsin. She was/is a person of great charm and immense energy, and when we first met her, she was chosen to lead a party to go on a four week tour of China.

To enter China, we had to pass though Hong Kong and I found that, with much effort, I could climb up to the top of the island. I preferred the island off Hong Kong, which we visited while waiting for our entry permits to China proper. After taking the train from Hong Kong, our first stop was Canton where another jogging enthusiast in our party and I found that avoiding the streams of cyclists on the road we could climb up into parkland to run. We repeated the same procedure in even more traffic in Shanghai after our flight there, finding a park to run round. When we left Shanghai for Nanyang at the foot of the mountains we were in very heaven, with great fields of rice between canals we could run along lined with walnut trees for shade.

We much regretted leaving the mountains by train for Beijing. We had visited a succession of town hospitals and village clinics, and got a very relaxed response from our male interpreter to questions about Mao Tse Tung's cultural revolution. He didn't mind taking time off to discuss political questions, but he thought it wasted the time of his foreign tourist visitors. It was a moment of relative tranquility between the Gang of Four and the new regime of Deng Xiaoping.

Nancy decided to press such questions of succession and the issue of women's rights, in discussion in one carriage with other women members of our party and with the female interpreter we had, who was coming with us on the train to Beijing. I never heard the result, but our reception in Beijing was marked by the most careful consideration of the interests all the members of our party, male *and* female. We saw some astonishing operations, including the removal of a brain tumour, under acupuncture, and talked to surgeons who had returned to China after some years living and working in the US.

We visited the Great Wall of China and realised its immense length but, more

China's Great Wall

important, how near it was – a day's horseride out from Peking – an army could get there quickly to meet Mongolian invaders. The temples in the city and Tien An Men Square were, as expected, and something to remember when the massacre took place there in 1990.

Two years after our Chinese visit, Nancy Worcester arranged a visit of a similar medical group to Cuba, which again I joined with Eleanor. Some of the women members of the party, not Nancy, commented on the beautiful clothes which Eleanor always wore and expressed doubts about her feminism. This was soon dismissed when we were shown a poster of a man, a soldier, with a gun in hand, protecting an elderly woman, and Eleanor said that she would like to see one of a woman with a gun in one hand and a baby on her back. There were no more snide remarks after that! I found plenty of places to run in Cuba, along the long beaches and inland among the fields of maize and tobacco. The tobacco, unlike other crops, was grown in private plots.

Nancy endeared herself to us all when she criticised the enthusiasm being shown by our guides for the production of Cuban cigars, and even more when she questioned the obvious colour hierarchy of white doctors, brown (Indian) technicians and nurses, and black cleaners. We were all deeply impressed, however, at the quality of the health service and the contribution which Cuban medical workers were making by their work in less developed African countries. We noted that visitors from Canada, and even on day trips from the United States, were being encouraged, despite the trade bans imposed on Cuba by the US.

My trips to China and Cuba led by Nancy Worcester were followed by two lecture tours in successive years to Papua New Guinea and Toronto, Canada, organised by Pat Healey. Pat had married Joss Murray, whom we had sort of adopted in Chesterfield and assisted to study as a nurse. Pat was studying at Essex University, and obtained a lecturing post in Ulster, followed by a more senior post in Melbourne, Australia. This was followed by an appointment in Port Moresby, Papua New Guinea.

One year, Eleanor and I visited Eleanor's Bailey relatives in Australia. We stayed near Sydney with our old Colchester friend, Peter Gracey. He was managing a firm of IT consultants, but continuing his musical interests. He played several wood instruments, and his wife played the double bass in the Sydney opera house. They had several musical friends, including a soprano singer, who became world famous, Joan Hammond, who we met again when she came to London. Jogging from Peter's house in East Killara was delightful, through a wooded valley and up onto a large playing field, where brightly coloured parrots flew about.

Eleanor's Bailey relatives lived in Canberra, the Australian capital, and had important jobs, one an ambassador, another the secretary to the cabinet. They lived in villas on the perfectly planned and designed garden city lying beside a lake and below a small hill. We were taken to the top of the hill to observe the city, and we asked where the workers lived. Eleanor's relatives pointed vaguely

Michael at Uluru, Australia

to the north and said 'over there!' They were very generous with their time and took us into the outback. When we had passed the lovely green of the golf links – all carefully watered despite a serious existing drought – we came to rough bush, where we saw wallabies and kangaroos grazing. We sat down on sheets to eat our lunch, and found our sandwiches being nibbled by inquisitive animals over our shoulders. We were most impressed by the tidiness. All rubbish was collected up and taken for disposal in bins in the city. I was, however, a bit frightened running in Canberra, because I had to cross a dual carriageway to get into parkland from the homes of Eleanor's relatives. Inside the door of our hotel the floor was slippery and I shot across it, landing up with a bump against the receptionist's desk. 'A lot of people do that,' she said!

In Sydney, when we were staying with Peter Gracie, Eleanor had a most unfortunate fall and cracked her kneecap. I took her to the local hospital. It was a Sunday, and I had to get the stretcher trolley to put her on and take her past a cash register to pay for entrance. I was told to see the Almoner, who wanted to know my occupation. I explained that I was looking for help for my wife, not for me. She repeated the request for my occupation, because I would have to pay. But when I said that my wife was a doctor, her attitude totally changed and she said she would call a surgeon at once from the tennis court. He came and put Eleanor's leg in plaster and told us to return the next day to see the consultant. I loaded Eleanor back onto the trolley and found a taxi to get back to Peter. We left Australia and when we got to Singapore, some weeks later, it was time for the plaster to be removed. I found the name of a surgeon by consulting the head of extra-mural studies at the university, to whom I had an introduction. The plaster was removed and I was sent out to a Chinese emporium to buy Eleanor a stick. I came back with one, but it was too long. By chance, there was a carpenter in the hospital lift, who cut it to the right length, and Eleanor used it thereafter, becoming known as the 'lady with the stick'. The physical exercises required to re-use the kneecap were not so easily arranged. We had some days to spend in Delhi, and went to the orthopaedic hospital. There the doctor insisted on giving Eleanor instructions by talking to me; he evidently did not believe that a lady, even a doctor, would understand! It was a relief to get to the UK National Health Service after experiencing medicine in Australia and India.

On another visit to Australia, from Sydney we went on to Port Moresby in Papua New Guinea. There I had to lecture at Pat Healey's summer school on 'Problems of Economic Development' and was able to make a tour with Pat of the mountain region. We visited a coffee farm co-operative that Pat had helped to found. Forty years later, I heard that it was considering selling its coffees to the fair trade organisation that I had helped to launch in London. I was somewhat alarmed inland from the coast by the presence of native Guineans in the mountains, half naked with long necks and masks on their heads. We next visited the Solomon Islands and, by contrast, the beaches seemed to be occupied by the most beautiful long-haired black women I had ever seen. I also found where the lovely Mediterranean bougainvillaea climbing plant comes from – a Pacific island discovered by a French admiral, called Bougainville.

I have to say more about Pat Healey. After some time in Papua New Guinea, he worked in Madagascar and Sudan and then in London, and finally rose to a highlevel job in the International Red Cross in Geneva. When Joss's health and his own deteriorated, they had to return to England for treatment. Pat for a time ran a restaurant in Tavistock, where we visited him, and they retired to Cheltenham where he died. He was one of the most imaginative and creative of all the people I have known, and, but for ill health, would have been a leader of the movements for aid to the developing countries.

Back in England, I continued my running in Derbyshire with my faithful companion, my Labrador dog Gillie. When she died, I still found myself calling for her on my runs. We started visiting Eleanor's nephew, Bastien, in London and going to the concerts in his living room,

Bastien Gomperts

performed by his friends, the Fitzgerald Quartet, who became our friends, too. From Bastien's house I could run round Holland Park, a delightful trip, and, if I was very energetic, go on into Kensington Gardens and Hyde Park.

Bastien Gomperts should have an important place in this book. We first met him with his Pakistani girlfriend in Essex. We went to their wedding reception, and agreed with Eleanor's brother in law, Professor Daryll Forde, who presided, that the mixing of the genetic pool was wholly desirable. They had three beautiful girls. One was tragically shot on a visit to the Hindu Kush. The other two became successful professional people with fine children. Bastien, like his mother, was musical, playing the French Horn in the National Youth Orchestra. But he was also a biochemist, who was made a professor at University College, London, and had several well-known textbooks to his credit. When Eleanor died he took me to his heart, and I spent many happy days with him in London, Derbyshire and Scotland. On his retirement, he took up cabinet making, and provided his house and his children's homes with the most elegant furniture. The picture shows one of his cabinets.

I have already said that, when Eleanor died, I found much companionship with her two nephews, Bastien Gomperts and David Donnison. David was the son of Eleanor's elder sister, Ruth; Bastien, of her younger sister Barbara. I had already found refuge in going fishing and sailing from our Scottish house in Ardnamurchan, and found that on the way I could stay not only with the Alexanders at Callander but also with David and his new wife, Kay Carmichael, in Glasgow and on the island of Easdale, where they had a holiday home, just

Bastien's joinery

south of Oban, and always went to for Hogmanay. David had been a professor at
LSE and then chairman, under a Labour government, of the Supplementary
Benefits Commission. He then left his wife and children and married Kay
Carmichael, who had been a Benefits Commissioner. Kay was divorced from
Carmichael, when he ceased to be an MP and became a Lord. She was born in
Glasgow's Gorbals, but had been evacuated during the war to a middle class
family in Ayrshire. I had met her as an external examiner at Ruskin College, and
been very impressed by her approach to the social services. The photo of her with
me is on Easdale Island.

Kay Carmichael and Michael at Easdale Island

David and Kay went to live in Glasgow when David became professor of
regional studies at Glasgow University. I much enjoyed the runs I did with David
round Kelvin Park in Glasgow and on Easdale Island. But what was most
important for me was the celebration of Hogmanay on the island. As we crossed
by boat we were given a list of the parties being held, to tick the ones we wanted
to attend. All that drinking was a bit much, but there were concerts each night,
when David played his squeeze box, a football match, and an annual general
meeting of the management committee, of which David was a member, to make
its report. A number of interesting people had second homes on Easdale and
neighbouring islands. These included the mother of Diana, Princess of Wales, the
ex-chairman of the Midland Bank, the one-time British consul in Sarajevo, the

Governor of Brixton prison and his wife, who was a peeress and head of the ex-prisoners association, and also a crazy man who had written a book purporting to show that there had been no American landing on the moon. He said it was all a fake. I was quite convinced by the argument, but that was probably wishful thinking. Apart from Diana's mother, I got to know all these people rather well. David and Kay and I enjoyed long political discussions. On the political spectrum I stood somewhere in between Kay's Scottish socialism and David's Labourism. I went once with Annette to Easdale, but not at Hogmanay, too cold!

It was some time before I travelled out of Europe again, after the 1960s, but journeys to our house in Spain and to Mallorca were complemented by visits to Czechoslovakia, to Hungary and to the Soviet Union, as Communist rule was relaxed. Running over the bridge in Budapest to meet my friend Bertha Gaster, who was working there, was no problem. But I went to Prague earlier, in 1968 in the Prague Spring, when it was far from clear where and when the Red Army might reappear to occupy the city. In Moscow I could run along the side of the Moskva river, but it was winter, and extremely cold, as it had stopped snowing. These European trips were initiated by Ken Coates, and that brings me to a whole new chapter of this book.

Before I get there, however, there is another continent where I have jogged – the USA and Canada. I have been to Washington and New York to visit relatives, to California to lecture in Los Angeles, and to San Francisco to see my niece get married. Central Park in New York provides perfect jogging, so long as you remember to go round anti-clockwise, and there are paramedics at the gates in case you have trouble. There are parks in Washington, but also quiet roads in the leafy suburbs. LA has Hollywood, but I stayed mainly with friends near Santa Barbara. There you can run up into the hills, bright blue in the spring from the mass of ceanothus bushes.

My friend Dennis Dunn lived there. He was the producer in the Santa Barbara theatre and author of several Shakespearian commentaries. We were introduced to him by an old Berkeley friend of Eleanor's, Helen Hosner, who was suffering from a lung disease and needed a respirator. When her medical insurance ran out we paid for its supply. Such is the nature of the US health service. Dennis visited us in Derbyshire and went with us to the pageant in Chatsworth Park, to celebrate the 300th anniversary of the Devonshire dukedom. He died soon after.

In San Francisco, I have also run up into the hills, but the best runs are round the bay towards Berkeley and on beautiful roads through the vineyards of Vallejo. There is always a temptation to stop at the vineries on the way. Moving north beyond Oregon and Washington State, my favourite running ground in the New World is on Vancouver Island. There I lectured at a summer school at the campus of Victoria University, on the invitation of my friend Greg Blue, and could run wherever I wanted into the hills or along the bay.

One day I was taken up the Pacific coast by a lady lecturer who was descended from the Chinese navvies imported to build the railway. When I was there, the governor of Vancouver was of Chinese origin. My lecturer friend took me up and down the rocks along the shore to a place where there was some Neolithic rock art. It took several hours to get there, and on the way I suggested a stop for our picnic lunch. I explained that, as I was over 80, I was getting tired. She was appalled at her thoughtlessness, but had not dreamt that I could be so old.

My other visit to Vancouver Island, in 2000, was to see my niece, Liz, who was staying in a friend's house, very pregnant with her first child. The house was near a lake among fir trees, and if you ran into the woods, the tapping of the woodpeckers was what you heard. I went on several runs with Liz's husband Bos, round the lake and through the woods. In nearby Victoria I was shopping one day and mentioned my name to someone who asked if I was related to Liz, and I had to explain that I was Liz's uncle. 'But she is famous!' the woman said. Liz is famed on Vancouver Island for her work in stopping the loggers destroying great swathes of the forest.

In 2004, I went with Tony Simpson to the Boston Social Forum at the University of Massachusetts campus. I could run round the playing field, which had rows of boots set out in memory of local soldiers who had been killed in Iraq; a most moving sight.

Hilary Barratt Brown

The Bertrand Russell Peace Foundation, European Nuclear Disarmament and the Independent Labour Network, 1980s-90s

The period covered by this chapter is 1980 to 1999. The 1980s witnessed the last years of the Cold War between the Capitalist West and the Communist East, with the rise of Gorbachev in 1985 to lead the Soviet Communist Party. By 1989, there began the collapse of the Soviet Union along with the Berlin Wall during that year. The massacre of protesters in Beijing's Tiananmen Square in China took place in June. Gorbachev had taken over in the Soviet Union and reached agreement with US President Ronald Reagan on nuclear arms control. In the UK, the Labour leader, Neil Kinnock, attacked the 'Militants' in the Labour Party, a Tory Government was re-elected in 1992, but under John Major in place of Mrs Thatcher. The IRA bombed the City of London and destroyed many buildings. The insurance companies demanded that the UK Government should make peace in Northern Ireland. Clinton was elected US President in 1992. Late in 1991, Gorbachev was ousted by Yeltsin in Russia.

Hyper-inflation had started the break-up of Yugoslavia, leading to civil war and the destruction of Sarajevo and Mostar. A sort of peace was imposed on Yugoslavia in 1995 through US intervention, but massacres of Muslims at Srebrenica and of Serbs in Croatia led to further civil war, and the separation of the several states, Slovenia, Croatia, Bosnia and Macedonia from Serbia. The position of Kosovo remained undecided, until the NATO bombing of Belgrade in 1999 established Kosovo's independence from Serbia. Tony Blair became Prime Minister in the UK in 1997 with a massive majority for what he called 'New Labour'. On 31 December 1999, Vladimir Putin replaced Yeltsin in Russia, following fighting in Chechnya and economic crisis in Russia, East Asia and Japan. In 1999, Hong Kong was returned to China. The first stories of the effects of climate change resulting from growing releases of carbon dioxide into the atmosphere were gaining credence. There was much work for radical movements everywhere to defend the welfare state. These came later to make use of the internet and new methods of worldwide communication, email, Twitter, and Facebook, especially to meet the growing worldwide inequality and increasing rates of unemployment, following Mrs Thatcher and President Reagan's reductions of state regulation.

Bertrand Russell had taken the major initiative in the Cuban missile crisis of 1962, of appealing to Khrushchev and Kennedy for a peaceful solution. Following this initiative, Bertie agreed to establish a Peace Foundation in his name (the BRPF), in 1963. From an early date, Ken Coates became involved in the Foundation and, some years after Bertie's death, its chairman. I was a member of the Board, along

Bertrand Russell

with Ken Fleet as Secretary, John Daniels in the print works, Tony Simpson who had worked on European Nuclear Disarmament (END) and was responsible for publishing, and Regan Scott of the Transport and General Workers' Union.

During the 1980s, the Cold War between the Western powers and the Soviet Union intensified. In 1979, the US decided to deploy nuclear armed cruise missiles in the UK and several other European countries, aimed at Soviet targets. A large British feminist movement occupied Greenham Common in Berkshire, where some of the missiles were to be based. Later, some women succeeded in breaking into the US compound and were arrested. It was also mainly women who broke into the pens in Faslane, Scotland, where US and UK nuclear-armed submarines were based. These Scottish women included Kay Carmichael, the wife of Eleanor's nephew, David Donnison. She was arrested and sent to prison for six months. She told us a nice story of this imprisonment. Hundreds of bouquets of flowers were sent to her in prison and the governor refused her request that they should be distributed to the cells of each of the prisoners. She had already had a fracas with the Governor, because she had complained that she was called by her first name, Kay, while all the male prisoners were called by their surnames. This spell in prison did not stop her or other women from further break-ins to US nuclear arms and other establishments in Scotland and in North Yorkshire.

The response of the Bertrand Russell Peace Foundation to the proposed deployment of US Cruise missiles and Soviet SS20s was initiated by Ken Coates, in 1980, with the launch of the Appeal for European Nuclear Disarmament. In 1981, Eleanor and I attended a preliminary meeting of signatories in Rome, along with Ken Coates, Stuart Holland, Ken Fleet and Tony Simpson. Subsequently, beginning in Brussels in 1982, large END Conventions (conferences) were held, drawing men and women from all over Europe, East and West. Conventions which I

Bertrand Russell by Kapp

attended took place in Berlin, Perugia, Amsterdam, Vitoria-Gasteiz in the Basque Country of northern Spain, Coventry, Helsinki/Tallinn, and finally Moscow, in 1991. Coachloads of participants were bussed from England, notably large parties from the Midlands to Berlin, organised by Ann Kestenbaum and Tony Simpson, and from the north of England to Perugia, organised by David Browning and Lydia Merryl.

Ken Coates was undeniably the leading force in this movement, but much support was provided in the speeches and writings of Edward Thompson, who became a popular speaker at conferences. I had a memorable last time with this old friend on a boat travelling from Helsinki to Tallinn for an END meeting. Edward was speaking of

Ken Coates

celebrating the Latvians' success in freeing themselves from Stalinist repression, and explaining how he would bring this into what he had to say. But when we

Coventry by John Piper

landed at Tallinn, we were met by a military parade complete with swastikas and Hitler salutes. Edward had to re-write his speech.

For me one of the most moving of the END gatherings was in Coventry, in 1987, held just next to the restored cathedral. The atmosphere created by the great glass windows and ruined walls pervaded the whole occasion. Lydia Merryl had gathered together a remarkable number of active feminists, including a leading Australian aboriginal activist. From the seminar which they had conducted they delivered a most impressive report on the very special concerns of women at the threat of radioactive damage to children, as had been experienced at Hiroshima and Nagasaki.

In the 1990s, when Ken Coates became a Member of the European Parliament, I was much involved with him in the Bertrand Russell Peace Foundation as temporary chair and author of several books and pamphlets for the European Labour Forum (ELF) and Socialist Renewal, published under the Foundation's Spokesman imprint. In 1996, more than one hundred years of Labour's May Day was celebrated with a Socialist Renewal pamphlet by John Gorman which particularly pleased me because it contained a reprint of a poster printed in Dartmoor prison in 1917 by conscientious objectors there, of which my father was one, advertising a Demonstration in the Communal Hall at 7.30pm on May 1st. In 1991, I had written an ELF book, *European Union – Fortress or Democracy?*, which asked how we were to defend planning against the market and protect the weaker eastern and southern states. This was followed, in 1993, when Ken Coates and I edited for the European Labour Forum *A European Recovery Programme*, in which each of us wrote chapters along with others, including Jaques Delors, Sir Donald MacDougall, Stuart Holland, Francis Cripps, Peter Townsend and John Hughes – a truly powerful collective!

In 1995, we responded to the Blair initiative, 'revising socialism or rejecting it?', in a book on *Common Ownership, Clause IV and the Labour Party*. We followed that with another ELF book, *The Right to Work*, written with John Hughes and John Wells. The next year, just one year before Blair was first elected as Prime Minister, Ken and I expanded the argument with Blair in a major book, *The Blair Revelation: Deliverance for whom?* In it we predicted many of the disasters for Labour's welfare state and the ending of peaceful international relations that were to follow. What did follow, I spelt out in an ELF Socialist Renewal pamphlet, *Where Blair Went Wrong.* By 1997, we were moving onto the defensive with a detailed study of unemployment in the British coalfields, *Community under Attack*, and in 1998 I wrote the first part of a *May Day Manifesto* with a Preface by MEPs, Ken Coates and Hugh Kerr, and the sponsorship of 38 others, including Professors Gerry Cohen, Chris Jones, Robert Moore and Malcolm Sawyer, as well as John Palmer and Hilary Wainwright. In the same year, I added a Socialist Renewal pamphlet written with Hugo Radice, *Democracy versus Capitalism - A Response to Will Hutton with some Old Questions for New Labour.* But by this time, I had turned my attention to the plight of my old friends in Yugoslavia suffering from NATO bombardment of Belgrade, which had Blair's support and no UN endorsement. I made my contribution to the struggle an ELF Socialist Renewal pamphlet on *The Yugoslav Tragedy: Lessons for Socialists.*

Events in Yugoslavia involved me in much activity in the 1980s. I had been going each year to attend with Ken Coates the international 'Round Table' meetings at Cavtat in Croatia. They were attended by delegates from all over Europe, Canada, the USA, the Soviet Union and China. We brought several delegates from Britain, including David Blunkett from Sheffield. In 1981, I went from Cavtat with Eleanor to visit our Slovene friends, Nada Kraigher and Robert

Neubauer. I had been asked to speak on the way at a Communist Party conference in Zagreb. I spoke on the limited British experience of the decentralisation of government to Scotland and Ireland and on the lessons that might be learnt for Yugoslavia, where the problems created by nationalism were much more serious. How serious became clear in 1990, when hyper-inflation led to the threat of a break-up of the whole federal system which Tito's Government had bequeathed to Yugoslavia.

Inflation was brought under control, but outside pressures were at work on the Yugoslav federal system. Clinton in the US, anxious to improve his credentials with Islam, was supporting the claims of the Moslem Bosnians for independence. Germany, with major investments in Croatia, was beginning to see the Republic as a German colony. Some Croatian forces had fought alongside the German army in the Second World War under the same checker-board flag that Croatia flies today. Slovenia, with the highest standard of living in Yugoslavia, could recognise the value of independence, when aid would no longer be required for the poorer states in the federation. Serbia was still regarded as an ally of Russia but had attracted some European capital investment.

Rival armies, respectively Serbian and Croatian, attacked Sarajevo and Mostar in 1994, and bombing continued until 1995, when a temporary peace was arranged under the so-called Dayton accords, signed with the Serbian president Slobodan Milosevic by Clinton, who renewed his US presidency in 1996. It was evident that these 'accords' would not last, despite the support of the UN special envoy Cyrus Vance and of the European Union representative, David Owen, upon whom I and others rested a great measure of faith. The accords were broken by a mass Croat attack expelling the Serbs in the Krajina of Croatia and by the Serbian massacre of Bosnian Muslims at Srebrenica. Alija Izetbegovic, the Bosnian President, had left that city open to attack and Bosnian forces had been harassing Serbs around Srebrenica, but this hardly excuses the scale of the killing of men and boys by the Serbian Army.

I joined with others in several northern English universities in a campaign to encourage a peaceful solution to the situation that arose in Kosovo, still a province of Serbia. Kosovo had a mainly Albanian population of Moslems but had a long Serbian tradition as the centre of the 6th Century Christian monasteries and still had a large Serbian population. A Kosovo Liberation Army, largely financed from outside powers (including the US, Switzerland and Germany), was challenging the local government, led by Serbs, and unemployment had risen to 40%. A story of a massacre in a supposed Serb army attack on civilians at Racak, later shown to be on army units, not civilians, became the pretext for NATO bombing. This was without UN support, and aimed at Kosovo and then at Belgrade, to stop Milosevic in his tracks.

Until this time, there was a veto on unprovoked military offensive by any nation on another nation without the explicit authority of the United Nations

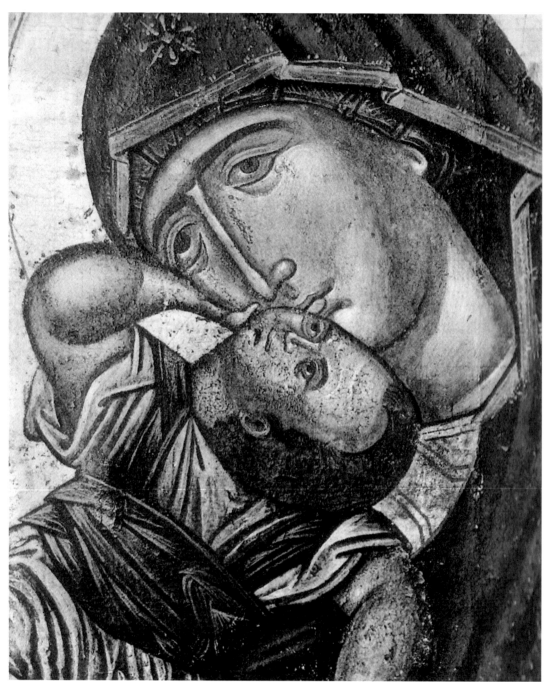

Kosovo Decani icons

Security Council. The concept had, however, grown that great humanitarian need could justify military intervention. This was invoked to justify the NATO bombing of Belgrade. Two bridges over the Danube were destroyed and several important buildings including the radio/TV centre, a power station, several factories, a hospital and many blocks of flats and houses. This bombing was claimed as a success in bringing Milosevic to withdraw Serbian troops from Kosovo, but a major reason for this must have been the withdrawal of Russian support for Milosevic.

The Russians had rushed an army from Bosnia to Kosovo to relieve Milosevic, and the US NATO General Wesley Clark had ordered the British General Mike Jackson, present on 'Bloody Sunday' in Northern Ireland, who was in Kosovo with a NATO force, to block Priština airport to the Russians. He had received the following reply from Jackson, 'I am not going to start the Third World War for you'. Clark had obtained Tony Blair's support for going beyond bombing to introduce a land army to bring Milosevic to heel, but had switched his thinking to high level bombing of Belgrade. 'I will systematically attack, disrupt, degrade, devastate and ultimately destroy' Milosevic's fighting capability, he swore. The Russians withdrew when Clark started on the bridges, refineries, electric grid, motor factories and basic infrastructure of Serbia.

The bombing lasted for 78 days. An estimated 12,000 tons of NATO munitions were used, including scatter bombs and depleted uranium weapons, causing severe cases of cancer. The Bertrand Russell Peace Foundation published a special pamphlet exposing this horror. Altogether, 500 Yugoslav civilians were killed and many thousands injured. The loss to the economy was estimated at 20 billion Euros, setting back Yugoslavia's development by a decade or more.

Milosevic survived for a time as the president of Serbia and reached agreements on behalf of Serbia with Croatia and Bosnia for their independence but, in 2002, he was captured and brought before the International Criminal Court for Former Yugoslavia. I obtained and read the thousands of pages of the trial, which only ended with Milosevic's death from a heart attack, in 2006. He was refused permission to go to a specialist hospital for his illness. I wrote up the whole story with the background of my experience over many years from 1945 in Yugoslavia in a book published in 2005, *From Tito to Milosevic – Yugoslavia, the Lost Country.*

The NATO attack on Belgrade was used as a precedent for further so-called 'humanitarian' military interventions by the western powers in other countries. The first Gulf War against Saddam Hussein was justified by the UN as Saddam had invaded Kuwait. Mr Blair's and president Bush's second war against Saddam, on the claimed humanitarian grounds of the oppression of the Kurds and others, as well as non-existent weapons of mass destruction, but in reality to preserve control of oil supplies, had no such authority. Afghanistan was invaded ostensibly to catch Osama Bin Laden, the perpetrator of the September 2001 attacks on New York and Washington, and there are likely to be similar questions raised about military support for the rebels in Libya and Syria. US use of unmanned drones to kill individuals in Pakistan, Yemen and elsewhere raises further questions of legitimacy.

Truly, the end of the 20th Century and the beginning of the 21st have set major problems for any organisation like the Bertrand Russell Peace Foundation to respond to with its tradition of human rights tribunals and conferences in the European Parliament. And on top of this is the question of climate change and the using up of scarce mineral resources in the drive for rapid economic growth. Spokesman Books, the imprint of the Bertrand Russell Peace Foundation, first raised this issue of climate change in a seminar on *Liberation and the Environment,* in 1972, and in subsequent pamphlets in 1978 and 1983 on *Resources and the Environment* and *Socialism and the Environment.* The Foundation publishes many books as well as a quarterly journal, *The Spokesman,* to which I contribute regular book reviews. Until his untimely death in 2010, Ken Coates was the driving force in the BRPF and, as a Member of the European Parliament for ten years, he was an influential international figure.

Ken had four particular areas of interest and activity in the European Parliament, which those of us who worked with him all to some extent shared. The first was the Human Rights Committee and the conferences on human rights issues, which Ken organised in the Parliament. The second was the Pensioners' Parliaments and the Disabled Peoples' Parliaments, which Ken mobilised and which produced important recommendations for state provision for old people and the disabled. The third was the continuing struggle for international nuclear disarmament. The fourth, which consumed much of his time in close collaboration with Stuart Holland and Jacques Delors, was working for full employment in Europe. Despite the active opposition of a senior British civil servant in the European Parliament, Ken convened large conventions of unemployed people and their organisations in the Brussels Parliament, on one occasion with the help of President Santer's own team of translators. It was a tragedy when the Labour Party disfranchised Ken with some other left-wingers from their representation in the European Parliament.

The emergence of Tony Blair's 'New Labour' after the death of John Smith was a disaster about which Ken Coates and I issued a clear warning in our book *The Blair Revelation,* which we published in 1996, before Blair became Prime Minister. Tony Blair was the natural son of a Communist, Leo, who himself had been adopted by the Scottish secretary of the Young Communist League, and later became an army officer, lawyer and university lecturer, ending up a Thatcherite. Tony Blair was sent to a choir school, Fettes College and Oxford University, where he fell under the influence of an Australian Anglican and married a Roman Catholic. In seeking selection to stand for Parliament, Blair claimed membership of CND. When elected, he dumped Gordon Brown, his chief rival, as an early successor as Prime Minister. Blair's was not a career to encourage any expectation of a principled Labour leader.

After he was expelled from the Labour Party, Ken Coates's response to Blair's Thatcherite offensive against the Welfare State was to launch the Independent

Labour Network and recruit a working group of politicians, economists and other experts to advise on the preparation of a 'May Day Manifesto'. I was given the task of writing, with the working group's help, Part One of the Manifesto, 'Defending the Welfare State'. This was illustrated with cartoons from Steve Bell showing Blair in nappies with a gobstopper and a tiny policeman's helmet, and also in a large car driven by a poodle-like John Prescott, advertising the 'Welfare Reform Road Show' watched by cheering fat cats with union jacks. My contribution was ten chapters of careful statistical analysis of what had happened to the Beveridge principles under Tory governments. Unemployment had risen, and with it the proportion of the population in poverty.

Manufacturing and mining were in decline and only the financial sector was booming, with obscene incomes and bonuses going to the speculators. Blair's 'reforms' were not concerned to address these distortions. Moreover, when UK performance was compared with that in the rest of Europe, only Spain, Portugal and Ireland had a higher proportion of unemployed, more poverty, and a lower proportion of national income spent on welfare. Blair's 'reforms' were shown to have been designed to offer to trans-national capital the most skilled financiers, the cheapest labour, the lowest taxes, and the least regulated environment, including weakened trade union, as well as physical and ecological controls, of any competing state economy. Mr Blair argued that he was choosing a 'middle way' between an over-regulated public economy and an under-regulated private economy. But this balance had been much more effectively achieved by the Scandinavian countries and in the Netherlands with more, rather than less, public intervention.

What was most important was that such public action required agreement among the members of the European Union, which Ken Coates and Hugh Kerr had been advocating in the European Parliament, and not a competition to be the economy most amenable to the giant international corporations. In 1997, at the European Parliament in Brussels, Ken Coates convened the first European Convention for Full Employment, with a follow-up second convention in 1999. Jacques Delors, President of the European Commission, whose vision inspired this sustained work on full employment (closely assisted by Stuart Holland) was replaced. Ken and his friends lost their seats in the Parliament in 1999. In the UK Elections of 2001, Blair's appeal to the private personal interest of the electorate, rather than to their common pubic interest, prevailed. The poorest among the electorate tended not to vote, and the increasing availability of jobs for women especially in retailing, however badly paid, led to a sense of economic satisfaction. But how long would that last? The world wide financial crisis of 2007 gave the answer, and resulted, in 2010, in a Tory-Liberal Democrat Coalition.

It is impossible to complete a chapter on the Bertrand Russell Peace Foundation without paying full tribute to Ken's wisdom, encyclopaedic knowledge, socialist conviction and energetic devotion to the cause of peace and human freedom. It was a privilege to work with him, and a pleasure to share in his enthusiasms.

After Ken's death, Tony Simpson took over not only the editorial responsibility for *The Spokesman* and book publications but also representing the BRPF at important meetings of the Russell Tribunal on Palestine and elsewhere, as well as joining delegations to Greece, Japan and Turkey, to take recent examples. What the BRPF had done under Ken's leadership had been to establish in an evil world a major influence for good, of which Bertrand Russell would have been proud. It is my privilege to have shared in a small way in that process.

I cannot end my writing about this period of my life without saying something more about my wife Eleanor, who died in 1998. She may appear in these pages as just my spouse, but she was much more than that, as her obituary in *The Guardian* made clear.

Eleanor was much influenced by the example of her two aunts. Her mother kept her suffragette colours in a drawer in her desk, but her mother's sisters wore them openly. These two became well known on political demonstrations as the 'umbrella sisters'. They were very small, but fought off policemen who were chasing protesters at demonstrations by wielding their umbrellas. Simmie, the youngest sister, who was brought up in Portugal, kept her maiden name, Seruya. Eleanor and I, on our way to our house in Spain, often stayed with the Seruyas in Lisbon. According to Eleanor, Simmie lived on a diet of nuts and dried fruit. When she came to England, she had a child by a leading trade unionist, a member of the British Communist Party, who then left her. The son became the manager of the Hampstead Communist Party book shop, after being arrested for hanging around the garden of the house where

Ramsay MacDonald lived, apparently with the purpose of planting a poster critical of MacDonald's decision to form a National Government in 1931 with Tories and Liberals. Simmie was for a time secretary to Keir Hardie, and helped to finance his political campaigns.

Eleanor's acts of disobedience were limited to throwing marbles onto the road in front of police horses chasing anti-fascist demonstrators in London's East End, in the 1930s. Fortunately, she was not arrested. When she worked in the United States, a friend gave her for self-protection a pistol with some bullets, which she kept in a

Eleanor, 1905 and 1995   drawer in our bedroom. Eleanor felt that in our isolated house in Derbyshire, when I was often away, she needed the protection, but we should have declared it. When our house was burgled, the only thing the thieves took was the gun. We confessed the theft to the police, but I always felt worried afterwards that someone had a gun who might use it to kill.

I have often wondered how Eleanor came to have the two carved wooden figurines that we always had on either side of our fireplace, and I still have. Eleanor said that the anthropologist, Bronislav Malinovski, brought them back from the Pacific Trobriand Islands. The figurines are about two feet tall, a man and a woman, the woman carrying a wooden bowl on her head. There was once a large bowl, but it was lost. I call the figurines by the Latin name for the household gods, Lares and Penates. I think that Eleanor said that Malinovski gave them to her when he was at the London School of Economics, but I don't remember why or just when.

Eleanor was trained as a bio-chemist, having been turned down for medicine on account of illness, though she played lacrosse for London University! She worked for Sir Jack Drummond, the chief adviser to the UK Government on food questions in the Second World War. As her health improved, Eleanor trained to do medicine at the Royal Free Hospital, becoming the students' president. At Hammersmith Hospital she got her diploma in public health, and went on to work at Queen Charlotte's Hospital and the Wingfield Isolation Hospital in Oxford. There she was the first person to use penicillin on a patient, when it was discovered by the Oxford scientist, Howard Florey, who asked for her collaboration. In 1943 she joined the Save the Children Fund and went to Cairo to lead a mobile medical and hygiene unit, destined for Yugoslavia. This is where I met her, running a clinic in Sarajevo. For a time after that, she worked in a clinic in Belgrade. When we returned to England, and married, she became an assistant county medical officer in Essex, with responsibility for child patients in the Colchester Isolation Hospital. There were in those days before inoculation many children suffering from polio and from measles encephalitis, which Eleanor had to treat. Fortunately, inoculation against both polio and measles rendered this work unnecessary, just as I decided that I wanted to move on.

When we moved to Derbyshire, Eleanor was again an assistant county medical officer, this time with responsibility for schools' health and some children's clinics. But she also took on two extra responsibilities. The first was starting a family planning clinic in Sheffield for young people, who at that time were not supposed to engage in sexual activity. The second was to conduct a survey of cases of goitre, what was called 'Derbyshire neck', a swelling of the neck prevalent in Derbyshire. She found that in all cases the illness was associated with drinking water from artesian wells. This water lacked iodine, and thereafter extra iodine was added to the water supply. The fact that she was a loving mother to Daniel and Deborah and my beloved wife for 51 years adds up to the story of a remarkable woman.

Eleanor's pottery

And this says nothing about her cooking or needlework or pottery. I did no cooking until the last five years of Eleanor's life, when she taught me to take over. I was once asked why I did not cook, and I replied, 'If you were married to Picasso, would you paint?' Eleanor's work at her old Singer treadle machine in making clothes for the children and turning sides to middles on the sheets was part of an all round capacity to manage. For years we used the tray with the sampler she had embroidered at 17. Eleanor made beautiful pottery, which she worked on dressed in her white starched medical coat, and some of the pottery she gave away on her ninetieth birthday, as is shown in the picture. She loved especially the feeling of the clay rising and shaping on the wheel between her fingers, and then painting her handwork to her own designs. Her energy was amazing. When she went shopping in Chesterfield, they called her 'the running shopper', as she ran from shop to shop, even in her 70s. But it was her warmth that will be remembered longest. In Essex we had an *au pair* girl from France, who arrived a dejected waif and blossomed – and more – under Eleanor's warmth. Janine had a special greeting for me if I arrived home from work before Eleanor, *'Non, monsieur, le soleil n'est pas encore retourné'*. Having children and then grandchildren was a profound emotional experience for Eleanor. Under that white medical coat that seemed so clinical, you could hardly miss 'the fire that in the heart resides'.

CHAPTER 12

The Fair Trade Movement
in the 1980s and beyond

This chapter covers the years from 1983 to 2012. In 1981, the Greater London Council (GLC) was taken over by the Labour Party under the leadership of Ken Livingstone, while the UK was still ruled by Mrs Thatcher. When I started to work at the GLC with Robin Murray in 1983, the Council was introducing a range of innovative economic policies, including a Greater London Enterprise Board (GLEB), which was encouraging the development of co-operative enterprises. It was not a favourable period for a Labour local authority. In 1992, the Tories returned with John Major as Prime Minister, in place of Mrs Thatcher. The break-up of Yugoslavia had begun, as Clinton was re-elected to the US presidency in 1996. Tony Blair, however, won a landslide victory in the UK in 1997 for 'New Labour', whose triumph Mrs Thatcher later cited as her 'greatest victory'. Certainly, Blair continued Mrs Thatcher's running down of mining and manufacturing industry in Britain, and supported the rise of financial services in the City of London, as Ken Coates and I predicted in our book The Blair Revelation. *It led to disaster. A financial crisis of over-lending in Japan, East Asia and Russia, in 1998, nearly led to economic collapse in Europe and the US. With the help of my grandson, Elliot, I wrote* Young Person's Guide to the Global Crisis, *with a glossary of economic terms that you can tear out and use to consult when reading the book.*

The first Gulf War, in 1990-91, led to the defeat, but not to the removal, of Saddam Hussein, and to Blair's belief in military action in Yugoslavia in 1999. Blair was returned to power in 2001 with another huge majority, despite stories of Indian sleaze and less than total affection for the Millennium Dome. George Bush confirmed his presidency for a first term. In that year, 2001, on September 11, the World Trade Towers in New York and the Pentagon in Washington were attacked by hijacked aircraft, and the blame laid on Osama Bin Laden, leader of Al Qaeda, from Saudi Arabia. He was supposed to be hiding in Afghanistan, so the US and its allies began another Afghan war, which has lasted until 2013. But Bush also took the opportunity to launch a further massive 'shock and awe' attack on Iraq, which was supposedly concealing weapons of mass destruction and supporting Al Qaeda, contrary to some intelligence, but which certainly had large oil supplies, which the US wished to control. This war did not have the sanction of the UN, but Bush won his second term as US president, with support from Blair. Elections in Iraq in 2005 produced a government apparently acceptable to the US, but violence continued and oil supplies were still reduced. Civil war took place in Rwanda between Hutus and Tutsis killing millions and there was fighting in other parts of Africa, notably in Liberia and the Congo. But in South Africa Nelson Mandela had been released from prison in 1990 and served as the country's President from 1994 to 1999. War erupted in Lebanon in 2006 and, in 2011, NATO air strikes were authorised to support the rebels against the rule of

Colonel Gadaffi, President of Libya, another African with control over large oil supplies.

2007 saw the most serious worldwide financial collapse since the 1930s. It began in the USA, but soon spread to the UK, Europe and the East. Banks were bailed out with public money leaving heavy state debts everywhere except for China. The recession became global in 2009. Gordon Brown succeeded Blair, and did something to rescue the British economy, but did not give up New Labour's love for the banks, bailing out several more. In 2008, Obama was elected to the Presidency in the US, the first black president in US history. In 2010, Labour was just defeated in a general election, but the Tories did not win an overall majority in the House of Commons and formed a coalition government with the Liberal Democrats. This government was committed to austerity and cuts in public spending, partly required by the huge state debt, but also politically part of fundamental Conservative beliefs. Obama was just re-elected in 2012, having failed to do much to revive the US economy as he had originally promised to do. He still faced a Republican majority in Congress.

This history of the period does not suggest an easy life for an organisation committed to building international fair trade, such as we had founded in 1985, nor a happy future for all but the very rich in developed countries and in China, whose businesses were buying up land for their needs, at the expense of small farmers everywhere. The rich countries' use of chemical fertilisers was becoming a threat of disaster for the planet, as was more widely recognised by the early years of the 21st century – a 'collision with nature', as it has been called.

Retiring in 1983 from full time work at the Northern College, I went to see my very old friend, Robin Murray, who was then head of the industry and employment department of the Greater London Council (GLC). He suggested

Robin Murray and Michael

that there was need for a full study of the work that the Council under Ken Livingstone had been engaged on together with an examination of the way London's co-operatives, assisted by the Greater London Enterprise Board, might be developed – two big tasks. I started, and over time completed, work on the first, but the second attracted me more. I had written books about international trade, but here was a chance to put some alternative ideas into practice.

Robin was anxious to encourage two new developments in the GLC: the first was to organise the recruitment of more black officials through an apprenticeship scheme – there were plenty of black cleaners and messengers. The second was to build relations with revolutionary governments. Robin and I still believed in revolutionary political and economic change. Delegations from the Vietnamese, Cuban, Nicaraguan governments and from Zimbabwe were invited to the GLC, and I was encouraged to see my ideas for trade development going in that direction. It got to the Prime Minister, Mrs Thatcher's ears that Ken Livingstone at the GLC was developing a foreign policy, and with her Foreign Secretary, she determined to close it down, along with the banner on the GLC building that reminded all who passed of the current number of unemployed people.

With the help of Olivier le Brun at the GLC, in 1983, we organised a conference of co-operatives from Britain and representatives from developing countries to consider forms of future co-operation. We had the strong support of Ken Livingstone and of Michael Ward, chairman of the GLC Industrial and Employment Committee. I made a speech arguing *inter alia* that we had had enough of unfair trade, and it was time for some fair trade. I had in mind forms of international planning, based on the GLC experience. This led to the idea of establishing an organisation in the GLC to promote such co-operation. The GLC already had a Greater London Enterprise Board (GLEB) and one of its leading members, Vella Pillay, chairman of the branch of the Bank of China in London, joined me in pressing our case.

The first idea was to help developing countries with progressive governments by encouraging planned trade exchanges, as recommended by the Norwegian Nobel prize winning economist, Professor Ragnar Frisch, whom I had met at a London conference to consider alternatives for Britain to a European Union. A start could be made, we thought, in those countries being boycotted by the rich countries. Cuba, Nicaragua and Vietnam were our first choices, and Dick Day and Olivier Le Brun went to Vietnam to develop pineapple production for canning and export in exchange for British engineering products. Dick organised the production for export from Cuba of certain precious metals, textiles and rocking chairs, which had to be assembled from the separate pieces that arrived.

As for the textiles, we had a great success. A friend of mine, John Laflin, was a manager at Liberty's store in Regent Street. John was married to Felicia, the daughter of my good friend, Don Sproule. John arranged for the beautifully coloured printed textiles, which could be made into dresses, curtains or cushion

TWIN Staff, 2003

covers, to be exhibited in Liberty's shop windows. Four Cuban ladies arrived to display the textiles draped around them, but as they appeared in the windows they had no clothes on, having covered themselves in paint. The result was sensational, and seriously affected traffic flow in Regent Street. The textiles were soon sold out. I am now sitting on a cushion made by Eleanor from the lovely bright materials with 'Mendive', the signature of the Cuban designer, at the centre. When the Sandanista Government came to power, we added Nicaragua to our list of possible trading partners.

Unfortunately, Mrs Thatcher, then UK Prime Minister, decided that the GLC should be closed down within a year. However, in 1985, we obtained a guarantee of funding of an organisation for three years, to be called 'Third World Information Network' (TWIN) with a trading arm, Twin Trading. Vella and I signed the necessary documents for setting up the trust fund on the evening before the GLC's closing date for new activities.

We hired a staff of seven, headed by Olivier Le Brun as director of TWIN and Twin Trading and Dick Day as our development officer. We started on TWIN's programme of conferences, launched the newsletter and implemented some of the numerous projects emerging from the GLC trade conference, including:

a) technical and financial support with EEC funds for an irrigation scheme of peasant village associations, running vegetable gardens, to supply neighbouring towns and hotels. This scheme functioned for more than ten years.

Vella Pillay and Michael

b) a fair trade project with coffee producers in Nicaragua. This coffee, branded as 'Twin Trading Nicaraguan Coffee', sold mainly to organic shops and students' unions, was a seed that later grew into 'Café Direct'.

c) barter trade with Nicaraguan enterprises, exchanging computers against rocking chairs and other handicraft products.

d) import and sales of several Vietnamese products (spices, silk, kimonos) for state companies in Vietnam.

e) importing Mozambican wood to be transformed into beds by a London carpentry enterprise.

f) technological support for various projects, e.g. for a pineapple canning company in Vietnam and an organic vegetable growing scheme in Eritrea.

Vella joined our managing board, and stayed to help us until he was called back to South Africa by Nelson Mandela to advise him on financial matters. Basil Davidson came onto the Trust as an advisor. I shall not easily forget the day when Vella and I were chatting in his Highgate home, and the phone rang. Vella said, 'Nelson, Nelson! I don't believe it!' After 26 years in prison on Robben Island, Mandela had been released and one of the first people he wanted to speak to was Vella, whose family had helped him before his imprisonment. Mandela had recalled the name of Vella's wife, Patsy, and the names of his sons and wanted to be remembered to them.

Vella went back to South Africa, and put forward constructive economic and financial planning proposals for Mandela to introduce, but the international monetary authorities had got South Africa in their sights, and nothing was done that Vella had hoped for. I saw him briefly with Olivier Le Brun on his return to England, as can be seen in the photo, taken by Olivier. We celebrated his 70th birthday, but he was not well and died shortly afterwards. I was asked to make the oration at his funeral and sat next to his wife, Patsy. 'Give it them hard and strong!' she whispered. I had prepared a rather quiet, factual story of Vella's life and work in China, ending with TWIN and Mandela, but an idea for a conclusion came to me and I quoted from the song of the left-wing American trade union, the Wobblies:

> *Freedom doesn't come like the rain from the sky!*
> *Freedom doesn't come as a gift from on high!*
> *You have to work for it, fight for it, day and night for it!*

As I finished, I threw out my clenched fist, and by mistake hit the microphone. The noise in the crematorium and in the overflow meeting outside in the garden was shattering. Everyone thought that I had done it intentionally. When I sat down amid the din, Patsy said 'Wonderful, Michael, just wonderful!' I was pleased because there was no doubt about our celebration of Vella's life, working and fighting for the cause of African liberation and for TWIN as a part of that new Africa.

My interest in Africa, begun in 1942 by my boat trip along the West African coast to Cape Town, train journey across the Kalahari desert to Durban, and seaplane flight all the way back up the East coast of Africa to Cairo, led me to think at once, when we founded TWIN, of TWIN working with African organisations. We decided to arrange in Africa a follow-up international conference of co-operatives. Several African co-operatives from Zimbabwe and Tanzania had attended our GLC conference in 1983, and I had a good friend managing a sugar factory in Kenya. I set out to travel with Eleanor to our friends in Kisumu, Kenya, and went on to Zimbabwe. Mugabe had just established himself as the President of Zimbabwe, and our co-operatives were being brought under his control. Despite much support from Professor Terry Ranger, whom I had met in Manchester, we failed in Zimbabwe, but a much earlier English Co-operative College contact I had with co-operatives in Tanzania gave us a start in Africa.

Our work with coffee farmers in Africa had been preceded by imports of coffee from co-operatives in Mexico and Nicaragua. The Mexican Government relaxed control over coffee exports so that small coffee farmers' co-operatives could choose how to export. Teodor Shanin, who I had persuaded to join our TWIN board, had contacts in Mexico among the co-operatives, which led to our importing the first container load of Fair Trade coffee from Mexico, despite its reactionary government, for sale through Oxfam, Equal Exchange and other charity shops in the UK. The export of this container had been held up by our refusal to pay bribes to the officials at the port. When this was reported to the dockworkers, they showed their solidarity with the small farmers by stopping work until our coffee was loaded. The Mexican Government then jailed some of the farmers for supposedly getting round their legislation. I got Ken Coates, as a Member of the European Parliament, to persuade the European Union representative in Mexico to intervene, and we got a cable from the Mexican co-operatives, thanking us for the improvement of the food in prison. I told this story in my book, *Fair Trade.*

The addition of Nicaragua to our list of favoured countries was brought to an end by the United States' military intervention and overthrow of the Sandinistas. When that happened, our agent there had a bar of gold for export, as part of our plan to offer an alternative to gold for wedding rings supplied from *apartheid* South Africa. As our agent's house came to be inspected by the new government authorities for evidence of collaboration with the Sandinistas, he hid the gold in the chamber pot under his bed and got it away to his sister in Peru, who forwarded it to us. It so happened that at that time my wife lost her wedding ring in our strawberry patch at Robin Hood Farm, and she replaced it with one from Nicaraguan gold. My granddaughter Sarah still wears it on her right hand.

Once TWIN's association with co-operatives of coffee farmers in Tanzania and Uganda, cocoa farmers in Ghana, and cotton farmers in Mali was established, I met Adebayo Adedeji, the Executive Secretary of the UN Economic Commission for Africa on a visit to London, and had long talks with him. I also talked with my friend Victoria Bawtree, who was editing the Food and Agricultural Organization magazine of the Freedom from Hunger Campaign, and with my old friend Basil Davidson, who had broken into new interpretations of African history. I decided to launch myself into writing a series of books on Africa. The first, published in 1992, was called *Short Changed,* a major statistical study of Africa's world trade, on which I had the assistance of Pauline Tiffen. I followed this up in 1995 with a comprehensive study of *Africa's Choices – After Thirty Years of the World Bank.* This was published by Penguin, with an American edition from Westview Press and a Japanese translation. Finally, in 1997, I delivered the 'African Studies Lecture' at Leeds University, under the presidency of my friend Lionel Cliffe. In this I emphasised, with much historical support, that my belief in the possibilities of developing fair trade was not just a romantic illusion but a real basis of hope for the future.

Having begun on TWIN's programme of conferences, and launched the newsletter, we opened a shop in London for Third World co-operatives' products, especially from countries suffering trade embargoes such as Vietnam and Cuba. Dick Day, as development officer, explored trade openings in Africa and was soon joined by Pauline Tiffen, who became his partner. Pauline organised a co-operatives conference under the rubric 'Whatever happened to Fair Trade?' She realised that our shop and the small markets of voluntary organisations such as Oxfam were quite inadequate to sell the produce of the co-operatives we were in touch with. She proposed the formation of a company made up of TWIN, Oxfam, Traidcraft and Equal Exchange, that would be capable of marketing small Third World co-operative producers' coffee to the UK supermarkets.

So it was that Cafédirect was born, in 1993, and we had advertising posters on the railway stations, promising a fair deal for Third World producers – 'You get excellent coffee, and they get schools and clinics'. The first supermarket to take some of our coffee was won over by Equal Exchange in Scotland. This was followed by the Co-op and, after three years of agonising delays, all the UK supermarkets, except ASDA, were putting Cafédirect on their shelves.

Pauline and Dick Day went on to work with a newly formed Ghanaian cocoa co-operative to make chocolate for marketing in the UK and in Japan. A company was formed with the involvement of Sophie Tranter and Sandy Balfour to market chocolate in the UK. Originally, after Dick Day's death, it was called 'The Day Chocolate Company', but when it was converted into a joint Ghanaian-British company, it became 'Divine Chocolate', a direct translation of the Ghanaian *Kuapa Koko*.

Dick's death from a brain tumour was a terrible loss. He had done so much from the very beginning to build TWIN. I had once again to speak the oration at a funeral. Our Japanese co-operative colleague came all the way from Tokyo to be present, and there were delegates from co-operatives in Africa and Spanish America. I ended my tribute to Dick's work with the Spanish challenge, *Venceremos!* (We shall overcome!) and *La lucha se continúa!* (the struggle goes on!) I sat down, shaking with emotion. Happily, I had sitting next to me, Barry Munslow, a huge man, African expert and Professor at Liverpool University, who had been one of our most loyal supporters. He took my hand in his great paw, and calmed me down.

An early success in establishing TWIN as a major force in Third World Trade was at a conference organised partly by TWIN and partly by the World Association of Fair Trade, held in Kilkenny, Ireland, in 1988. Mary Robinson, the Irish President, presided. She later became the UN high commissioner for human rights. I had to make a major speech about TWIN and the principle of fair trade and had strong support, speaking in Erse, from my friend Mike Cooley, the author of the *Lucas Plan* to replace arms production at Lucas Aerospace. The conference was the first to bring together a number of Third World small farmers' co-operatives with European non-governmental organisations under the inspired leadership of Carol Wills from Oxford.

One very important role that TWIN played in the advancement of ideas for diversifying the trade of developing countries was by attending at conferences on the role of non-governmental organisations (NGOs), organised by the UN

Commission for Europe in Geneva in the late 1980s. I attended several of these on behalf of TWIN and had the support of John Denham MP, later a Labour minister, for establishing fair trade principles in international trade. However, the increasing acceptance worldwide of free market 'neo-liberal' trading practices unfortunately brought these valuable discussions to an end.

One great occasion was the public launching of TWIN's products in London. We assembled representatives of nearly a million farmers from several hundred co-operatives in 26 different Third World countries. I wrote the book with Pauline Tiffen, *Africa Short Changed*, which was published by Pluto Press and we started a regular information service, the *TWIN Café Bulletin*. This still appears every fortnight, informing our coffee-growing members of the movement of arabica and robusta coffee world prices. One of our first tasks had been to supply computers to all our members so that they could receive e-mails and get internet communication.

As well as my earlier visits for TWIN to Kenya and Zimbabwe, I made one memorable visit to Peru to visit our coffee co-operatives there with the support of Rebecca Morahan where we could witness the buying skills of John Wheeler of TWIN. We went to Lima and then to Cuzsco and climbed up into the mountains to Machu Picchu, which I visited with the representative from the Japanese co-operatives to whom some of our Peruvian farmers were selling their coffees. You

At Machu Pichu, Peru, with a Japanese delegate

can see her with me in the photo. Machu Picchu is an amazing site, with the remains of a large settlement of houses dating back to the 11ᵗʰ century between the peaks. On the mountain climbs some of our party suffered from altitude sickness. But for me it was pure joy. I could hear without my hearing aids, because the air pressure was less and my Eustacian tubes opened, which high board diving had closed. I once asked my wife while we were staying in the Pyrenees why lovemaking was so good in the mountains. 'You can hear me!' she said.

Climbing up into the mountains from Cusco, I had an extraordinary experience. It was 12 November, and I was just thinking that it was Eleanor's birthday when I noticed that the village we were approaching was called 'Eleanora'. As we left the village, I looked out for the sign that gave its name, and it was true – truly remarkable. When we returned to Lima, I stayed with relatives of Robin Murray's wife, Frances. My hostess and her daughter were both well-known Peruvian dancers. They took me to a dance, and to my amazement I found that, when they led, I could follow their movements in accord with the music. Before leaving Lima, I bought two jersies of llama wool, each having the outline of two llamas woven into the pattern. They are warm without being heavy. I still wear them; indeed, I am wearing one now, as I write. It now has little leather elbow pads, where I wore out the wool at the elbows. The Peruvian trip was a real summation of my whole TWIN experience, not only the products we bought, but the splendid people, the mountain countries they came from, and their evident gratitude for our help.

After twelve years as TWIN's chair, I stood down in 1995, retaining my board membership. Robin Murray, returning from several years' work in Canada, took over. Pauline Tiffen resigned and took on a high profile job in the World Trade Organisation in Washington. Robin completed the chocolate negotiations with finance from the Body Shop, and launched initiatives with tropical fruit producers in AGROFAIR, and nut producers in a new organisation, obtaining nuts from Peru, Malawi and Kerala. AGROFAIR became a major UK supplier, first of all in the Co-op, of fair trade bananas and other tropical fruits.

The financing of a nut company proved more difficult and required a major contribution of funds from TWIN's reserves. In the end, a company called 'Liberation Nuts' was launched through Sainsbury's. After starting initiatives for fair trade cotton from Malawi and rubber goods from Malaya, Robin resigned from the chair in 2010. It is impossible to exaggerate the importance of Robin Murray's contribution to TWIN and Twin Trading, from the founding in 1983 at the GLC to his retirement 27 years later, all combined with most important work done with London boroughs and books written on waste disposal and co-operatives, and most recently on the whole social economy.

TWIN continued under the chairmanship of Catherine Cameron, the environment expert, and then of John Boase, the director of the Co-operative

Society in Cumbria, who sadly died after only a year, having written a key book, *The Fair Trade Revolution.* Finally, Michael Ward took over the chair. He had been the chair of the GLC industry and employment committee, which had first launched TWIN and Twin Trading in 1983. It cannot be said that the TWIN experiment has changed the unequal economic relations of developed and developing countries, but a beginning has been made.

Especially remarkable has been the growth in public understanding in Britain and more widely of the concept of fair trade. Even giant corporations such as Nestlé and Kraft have sought to carry the fair trade logo and guarantee on some of their products, notably Ethiopian coffee

Catherine Cameron

and KitKat chocolate. Their huge scale of supply means that they can be offered at prices that the products from our small-scale farmers cannot compete with on the supermarket shelves. The creation of a level playing field in international trade is still a long way off.

A new problem that affects our farmers is the result of climate change. Some areas of production are suffering from continued droughts, others from torrential rain. My friend Catherine Cameron, a well-known expert on climatology, while she was the chair of TWIN for a few years after Robin, sought to address this issue. The problem of combining the finance of TWIN's ongoing responsibilities with new initiatives proved overwhelming and Catherine resigned. The issue remains. TWIN has attracted a succession of brilliant leaders, but many of its problems remain intractable in a world of giant corporations.

International trade in a time of continued recession, not just a double dip, but a threatened treble dip for the UK and most of southern Europe, is bound to be sluggish. It can be said that fair trade principles applied to the produce of small-scale Third World co-operative farmers have slightly increased the price they receive and improved somewhat the quality of their lives. But when I drink my cup of coffee in Starbucks or Costa, or buy a bar of chocolate in the Co-op, perhaps 10 pence of the £1 I pay goes to the producer, even if what I buy has the fair trade and organic logos. Apart from the milk and sugar, which may or may not be fairly traded, the money is made in the roasting or processing, the packaging and the retailing. Very few farmers' co-operatives and hardly any fair trade suppliers do their own upstream roasting, processing, packaging and, least of all, the retailing. TWIN has never had enough capital to be able to do that and compete on price with the giant companies that control the markets, but fair trade has greatly enhanced the power of the small farmers in the international commodity markets which these companies dominate.

The whole history which we reviewed at the beginning of this chapter is a history of leaving it to the market and of a market dominated by ever fewer and larger international companies. Even some of the great fair trading Quaker companies such as Rowntree's and Cadbury's have been taken over by such giants as Kraft and Nestlé. They advertise some of their products as 'fair trade', but these make up less than 1% of their sales. You can buy fair trade coffee at Starbucks, but only a few people do. This few is growing every year, and that is where some hope lies. But the future for fair trade has to lie in a real movement from below to build an alternative social economy, which reduces inequality and protects the environment. And that implies a major challenge to the capitalist market, using all the new means of communication – the Internet, Twitter, Facebook, and email links. It is a massive task, but that alone will save the planet, which we all depend on for our very lives. And it means resisting the great land grab by the rich that is taking place in Africa and Latin America to take over land for large estates to feed the rich with sugar, soya, beef and maize, at the expense of the millions of small farmers growing their mixed crops – a disaster for the planet.

Epilogue

I have to add a word of historical introduction to an Epilogue, which was written in the years 2011-2013. During those years I became increasingly aware of the disaster course which the planet earth and our lives were following. The global economic crisis of 1998 was followed by a much deeper crisis in the 'housing bubble' and banking collapse of 2007, continuing into 2013. All nations, except China, and most families, except the very rich, were running larger and larger debts, borrowing far above their incomes and not saving – and this could not last. At the same time, the energy, on which all economic activity depends – oil, gas, coal – and the minerals for production, were running out and alternatives of solar, wind and wave power and nuclear were inadequate to fill the gap. Peak oil, that is the year when new demand for oil begins to exceed new supplies, occurred in 2013. After that, prices of oil and minerals will rise, and shortages will occur. Frac oil uses more energy and cannot be sustained. But that is not the end of human problems on the planet. World population is growing, but it is more and more difficult to grow the food that is needed for the increase. The soil is being depleted and needs more and more fertiliser – from oil – to produce crops. And then we have said nothing about the effects of the burning of more and more energy on the climate, which is steadily warming up, to melt the polar ice and flood our lands with the sea. There are still things we can do – to consume less, to waste less, especially food, to save energy in our housing and travel, to use technology more effectively, to stop increasing the population, but there is not much time left. We had to begin, I realised, from reading Chris Martenson's The Crash Course, *with little changes to alter our habits and build on such small changes, with our families, neighbours and communities, to make the big changes that are needed. I could only do a very little, but I could encourage others, family, friends and neighbours, to act in the economy of co-operative learning by the digital networks of our increasingly knowledge-centred society with a new cognitive division of labour, using what one writer (Yan Moulier Boutang in his* Cognitive Capitalism) *has called our new 'collective intelligence' based on the Internet,* Tweets and Facebook, *etc.*

But I was engaged in more personal problems. In 2005, I met up again with an old friend, Annette Cooper, whom I had known in the Friends Ambulance Unit during the London Blitz, while we were living at the students' hostel of the London Hospital in Whitechapel. The painting reproduced here is of her at that time. She married my Oxford friend, David Caulkin, and I went to the Middle East. We did not meet again for 65 years, but in 2005 Annette got in touch with me, and we lived together for seven years after that. Very sadly, these lines were written on the evening before she died peacefully in her sleep.

I must here add a few words of tribute to a remarkable lady. Annette had to respond to a succession of disasters that would have destroyed most people – orphaned at the age of seven, she was sent by her aunt and uncle, her foster parents, with her sister to a Catholic convent in Belgium, where she learned to

Annette Caulkin

speak French before returning to England and finishing her education at Ackworth, a Quaker school in Yorkshire. After working for a while in the school bursar's office, she joined the Friends Ambulance Unit when the war broke out, where we met and she married David.

When David was killed a week before the end of the war, Annette took her two babies to a cottage in mid-Wales. When they were old enough to go to school, she went to live in Maidenhead and worked at the Canadian Red Cross hospital in nearby Taplow. With the help of friends she got her children to boarding school and universities and launched them on professional careers. Thereafter she shared in their lives, but then, without higher education, she took on a most demanding job – the editing and assessing of scripts for possible films at the National Film Finance Corporation, for which work she received the MBE. But she hadn't finished yet. When her sister died in 2005, in her 80s, she looked for new companionship and, luckily for me, thought of our friendship in 1941-42. It is an amazing story. She happened to travel on a bus and talked to her next door passenger, who said she worked at the library of Sheffield University. Annette then asked if, by chance, Michael Barratt Brown still worked at the University. The lady knew me and had my address, and Annette wrote to me.

Eleanor had died seven years earlier and I had failed to find a possible new partner. I was eager to see Annette again, after 65 years. We met in London over a glass of champagne and went to Lemonia in Primrose Hill, her favourite restaurant, where they called her 'Lady Caulkin'! From there we went together to St. Pancras to take the same train to Chesterfield, the station for both my house and for her sister Betty's, where she was staying. We talked solidly all the way about our past 65 years, and when we separated to take different taxis at Chesterfield, I said, 'Shall we meet again?' and Annette replied, 'Yes, I suggest tomorrow!' We did meet again that very next day and on several following days.

As Annette later told the story to my friend David Browning and to her friend Bea Thompson, we renewed a friendship that had begun in the early 1940s in the Friends Ambulance Unit in the blitz. It was truly a loving reunion. After 65 years unknown to each other, we came together as if somehow we had never been apart.

Annette

Annette and I often used to talk together in French. We even wrote letters to each other in French, as we had done seventy years earlier. We went to several French films, including *Cyrano de Bergerac* at the Institut Français in London. Annette for some time read and discussed her favourite French historical novels. Shared French was an important part of our lives before she lost her memory. I was able to tell Annette's son and daughter about their father, who was my friend at Oxford and joined the FAU with me, but was killed at the end of the War before his children knew him. This is a sad story, but Annette brought them up wonderfully well.

And so began a loving relationship that lasted for seven years, until Annette's death. The first year was difficult. To see each other we had to travel between Derbyshire and London. When we were apart, we phoned each other several times a day, not all calls started by me! But I was very impatient. I wrote out plans of meeting times and places, but Annette didn't like plans, and wished to preserve her independence. Then she felt responsible for the work being done on the roof of her house, though hers was only one of the four flats in the house. Because of bad weather this seemed to go on for months, and we could only see each other for two days at weekends.

Christmas came and I thought to join Annette at a party she was going to. But she said 'it wouldn't work'. I was very upset and drove off to Cumbria to join Robin Murray and his family. In the snow my car slid off the road below his house and nearly dropped into a deep ditch. By good fortune a farmer came past with a tractor to feed his cattle and pulled me out. I went on for Hogmanay at David Donnison and Kay's house on Easdale Island. I wrote a diary of this year and called it 'John and Mary' to conceal our identity.

The next two years were quite different. Annette and I shared a bed and found how to make love together. In London we went to films and theatres and exhibitions together, and met Annette's friends. In Derbyshire we saw my son Daniel and his two daughters, Sarah and Claire. We sat and talked in front of our wood fire, and went for long walks on the moors. We got to know each other's families. We went twice to Scotland to visit my sister, Deb, and to stay in our house on Ardnamurchan. We flew to Mallorca three times to be with my niece, Liz, on my brother's farm, once with sister Deb, who became very fond of Annette. Annette liked Liz's little children and they liked her. We were fantastically happy.

I had always been happy in female company, while still having good male friends. I had long lost my military, Titoist spirit, though I would never deny the good that Tito and the Partisans did in their strength of fellowship and brotherhood. Some wars have had their justification, but such wars are rare and least of all justified by claims of humanitarian interest. The heroism of a captain who goes down with his ship is so much greater than that of one who leads his men into battle and survives.

Although occasionally irritable, much less with Annette, I once more felt profoundly 'Quakerish'. Annette was no pacifist; she had a deep hatred of those who had killed her David. But she had a quietness of spirit from her Quaker upbringing that I found most comforting. Some friends commented that I never appeared riled by her repetitive questioning, when she became ill, but always quietly answered her questions once or twice or three times more. Early in this memoir I asked myself whether I was the same person, as my life progressed. In those four years, which Annette and I had together before the Alzheimer's ate into her brain, Annette made me feel truly once more a complete 'person', able in time to build that city which I dreamed of. Bless her! I did not lose my haunting sense of time passing beyond recall when Annette passed away.

In the third year everything changed. At first all was well. We made further visits to Scotland and to Mallorca, and I got to know Annette's son really well and two or three of her friends in London. Her daughter Anne very kindly planned a trip to France to celebrate Annette's 90th birthday in October, to stay in the house of the sister of the lady whom Anne's ex-husband had married. We went together as a family, Annette and me, Annette's son Simon and daughter Anne, and Simon's son George and his partner Caroline. It could not have been better company or a more perfect place, just outside Avignon, looking across to Mont Sainte-Victoire, which Cézanne had painted.

Unfortunately, on the very first day, Annette tripped on a bollard in the street, as we came out of a restaurant, fell and hurt herself badly. We saw a doctor who took an x-ray and said that she had cracked her pelvis, and must be confined to bed. We stayed in the house for the week marvellously looked after by the others, and Annette and I were flown back to London on my insurance policy by air ambulance. For six weeks, Annette had to stay in bed in her flat, while I cooked and catered. At the end of that time, she could walk again, and we could sleep together. But I was increasingly conscious of her failing memory. My friends Don Sproule and Basil Davidson had both suffered from Alzheimer's disease, and I feared that this was what had hit Annette. After some weeks, I persuaded her and Simon that she should have a brain scan. It confirmed my worst fears, and the doctors pronounced the verdict.

After that, the deterioration in memory and behaviour was continuous. We went to stay with my son, Dan, for the Christmas when snow and ice blocked the roads, and all that Annette wanted to do was to go out, which was far too dangerous. She had to be forcibly detained until the snows melted. As Annette became less and less able to cope, I had to have help in the house. We were very lucky and were able to have some of the time on three days a week of the lovely Brazilian lady who worked for Simon, and then Anne found a Columbian lady for another four to five hours on two further days, to cater and cook and clean for us. I was myself increasingly unable to do everything for myself, and began to find day and night caring for Annette quite exhausting. Annette could no longer manage the journey to Derbyshire. So, Robin Hood Farm had to be sold. Annette's flat was refurbished with a new kitchen, while we spent our last time in Derbyshire together.

It came to the point where I had to ask for time off, not just for a few hours on a Friday, but two weeks at a time, to get a break, to visit my sister, Deb, my son, Dan, and niece, Liz, in Mallorca. Anne and Simon had to look after Annette during those breaks. As time went on, Annette was less and less able to know what was happening and who was who. At the start of the day she would say to me, 'Who are you?' several times over, and repeat 'What are we doing today?', even after I had given answers. She could use verbs, adjectives, adverbs and pronouns, but not nouns. I developed a theory of the evolution of the brain. Apes can indicate their needs, know friend from foe, but have no language, which supplies nouns for names of people and places. That came later, and that part of the brain Annette had lost. If I guessed right about who or where or what she was thinking of, she would repeat the word with satisfaction. The most wonderful thing about Annette's illness was that she remained remarkably cheerful almost to the end, and always friendly to other people, even though this meant repeatedly asking them their names.

In our flat in London, Annette used to wake up when the horse guards passed our windows on the way from the barracks in Albany Street. She would say, 'turn your hearing aids on, Michael!', and whisper in my ear:

The king's horses and the king's men
They march up the street and march down again,
And when they are up, they are up,
And when they are down, they are down,
And when they are only half way up,
They are neither up nor down!

They are not out to fight the foe!
You might think so!
But, dear me, No!
They are out because they have got to go,
To put a little pep into the Lord Mayor's show,
The king's horses and the king's men.

Annette mixed up two rhymes, one about:

The brave old duke of York
Who had ten thousand men,
He marched them up to the top of the hill,
And marched them down again!

But, no matter! Such incidents made the sharing of a bed just pure joy.

I cannot leave this piece in the book about Annette without concluding that she was a quite remarkable person. I only saw her again after those 65 years for perhaps four years before her illness began to eat into her, but it was long enough to recognise a really splendid person. The smile on her face in the photo tells it all – questioning, thoughtful, generous, gracious, considerate and, above all, fun. I was indeed lucky that she found me, and wanted to live with me. Life without her is empty, but I have to say that I am profoundly relieved that the end was so easy and peaceful. We enjoyed a family Sunday lunch together at Anne's, we watched the 2012 Olympics and went to bed, she held my hand as always in bed, and after a time turned over and went into a sleep, from which she did not wake. Months after her death, I still wake up in our bed and put my hand out to find hers – but it is not there.

We held the funeral for Annette in the Congregational church in Hampstead under the beautiful William Morris stained glass window. There was a big attendance of both our families and Annette's many friends. Simon and Anne and George gave tributes and a pianist friend of Anne's played some Beethoven. Simon and Anne, George and Caroline, and Maysa took Annette to the crematorium, while we all enjoyed an excellent lunch at Lemonia in Primrose Hill. When Annette and I were in Derbyshire we regularly drove past Baslow church and the graveyard where Annette's mother, Nellie Cooper, née Hoyland, was buried. Annette often said that when she died she would like her ashes to be spread around her mother's gravestone and have daffodils planted there. We are still waiting for a good occasion for both our families to make the pilgrimage, to spread the ashes and plant the bulbs.

I should not have been able to survive these last few months if, as a result of the permanent move to London, I had not found a whole new circle of friends. First, I count Annette's son and daughter, Simon and Anne. Both are one-time journalists in their sixties, Simon specialising in issues of business management of special interest to me. When he was made redundant from *The Observer* nearly 400 people wrote in to complain. Fortunately, he has found slots for his writing at other publications. Simon and Anne have been most generous in giving us assistance and inviting us for weekend meals. In addition to their help, I am particularly lucky in having the helpers from Latin America, Maysa and Sonia, who have been shopping and cooking for us, dressing us, cutting my nails, and generally caring for us.

Three particular friends of Annette's have become close companions, whom we have been meeting regularly. They are Penny Wesson, who lives near us in Primrose Hill, and has just retired as an actor's agent, with many interesting clients. She now devotes her time to painting and yoga. Then there is Bea Thompson, a consultant psychiatrist, who is also a keen gardener and has been specially generous in giving us her time. Many years ago she was married to a Communist Party lawyer, whom I knew, and we can share our left-wing convictions. Finally, Anne's friend, Bol Stallard, has become a particular friend. He was an architect who worked with Ove Arap. We are about the same age and have similar memories of the Cotswolds (he was born in Cheltenham) and of York, where Bol worked for several years, and of Africa, where he was stationed in the war. We share the same degree of disgust and despair at the activities and inactivities of the Coalition Government. All these people I regard as people of real distinction.

Then I have my families and Eleanor's relatives in London. My son Daniel still gives me enormous help, looking after my finances and my general well-being, including my haircuts. His new interest is in cycling and repairing other people's bikes, and he has just bought me an electric motor scooter to increase my mobility. I see a lot of my granddaughter, Sarah, a solicitor now at Linklaters, who lives

Michael and Sarah, after her degree

quite near to me. Grandchildren Angelica, Elliot and Lewis are all in London, and Elliot and Lewis give me invaluable assistance with my computer, and Angelica has given me a tenth great grandchild. I see Bastien at his concerts, and his daughter Natasha, her husband Peter, and children, Zachary, Imogen and Adam give me much friendship and delicious meals in their Islington house. I am happy to stay on in London, but making visits to Derbyshire, Scotland and Mallorca. When in Derbyshire I can now see granddaughter Claire and her two lovely girls, Emma and Ruby.

I try to see my sister Deb and her son each year in the Scottish borders. Ardnamurchan is now beyond me. I make a yearly visit to my niece Liz and her husband, Bos, and their children, Barratt and Eliza, at what was my brother's farm in Mallorca, and rely on Liz for much wise advice about my life when she comes to London. I still occasionally see the good friends from my Sheffield days, David Browning, John Halstead and Pauline Harrison, and David Donnison in Scotland. I continue to read new books and review them for *The Spokesman,* with much support from Tony Simpson, its editor and co-ordinator of the Bertrand Russell Peace Foundation. Above all, I have my oldest friend Robin Murray and his family in London, to keep me living in London

When I get too depressed at the demolition of all that I have struggled for in my life – peaceful solutions to international problems, a National Health Service, comprehensive school education, full employment or training, I remind myself of Tennyson's vision of the future, written in 1842, that my father used to recite to us, and I can still remember, without looking it up:

> *For I dipped into the future, far as human eye can see,*
> *Saw the Vision of the world, and all the wonder that would be;*
> *Saw the heavens fill with commerce, argosies of magic sails.*
> *Pilots of the purple twilight, dropping down with costly bales;*
> *Heard the heavens fill with shouting, and there rained a ghastly dew*
> *From the nations' airy navies grappling in the central blue;*
> *Far along the world-wide whisper of the south-wind rushing warm,*
> *With the standards of the peoples plunging through the thunder storm;*
> *Till the war-drum throbbed no longer and the battle-flags were furled*
> *In the Parliament of man, the Federation of the world.*
> *There the common sense of most shall hold a fretful realm in awe*
> *And the kindly earth shall slumber, lapped in universal law.*

And, to confirm my own beliefs, I can recall what my father wrote in *The Friend,* on September 20, 1940:

'I believe in the power of Love that is mightier than the love of power. I believe in the spirit of Goodness and Truth and Beauty, of Love and Joy and Peace. These names are but signposts. Take them down, and I can still find my way even in the war-time black-out, to the places where they may be found.'

On many medical schools there is a Latin phrase cut in the stone – *Ars longa, vita brevis.* This is often wrongly translated as 'life is short; art lasts longer'. It should be 'life is short; getting the art of it takes a long time'. After 95 years, I am still seeking the way to that art, with other seekers.

Claire with Emma and Ruby

Envoi

This Memoir is based almost entirely on my memories, with practically no written evidence. All my papers, over a hundred boxes of them, carefully edited by John Halstead, are safely locked away in the Archives of Sheffield University Library, alongside those of Richard Hoggart and Royden Harrison. I seem to have very clear memories of my childhood and long life, but memories are notoriously fickle. We recall what pleases our ego, and suppress what does not. I have to ask myself some awkward questions. Did I really learn to read by the age of three or four, and to ride a bicycle on my sixth birthday? Did I really sit on Gandhi's knees and on Paul Robeson's shoulders? Did I sit on the floor with Bertrand Russell at his school? Did I discuss politics with Harold Macmillan at the age of 16, and argue with Fiorello La Guardia at 26? Did I really talk to the Duchess of Devonshire about hares, and was I hosted by Princess Margaret, and briefly held Marilyn Monroe's hand? These memories are all very clear in my head, but I have no written evidence for any of them. I have the good word of my friend Bol Stallard for the most unlikely story, that the pianist at The Prospect of Whitby really did play the piano with the backs of his hands.

Some important memories I have myself written down in official papers – I hope correctly – about the refounding, in 1939, of the Friends' Ambulance Unit, about the establishment, in 1945, of UNRRA in Yugoslavia, about the launching, in 1958, of *New Left Review,* about the formation, in 1961, of the Conference of Socialist Economists, about the founding, in 1978, of the Northern College, about the invention, in 1983, of 'Fair Trade'. I have consulted my friends Catherine Cameron, Robin Murray, David Browning, John Halstead, Hugo Radice, Simon Caulkin, Carol Wills and Pauline Tiffen on several of these educational innovations, and received invaluable advice. There remains only the pleasure of thanking all those who have worked with me over the years in seeking our way to make the world, that we were born into, a better, happier place for all those now and in the future who depend for their lives on the planet earth. We were all seekers, all liable to error and illusion, but not deterred by that.

'Yer not cooming fur me!'
Michael 2005

Index

Garnett, Angelica 107
  Bunny 107
  College 49
gas mask 97
Gaster, Bertha 151, 69
Geary, Frank 76
genes 22
genetics 2
Geneva 39, 57, 105, 127
general election 136
Geordies 99
George VI 62, 66
Georgia, Georgian 99
German, Germany 22, 35, 39, 52, 55, 68, 88, 100
  army 61, 63, 68, 89, 90, 93, 103, 105, 106
Gervasi, Sean 13
Gezira, Cairo 12, 104
Ghana 106, 122
Ghanaian 200
Gilbert, Leslie 55-6, 59, 110
  Martin 59
Gibraltar 99
Gill, Eric 63, 14
Gillett family 61, 62, 63
  Arthur 62
  Henry 55, 62
  Margaret 61
Gillie 174
Gladstone, William 16
Glasgow 161, 168
glass works 134
  Rockware 135
glass, stained 50
GLC 143, 184
  Industry & Employment Committee 185
GLEB 182, 184-5
global crisis 183
Globe theatre 91
Glouskin, Vladimir 101, 105

God 7, 19
Godfree, Jeremy and Vivien 70
Golnik 98
gold bar 188-9
gold standard 25, 143
Goliath 30
Gollan, Johnny 123
Gomperts, Barbara 154
  Bastien 166-7
  Coen 154
  Natasha 156, 202
Gonville & Caius College 116
Gorbachev, Mihail 146, 171
Gorbals, 175
Goring-on-Thames 66
Gorman, John 174
Gothic architecture 57
Gracey, Peter 125, 164-6
Gram Swing 67
Grand Canary 105
Grandpa Brown 30
grandchildren 25, 49, 139, 190
Grant, Duncan 107
Grant, Henry 112
Gray, Donald 63
great-grandchildren 25, 203
Great Democrats 63
Great Exhibition 122
Great Zimbabwe 148
Greater London Council 67, 70, 153, 183, 195,
Greece 93, 99, 125, 180
  bank of 8
  king of 91
Greek 7, 11, 13, 15, 19, 35, 93
  religion 8, 16,
Greenham Common 172
Greens 31
Greenwood Dennis 99
Grenoble 162
Griffiths, Jay 14
Grimond, Jo 102

Liz & Peter 141
Jacobs 50
James, Henry 20
Janine 182
Japan 39, 63, 90, 93, 151, 160-1, 179,
 180, 183, 190-1
 Emperor 170
 Japanese students 40
Jaynes, Julian 11
Jenkins, Clive 126
Jennings, Humphrey 112
Jerusalem 64
Jesus college, Oxford 88
Jews 20, 21
Joachim, Joseph 46
 Liesl 55
jogging 5, 51, 141,151ff.
Johns, Lyndon 16
Johnson, Amy 39
Jones, Jack 135
 Chris 174
Jordans 79
Joseph, Professor 44-5
Joyce, James 15, 20
Jubavu, Nontando 58, 90
'Jumbo', see SACMED

K
Kahn, John 69, 73
Kalahari 90, 188
Kampala 90
kangaroo 165
Kapp, Yvonne 107
Kashmir 168
Kauffman Angelica 145
Kay, John 55
Keats 123
Keble College, Oxford 70
Keble, John 14
Kelmscott 67
Kelvin Park, Glasgow 168
Kemp family 25

Kennedy, John F, President 127, 180
Kent family 41-2
Kenya 114, 197, 202
Kerala 161, 203
Kerr, Hugh 174, 179
Kestenbum, Ann 173
Keswick 74
Keynes, John Maynard 12, 107
 Keynesian 86
Khartoum 91
Khruschev, Nikita 99, 106, 127, 180
Kidlington Pageant 47
Kiernan, Heather 86
 Victor 86, 131
Kilroy, Bay 63
kindergarten 32
King Edward VIII, 58
King, Martin Luther 127
Kings College, Cambridge 115, 130
"King's horses" 200
Kinnock, Neil 171
Kintyre 90
Kipling, Rudyard 20
Kirremuir 77
Kisumu 198
Kit Kat 203
Klugman, James 94, 99
Knossos 84
Korean War 106, 122, 126
Kosovo 171, 175-6
 Liberation Army 175
Kraft 193
Kraigher, Nada 107, 125, 174
Krajina 175
Krakiutil 160, 170
Krauses 23, 74-5
Kremlin 76
Kuapa Koko 200
Kumaramalgalam Mohun 58, 90
Kurds 177
Kuwait 177

Martin, Kinglsey 100
Martyrs ' Memorial 69
Marvin, JL 14, 16
Marx, Karl 22, 125
Marxism 126, 136
Massey-Harris, Heather 131
Matthews, Sir William 96
Mau Mau 106
May Day manifesto 123, 174, 179
MBB teaching 141
MBE 207
Meacher, Michael 136
Meade, James 58
Medawar, Dr 93
Media Diversity Institute 157
medical officers 111
Mediterranean 53, 95
Melbourne 164
Melchett, Lord 135
Mellor, David 140
Melrose 155
memory 204
Mendive 186
MERRA 5, 93ff., 96-7, 104, 107
Merryl, Lydia 173
Merton college 76
   street 68
meteors 113
Metropolitan Police Force 124
Meynell, Francis 63
Mexico 92, 188-9
MHFAU 98
Michael the Archangel 28
Michelangelo 54
Midas, curse of 65
Middle Ages 125
Middle East 12, 52, 89, 90, 91, 93,
   101, 102, 113, 120
Midland Bank 75
Miliband, Ralph, David, Ed 125
milkman 29
militants 171, 179

Military Mission to Yugoslavia
   106
military service 14, 27, 66
Millennium Dome 183
Miller, Arthur 112-3
Milosevic, Slobodan 175-7
Milton, John 137, 148
miners 63, 111, 137
   Strike 143
Mining Review 121
Minister of State 86
minnows 39
Mitchell, Margaret 20
Mitchisons 53, 90-1
Mitford sisters 130
   Jessica 63, 130
Mitre hotel 81
Molotov 88
Mombasa 9
monasteries 183
Monday 11
Mongols 164
Monroe, Marilyn 113, 204
Montague, Ivor, Lord Swaythling 12
Montgomery, General 51
moon, months 10
Moore, Robert 174
   Miss Aubrey 32
Morahan, Christopher 133
   Rebecca 72, 202
Morin, Edgar 2
Morland, Geoffrey 29
Morocco 88, 25, 11
Morris cars 39, 40, 41, 46
   May 67
   William 19, 68, 14, 148, 200
Morrison, Herbert 67
Mortimer, Jim 156
Morton, Johnny 47
Moscow 83, 110, 169
   Metro 110
Moskva river 169

204
resident artists 156
library 121
principals 146
students 149
Northfield training camp 83
Northmoor Road, Oxford 44
North Sea 143
Norway 139, 185
Notting Hill 153
Nottingham University 144
nuclear arms 171ff
Nuneaton 41
Nunn May, Alan 120-1
nursery rhymes 36
Nuseirat 93
nuts 168
Nutter, Bridget 28

O
Oban 47, 142
Oberammergau 52
observe 87,
oil industry 153
  prices 15, 22
  rigs 143
Old Malt House 31-3, 39, 40, 66, 71
Olives 158-9
  oil 159
  picking 158
Olympia 84
Olympics 60, 131, 152,
O'Neill, Colette, Lady Constance
  Malleson 34, 67
Pat O'Neill 10
Open Colleges 150
  University 125, 138, 151
Organic 187
Organisation of African Unity 127
Owen, Bill 152
  David 182
OXFAM 50, 190

Oxford 27, 39, 45, 61ff., 71, 77, 88,
  110, 160, 189, 190
City Orchestra 149
Mail 50
Group 43
Peace Council 70
Saint Giles 120
University 68ff., 75-6, 79, 80, 160-1
Extramural department 126
Institute of Statistics 134
Union 70
and Asquith, Countess 76
Oxfordshire 39, 66, 67, 122

P
Pacific 169
pacifism 19, 21, 24, 47-8, 49, 95-6
Paine, Tom
packaging 204
Pakistan 19, 104, 161, 177
Palestine 19, 93, 126, 143
  Palestinians 119,
Palgrave, Golden Treasury 30, 31
Palladian 145
Palmer, John 174
Papua New Guinea 151, 166
Paris 108, 128, 145
Paris, Notre Dame de 57
Parker, Peter 134,156, 202, 204
Parsons, Dennis 77
Parson's Pleasure 69
Partisans, Bulgarian 74
  Yugoslav 74, 93, 96, 99
Pascale 142
Pataudi, Nawab of 109
pathology unit 109
Pavlov, Ivan 49
Peace ballot 40
Peak Park 132, 141, 153
Pearl Harbour 83
Pears, Peter 48
Pearsall-Smith 34

Q

Quakerism 54, 74, 98
Quakers 11, 17, 25, 30, 49, 50, 55, 57,
    61, 71, 85, 107, 116, 125
  businesses 49, 50, 52, 65, 95
  duty 22, 27
  meetings 50, 110
  schools 20-21, 50, 61, 207
  thee-thouing 53
  upbringing 20, 24
Queen Charlotte's Hospital 181
Queen Elizabeth 84-5, 132
Queen's Messengers 84

R

Racak 175
RADA 71
radar 162
Radica, Hugo 123, 204
radicalism 14
radio 60
RAF 19, 108
Raj, Professor 161
RAMC 91, 96, 07
Ramsay, Dr. Archbishop 123
Randolf hotel, Oxford 74, 81
Ranger, Terry 149, 188
Raven, Canon Charles 119
Reagan, Ronald 151, 171
reaper 204
rebellious 50
recitation 40
Reckitt, Eva 87
Red Army 176
Red Cross uniform 91
Regents Park 89
Regent Street 185
Regional Housing Association 139
Reith, Lord 149
relief work 92, 97
religion 49
Remembrance Day 49

Renaissance 118
Renishaw 128
Republicans, US 194
revolutions 148
Rex, John 131
Rheims 57
Rhodes scholars 146
Rhodesia 136
Rhum 47
ricefields 170
Richardson, Jo 50, 71
Richmond College 162
Rijeka 107
Rimsky-Korsakov 35
Robben Island 187
Robbins, Lionel Committee 144
Robeson Paul 33-4, 204
Robin Hood Farm 128-131, 138-9, 199
Robinson, Joan 86,123
  Mary 190
Rockware glass 143
Rod, Black 40
Roddick, Anita 160
Rogers, Ginger 59
Rolls Royce 153
Rollwright stones 39
Rome 116, 151, 160
Romilly brothers 59, 130
Ronald, 25, 64, 109
  Angelica 8, 25, 202
  Christopher 9, 25, 97, 102, 104,
    105, 110, 111, 117, 139-40, 148,
    149, 202
  Elliot 9, 182, 202
  Ivan 9
  Lorna 9
  Ken 9, 202
  Lewis 9, 182
Richard 9, 25, 50, 57, 117, 139, 202
Roosevelt, Franklin 93
Rostall, Max 154
Rotha, Paul 112

Warlock, Peer 109
Warriner, Doreen 43
wars 24
Warwick, Countess 68
  University 142
Washington 19, 160, 169, 193
  Consensus 151
watches 15
Waterhouse, Sir Charles 84
  Lady 84
Watt, Harry 112
Waugh, Evelyn 33
wedding rings 189
welfare officers 109
  "reforms" 179
  state 113, 178-9
Wellington, Duke of 17
  School 49
Wells, John 174
wells, water 30
Wentworth Woodhouse 146
Wesker, Arnold 133
Wesson, Penny 201
West Anthony 84
  Rebecca 84
West, Mae 81
Westerman, Jill 150
western powers 172
Westview Press 189
White House 137
Whitworth, Robin 97
WHO 9, 88, 96, 98
Whyatt, Rendel 57
Wilbrahams, Ann 121
Wilde, Oscar 44, 137
Williams, Raymond 123, 126
Wills, Carol 20, 105, 190, 204
Wilson, Dr Henry 85
  Harold 81, 113, 136, 143
  Roger 94
Windermere 74
wine, Californian 151

French 107
  society 122
Wingfeld Isolation Hospital 180
Winnie, Aunt 56
wireless, crystal, valves 30
Wisconsin 162
Wisher, Steve 150
Witham Abbey 48
Witney, Bevan 43-44
  Joyce 43-44
Wobblies 188
Wolstencraft 68
women 10, 11, 181
  suffrage 14, 37
  and war 23
  organisations 50
  studies 162
Woodbrooke College 30
Woodstock 39
woodwork 60
Woolf, Virginia (nee Stephens) 65, 107
  Leonard 65
woolsack 142
Woolton, Lord 84
Woolworths 35
Worcester College 39, 73
Worcester, Nancy 162, 171-2
Wordsworth, William 137
work hours 14
  safety 14
Workers Control 65, 136
  conferences 123
Workers Educational Association
  (WEA) 51, 106ff., 112, 122, 133
workers' self-management 10
World Association of Fair Trade 191
World Bank 114, 132, 189
World Federation of United Nations
  Associations 27, 165
World Trade towers 183
World War, First 9, 17, 18, 60
  Second 9, 18, 20, 27, 47, 66, 106-7,

160, 180
Third 183
Wormwood Scrubs Prison 25, 28
Wright family 107
   Peter 91-2
WTO 192
Wynn, Bert 133

X
xenophobia 15

Y
Yalta 10
Yamada, Hideo 161-2
Yeltsin, Boris 171
Yemen 177
York 19, 49
   Minster 49
   Station Hotel
Yorkshire 41, 59, 127, 152, 172

Quaker families 51
South, Socialist Republic of 153
Young, Michael 66, 84
youth 16
   Hostels Association 92
Yugoslavia 13, 19, 43, 93, 96-7, 110,
   112, 121, 125, 135, 174-5, 181, 183
   refugees 94-6
   Partisans 74, 93,96, 99, 101, 104,
   111

Z
Zagreb 175
Zambaco, Maria 96, 141
Zeno 12
Zeppelin raids 25, 28,
Zeus 8
Zilliachus, Stella 10, 97
Zimbabwe 188
Zinoviev letter 27